Somewhere Else

Four plays by

George F. Walker

Talonbooks
1999

Published with the assistance of the Canada Council for the Arts.

We acknowledge the financial support of the Government of Canada through the Book Publishing Industry Development Program (BPDIP) for our publishing activities. Canadā

Talonbooks
#104—3100 Production Way
Burnaby, British Columbia, Canada V5A 4R4

Typeset in New Baskerville and printed and bound in Canada by Hignell Printing Ltd.

First Printing: February 1999

Talonbooks are distributed in Canada by General Distribution Services, 30 Lesmill Road, Don Mills, Ontario Canada, M3B 2T6; Tel: (416) 445-3333; Fax: (416) 445-5967.

Talonbooks are distributed in the U.S.A. by General Distribution Services Inc., 85 Rock River Drive, Suite 202, Buffalo, New York, U.S.A., 14207-2170; Tel: 1-800-805-1083; Fax: 1-800-481-6207

Beyond Mozambique was previously published in *Shared Anxiety: Selected Plays*, Coach House Press, 1994 and in *Three Plays by George F. Walker*, Coach House Press, 1978. *Zastrozzi: The Master of Discipline* was previously published in *Shared Anxiety: Selected Plays*, Coach House Press, 1994 and by Playwrights Canada Press in 1977. *Theatre of the Film Noir* was previously published in *Shared Anxiety: Selected Plays*, Coach House Press, 1994, and by Playwrights Canada Press in 1981. *Nothing Sacred* was previously published by Coach House Press in 1988.

Canadian Cataloguing in Publication Data
Walker, George F., 1947-
    Somewhere Else

    Plays.
    ISBN 0-88922-402-1

    I. Title.
PS8595.A557S65 1999   C812'.54   C98-910730-2
PR9199.3.W342S65 1999

CONTENTS

Introduction

It seems to me that Canadian sensibility . . . is less perplexed by the question "Who am I?" than by some such riddle as "Where is here?"

—Northrop Frye

George Walker's title for this volume may be his paradoxical answer to the riddle posed by Northrop Frye in 1965. Walker launched his playwriting career in the early 1970s when the tide of Canadian theatrical nationalism was at its strongest. He subsequently served a six year residency at the Toronto theatre that billed itself "The Home of the Canadian Playwright" (Factory Theatre Lab). Yet at least until *The East End Plays* of the mid-1980s, Walker expressed *his* Canadian sensibility in settings that were resolutely elsewhere. And not just elsewhere in time and space. His African jungle with its motley band of colonials is situated somewhere *beyond* Mozambique. The European setting of *Zastrozzi*—"*Probably* Italy"—combines design elements from the eighteenth century and earlier with seventeenth century swordfights, even though Walker specifies that the play takes place in the 1890s. *Nothing Sacred*, set with apparent historical concreteness in Turgenev's 1859 Russia, could evoke for one reviewer "Marxist collegians of 1960s America" (*Time*, 3 Oct. 1988), while Walker himself insisted to director Bill Glassco that it was a Canadian comedy. "Here" for Walker comprises an indeterminate geography of the imagination, a somewhere else suffused with his often bizarre theatrical character(istic)s.

These are laid out vividly in *Beyond Mozambique* (1974), one of what critic Chris Johnson has termed Walker's B-movie plays. Cartoonish violence, perverse sexuality and a crumbling social order with chaos looming just offstage demarcate Walker's dark comic vision. His characters are obsessive, megalomaniacal: Rocco, the Frankensteinish Nazi doctor; Liduc, the drug addicted, pederastic priest; Lance, the demented Mountie; Chekhovian Olga and porn star Rita, as warped as the men. The corruption of Western medicine, religion, law and art is played out as monstrously grotesque post-colonial comedy, the whole deranged enterprise about to give way to apocalyptic collapse.

Each of these plays takes place in the midst of such a paradigm shift. *Zastrozzi* (1977), Walker's breakthrough as a popular dramatist, posits a "new age of optimism" against which the title character rages in his self-imposed mission to make everyone "answerable." But the real engine of this Grand Guignol melodrama is its elegant comic portrayal of sex, violence and nihilism. Zastrozzi's decaying criminal grandeur and philosophical eloquence find their perfect complement in Matilda's razor-sharp sensual power (she definitely does not suffer from rapier envy), Julia's ingenuous virginity and Verezzi's religious idiocy, aided by the cunning of Victor, the lapsed priest. Marrying John Webster with Oscar Wilde and Percy Shelley, from whom he took the Gothic story, Walker presents an utterly anachronistic metaphysical revenge comedy.

From swashbucklers and jungle flicks Walker shifted genres to the *film noir* in the late '70s. The dark visual style, ethical dilemmas and alienation, femmes fatales and malevolent urban corruption provide raw material for the North American settings of his three *Power Plays*, featuring the bumbling, cynical investigator Tyrone M. Power, and for *Theatre of the Film Noir* (1981). Its milieu is the moral chaos of recently liberated Paris, 1944. Using, shall we say, unorthodox methods, Zastrozzian Inspector Clair resolves the baroque entanglements of sex and survival surrounding the lovely, pragmatic Lilliane and her murdered brother. Walker transcends and transforms generic clichés with tremendous relish here, as in all these plays.

Nothing Sacred (1988) marked Walker's emergence as a playwright of international distinction. It not only won virtually every theatre award in Canada but was "Play of the Year" on the American regional theatre circuit (*Los Angeles Times*, 16 Oct. 1988). Adapted from Turgenev's novel *Fathers and Sons*, it may be seen as Walker's somewhere else version of his *East End Plays* in which the internal politics of a (Canadian) family recapitulate ideological issues in the society at large. At a moment of historical transition—the serfs have just been freed and revolution is on the horizon—the messianic nihilist Bazarov challenges received assumptions and has his own challenged in turn. Bazarov is more recognizably human in scale and complexity than his predecessors in Walker's drama. So are his contemporaries Arkady and Anna, and even the reactionary old men, Kirsanov and Pavel. But the world of this play—its themes and characters, language and wit—remains unequivocally Walkeresque.

You could never mistake it for anywhere else.

Jerry Wasserman
Vancouver, 1999

Beyond Mozambique

Beyond Mozambique was first produced at the Factory Theatre Lab in Toronto on May 11, 1974 with the following cast:

ROCCO Donald Davis
TOMAS Marc Connors
OLGA Frances Hyland
RITA Wendy Thatcher
CORPORAL Dean Hawes
LIDUC David Bolt

Director: Eric Steiner
Set Designer: Doug Robinson
Lighting Designer: John Stammers
Costume Designer: Marti Wright

Persons
ROCCO
TOMAS
OLGA
RITA
CORPORAL
LIDUC

Beyond Mozambique

SCENE ONE

Late evening.

The porch and surrounding area of an old, poorly maintained colonial house. Surrounded by jungle. Cluttered with discarded things: old tires, machine parts, magazines and newspapers strewn all around. To one side of the steps, a large picnic table. To the other side, DOCTOR ROCCO's *operating table. It has an umbrella attached to one end. Leaning against the roof of the house, a battered telephone pole, wires hanging to the ground.*

A whistle from the jungle. ROCCO *rushes out of the house in a lab coat, carrying his medical bag. He looks around. Another whistle.* ROCCO *goes off into the jungle towards it. Whisperings. Commotion. Branches breaking. Muttering. Muffled drums.*

TOMAS *comes out of the jungle. His head is bandaged, a trace of blood can be seen. Over his shoulder he is carrying a corpse covered by sackcloth.* ROCCO *follows him.*

TOMAS: Thélo ná nikyáso éna aftokínito.

ROCCO: Who cares. Just keep going. Wait. I hear something. I said. Wait.

TOMAS: O Kafés?

ROCCO: Shut up. Were you followed. No. You're too shrewd. Wait. No. Nothing. Get going.

He pushes TOMAS.

Get going.

They start off. ROCCO *looks under the corpse's sackcloth.*

Stop.

He grabs TOMAS.

This corpse. It's Old Joseph. I saw him yesterday. In good health. Put him down.

TOMAS *puts the corpse on the picnic table.*

I told you. Only dead ones. Out of graves. Graves, stupid. You murdered him, didn't you.

TOMAS *produces a switchblade. Runs it across his own throat. Smiles.*

No. The knife was only for cutting open the corpses' sacks. To check for decomposition. You've murdered Old Joseph. Look at him lying there. I taught that old man how to play dominoes. Oh God, he's missing a foot. Where's his foot.

TOMAS *shrugs.* ROCCO *points to his own.*

Foot. Where's Old Joseph's foot.

TOMAS *nods. Undoes his coat. The foot is strung around his neck.*

TOMAS: Good luck.

ROCCO: What's wrong with you.

> *He yanks the foot off.*

Have you no respect for human life. (*He throws the foot into the bushes*) I'm very sad.

TOMAS: Foot.

ROCCO: How many more of them have you murdered. Never mind. I don't want to know. What's done is done. At least it's for a worthy cause. He was a man of some wisdom. He might have understood. What's done is done. Off to the lab. Pick him up.

TOMAS: (*stomps his foot petulantly*) Foot!

ROCCO: Forget it! It's sickening. I'm sad. No. I must maintain my obsession. One day they will place a huge tablet in the foyer of the city hall in Naples. 'To Doctor Enrico Rocco, a native son. A man who had the courage lacking in all other scientists of his age. It was not that he thought that human life was cheap but that he believed that the advancement of medical science was divine.'

TOMAS *puts his hand on* ROCCO's *shoulder.*

Oh, yes. And a smaller plaque hidden in a corner. 'In memory of his clueless assistant. Tomas. Who was a scummy bastard of the first order.'

TOMAS: (*smiles*) Tomas.

> OLGA *comes out of the house, carrying linen and a basket full of silverware, plates, etc.*

OLGA: Oh, Enrico. I have to set that table for breakfast. Please remove the patient.

ROCCO: We were just leaving. (*to* TOMAS) Pick him up.

> TOMAS *throws the corpse over his shoulder. They start off.*

OLGA: Don't be out late, dear. The monsoons are coming.

> ROCCO *and* TOMAS *disappear around the back of the house.*

Ah. The monsoon season. A trying time. A trying time indeed.

> OLGA *begins to set the table, humming the 'Polovtsian Dances.' The sound of an approaching car is heard, screeching to a halt. The porch is flooded with light. Sound of door opening. Door closing.* OLGA *is oblivious, going about her business.* RITA *comes on, carrying a shopping bag. Her hands and arms are covered with blood. The rest of the scene is dealt with in the most casual of manners.*

RITA: Where's the Doctor.

OLGA: Out.

RITA: Goddammit. (*sits on the steps. Fingers her hair back*)

OLGA: Not so much activity please. You'll stir up the mosquitoes.

RITA: Goddammit. Have you seen the Corporal. I can't find him anywhere.

OLGA: No. What's that you're covered with.

RITA: Blood.

OLGA: From where.

RITA: His head.

OLGA: Whose head.

RITA: The priest. Father Ricci. Someone took an axe to him. I found his head outside my tent. It's in this bag. And I don't know what I'm supposed to do with it. I mean I can't carry it around forever. It's stupid.

OLGA: This joke is in poor taste, Shirley.

RITA: The name's Rita. Not Shirley. Rita. And it's no joke. Look.

She drops the head from the bag.

OLGA: Yes. That's Father Ricci all right. I recognize the disapproving look. Oh. Before I forget. You're invited to breakfast tomorrow morning. It's a formal affair. In honour of my homeland. Will you come? (*returns to setting the table*)

RITA: I'll see. I have some business to tend to.

OLGA: Well, if you can make it.

RITA: Yeah.

Pause.

Doesn't this scare you. (*pointing to the head*) This.

OLGA: My dreams are much worse. Much worse. When I see blood in one of my dreams it's like comic relief. Does it scare you.

RITA: Well, it doesn't seem real. I mean, no more real than the movies. (*looks at her arms*) Stage blood looks the same way. That's not what bothers me. What bothers me is why it was put outside my tent. I don't need the action. Question is, who's the one that thinks I do.

The CORPORAL *steps out of the bushes. Old Joseph's foot is tied around the blade of his machete.*

CORPORAL: The question is this. Does that head have anything to do with this foot.

OLGA: Lance. Have you been lurking around my bedroom window again. You know Enrico doesn't like it.

The CORPORAL *goes to the head. Kneels.*

CORPORAL: Different people. My guess is that the foot belongs to one of the sub species.

RITA: Oh, I get it. Two murders.

CORPORAL: Three murders. The guy who Father Ricci replaced. Father what's-his-face.

RITA: Carson.

OLGA: Oh, yes. I remember. The one who ran away.

CORPORAL: Wrong. I found his body deep in the jungle this afternoon. Nailed to a tree.

RITA: A priest killer. Oh, that's really bizarre.

OLGA: Lance, you're invited to breakfast tomorrow. And will you please dress.

CORPORAL: Uh-huh. This foot. This foot doesn't fit in. And I don't like that. No. I just don't like this foot. (*thinks*) Right. One thing at a time.

He throws foot into the jungle. There is mumbling from the bushes. They all react. The CORPORAL *draws his gun, walks into the bushes. We hear thrashing. Screaming. And finally two gunshots.* OLGA *and* RITA *are looking at each other, slightly confused, slightly disgusted. The* CORPORAL *casually returns, wiping blood from the blade of his machete.*

Subversives.

Everyone nods.

That keeps them away.

The ladies nod. They giggle just a bit.

Relax. You're in good hands.

They all look at each other. They all smile. OLGA *backs into the house.* RITA *begins to laugh loudly. The* CORPORAL *begins to laugh boyishly starting towards* RITA.

Blackout.

SCENE TWO

Morning.

Waiting for the guests. The table is set lavishly. ROCCO, *pacing back and forth on the ground in front of the porch, is wearing an old tuxedo.* OLGA *is sitting in her chair on the porch, reading a letter. She is wearing a full-length black dress with a collar.*

ROCCO: Like a boulder crushing my skull. Twenty-five years spent thrashing about in the wilderness. And then I wake up one day like a baby in its crib. Sucking my thumb and pissing my pants. Another wasted night. Twenty-five years long. Where are we?!

OLGA: I didn't say anything.

ROCCO: Neither did I.

OLGA: Masha writes such good letters. Social enough to satisfy the mind. Bittersweet enough to appease the memory.

ROCCO: Here. Really here. I don't believe it. And then there's the wasted time. The interruptions.

OLGA: London agrees with her. She writes her letters in English now. But somehow they still have a Russian accent.

ROCCO: Interruptions.

OLGA: Do you know how much I miss her.

ROCCO: Interruptions. Caring for the sick. Why for once can't the sick care for themselves. Don't they know I'm busy. Where am I. I'm not at the place I came to. The place I came to is somewhere else. It's quieter there. A man gets work done there without worrying about his conscience. My god. My poor conscience.

OLGA: Enrico.

ROCCO: (*to* OLGA) Woman. Why are you pestering me. What harm have I done you lately. Do I complain that you hum the 'Polovtsian Dances' in your sleep. No, I grant you your oblivion. And all I ask in return is that you bow completely out of the picture until my work is finished.

OLGA: You were raving.

Pause.

ROCCO: Tell me I am a genius. There's no one around. Olga. Tell me that if I had been born two centuries earlier and lived three times as long as anyone else I would have discovered all the cures now known to modern medicine. I don't ask much, Olga. But a mind like mine has a great appetite. It even needs flattery. Tell me. Am I amazing.

OLGA: Of course.

ROCCO: Somehow it doesn't seem like enough. Olga, I have something to tell you. No. Forget it.

OLGA: Would you like to read my sister's letter.

ROCCO: No. I can't stomach the way she manages to swoon even on a piece of paper.

OLGA: She misses Moscow.

ROCCO: Everyone misses Moscow. I miss it occasionally myself. And I've never been there.

OLGA: The letter contains good news.

ROCCO *gestures for her to continue.*

Your friend Livarno has won the Nobel Prize.

ROCCO: (*groans lightly. Bites his knuckles*) I know. We saw it in the newspaper last month. His picture covered the entire front page. Large vacant eyes. And a smile like a sheep. He didn't exist in Naples and even now, covering the entire front page of a newspaper, he does not really exist. His Nobel Prize for Science is a bad joke.

OLGA: You're jealous.

ROCCO: Stupidity fits you sometimes like a glove.

OLGA: (*getting up*) It's time for my nap.

ROCCO: Livarno is a mediocre mind. His accomplishments seem important only because he is surrounded by apes.

OLGA: Then maybe you should consider going back. You could always disguise yourself. And as for me—

ROCCO: And as for you, what. You have all you need.

OLGA: I don't know what I need. I do know what I have.

ROCCO: What do you have.

OLGA: My marriage. My history. And my original Renoir.

ROCCO: Exactly. Everything you need. The question is answered in the best way possible. By evasion. We stay here.

OLGA: For how long.

ROCCO: The world and I will collide at the proper moment. Everything in time.

OLGA: I don't like that expression! I blinked my eyes once and half a century passed. I found myself in a square in St. Petersburg surrounded by young men and women all looking exactly alike. I was wearing a ball gown and everyone thought I was about to perform an historical drama. Immediately I gave up.

ROCCO: I've always wondered what happened to your passion.

OLGA: What was left I gave to you.

ROCCO: Thank you.

OLGA: Not at all. I scarcely miss it now.

The CORPORAL *comes on in full* RCMP *dress uniform. Without speaking, he goes to the table. Takes his seat.*

ROCCO: What in God's name is that outfit all about.

OLGA: Lance was with the RCMP before he came to work here.

ROCCO: What's the RCMP.

OLGA: I'll explain later.

ROCCO: How'd he get here. I didn't hear his motorcycle.

OLGA: Some of the locals dismantled it. And Lance doesn't know how to put it back together.

ROCCO: The man is a clown. The only policeman in the area is a full-fledged clown. That is the most ridiculous uniform I have ever seen in my life.

OLGA: Shush. He's very insecure.

She goes to the CORPORAL.

Good morning, Lance. Nice of you to attend.

CORPORAL: Sure. (*quietly*) Am I over-dressed. It's the only formal thing I've got.

OLGA: No. You look fine. Almost dashing.

ROCCO: (*approaching them*) Come on now. Let's get this over with.

CORPORAL: Good morning, Doctor.

ROCCO: Is it. (*sits*)

OLGA: (*sitting*) Where is Tomas.

ROCCO: Sleeping.

OLGA: Well, who gave him permission to do that.

ROCCO: I did. I need him well rested.

OLGA: Unfair. The agreement was that I have him during the day and you have him during the night. Who is going to serve breakfast.

ROCCO: I don't know. Improvise.

CORPORAL: (*stands*) What do you and your boy do during the night anyway, Doctor.

ROCCO: (*stands*) We make house calls. Now take off your hat. My wife has gone to a great deal of trouble to create the proper atmosphere. (*sits*)

CORPORAL: (*removes his hat*) Sorry.

He sits. Pause.

OLGA: Enrico. The breakfast.

ROCCO: Be patient.

OLGA: But—

ROCCO: Be patient.

CORPORAL: Well now—

ROCCO: That goes for you too.

Long pause. OLGA *sits, restless; the* CORPORAL, *embarrassed;* ROCCO, *patient.*

OLGA: Excuse me.

They all stand OLGA *smiles. Goes into the house.* ROCCO *and the* CORPORAL *sit. Long pause.* ROCCO *is looking the* CORPORAL *over.*

ROCCO: How's your malaria.

CORPORAL: Comes and goes.

ROCCO: How often.

CORPORAL: More often all the time. I think I almost died last week from the fever. I was having visions of wheat.

ROCCO: Are you getting your transfer.

CORPORAL: My superiors say I have to prove myself here first. And with all these murders going on and that bunch of subversives running around blowing things up, well, it doesn't make me look very good. Why are you smiling.

ROCCO: I give you two months. Unless you can escape this climate. Two months at the most.

CORPORAL: You're joking.

ROCCO: I joke with friends. To people like you I dish out the ruthless truth. You're a dead man.

CORPORAL: Then cure me.

ROCCO: No.

CORPORAL: It's because I did your wife, isn't it. Don't hold it against me forever, for chrissake. I mean goddammit, man. She came to me.

> ROCCO *produces a switchblade with incredible speed and efficiency. Puts the blade under the* CORPORAL's *chin.*

ROCCO: I am not an impotent man, you son of a bitch. There are plenty of men who can't do their wives who aren't impotent. They just can't do their wives. For reasons none of your business. For reasons no one knows.

CORPORAL: Put the knife away, Doctor. I've got something to tell you.

ROCCO: Be careful, Corporal.

CORPORAL: I talked to Father Ricci the night before he was killed. He'd been doing a little investigating of his own. Seems he found out about this Italian doctor who was so good at his job that he became top dog in one of those fancy Nazi hospitals. They're still looking for him.

ROCCO: You repeat that once. To anyone. And I'll slice you up.

CORPORAL: Listen, Rocco. You can get away with robbing graves here. It's a petty crime. Just like the little bribes you all know I take. But anything more will upset the balance. Don't do anything to upset the balance. Understand?

> *They stare at each other.*

ROCCO: (*chuckles, puts the knife away*) Ah, mother of Jesus. I am only a simple country doctor. Leave me to my business in peace and you'll be fine.

OLGA *comes out with four glasses of orange juice on a tray.*

OLGA: I see that Shirley still hasn't arrived. A typical display of rudeness.

ROCCO: Rita will be late. She had a business meeting.

OLGA *is serving the juice.*

CORPORAL: What kind of business.

ROCCO: Ask her.

OLGA: Is it true that she's making pornographic movies with the natives.

CORPORAL: That's news to me.

OLGA: Well, perhaps it's just a malicious rumour. I hear so many.

ROCCO: From whom.

OLGA: Many different sources, Enrico. (*raises her glass*) To dear Russia.

ROCCO *stands. The* CORPORAL *knocks his glass over.*

What's wrong, Lance.

CORPORAL: Sorry.

ROCCO: The Corporal is having trouble coping with imaginary problems.

ROCCO *and the* CORPORAL *are staring hard at each other.*

CORPORAL: Two murders. Possibly three. People mucking about with government property. Strange comings. Strange goings. Mysterious sounds in the night. Add all that up and tell me what it sounds like to you.

OLGA: 'Les Misérables' by Victor Hugo.

They look at her.

Excuse me.

She stands. The CORPORAL *and* ROCCO *stand.* OLGA *smiles, goes into the house.*

CORPORAL: Victor Hugo my bassoon. It sounds like anarchy. It sounds like insurrection.

ROCCO: Why are you telling me all this.

CORPORAL: You were seen at three o'clock this morning sitting cross-legged in the jungle behind your house. Wearing an old army helmet and cradling a carbine in your lap.

ROCCO: What were you doing sneaking around my house at that hour.

CORPORAL: Subversives do their best work before dawn.

ROCCO: Ah. Are you a subversive.

CORPORAL: Just answer the question. What were you doing out there.

ROCCO: Maybe I was out there asleep. But I haven't slept for years. Maybe I was awake and can't remember. But that is unlikely. Or maybe I was mistaken for another. Which is probably too far-fetched. All right. I was really out there like you say. Wide awake. Suspiciously dressed. And armed to the teeth.

CORPORAL: Why.

ROCCO: (*standing*) None of your business.

CORPORAL: (*standing*) Now get this, you motherfucker. My life is on the line and no stupid wop quack is gonna ball it up for me.

ROCCO: Va fungu! (*producing his switchblade*)

CORPORAL: The same to you! (*drawing his gun*)

OLGA *comes out, carrying cups and a coffee pot on a tray.*

OLGA: Coffee?

CORPORAL: Sure.

ROCCO: Why not.

OLGA *pours the coffee. The weapons are put away.*

OLGA: Things aren't going well, are they. But then again they never do. If only Tomas was operating with all his faculties. I tried to wake him but he wouldn't budge. Enrico, where did he get that teddy bear he's sleeping with.

ROCCO: Rita gave it to him.

OLGA: Are they having an affair.

ROCCO: Anything's possible.

OLGA: Rumour has it that they are. But how many rumours can one believe. Very few. Very few indeed.

CORPORAL: (*opening his collar*) I don't feel so good. (*staggers a bit*)

OLGA: (*raises her cup*) Forever remembered. Forever lost. Those brittle Russian nights.

> *They drink. The* CORPORAL, *spits his out.*

Well, if you'd said so earlier, Lance, I would have served you tea.

CORPORAL: (*tears open his tunic*) Fever!

> *The* CORPORAL *falls on the ground, groaning, pulling at his hair.*

OLGA: Goodness. It does come on suddenly, doesn't it. (*to* ROCCO) Help him.

ROCCO: What's that.

OLGA: Help him. It's his malaria.

ROCCO: So it is. So it is. (*pours himself another cup of coffee*)

OLGA: (*starting towards the house*) I'll go get him a cold towel.

ROCCO: Get me my flask while you're in there, will you.

> LIDUC *comes out of the jungle, carrying a valise, covered with mud up to his chest. He is casually dressed in a windbreaker and slacks.*

LIDUC: Excuse me. Can you direct me to the mission? (*smiles*)

> *They all turn towards him.*

CORPORAL: (*pointing hysterically*) Assassin! Oh Jesus, an assassin!

> *He rushes at* LIDUC *screaming 'Assassin, assassin.' Throws him up against* ROCCO's *operating table. Turns him around. Frisks him.*

LIDUC: Please.

CORPORAL: Don't move.

LIDUC: (*to* ROCCO) Is this a mistake.

ROCCO: Corporal, what are you doing.

CORPORAL: (*to* LIDUC) All right. Strip.

LIDUC: I beg your pardon.

CORPORAL: Off with your clothes. I wanna see you naked.

> LIDUC *undoes his jacket. The audience sees his collar and his crucifix.*

OLGA: Oh, Lance. He's a priest.

CORPORAL: He ain't white. He's one of them. A mulatto or something.

LIDUC: No. Chinese. Half Chinese.

CORPORAL: Shut up.

LIDUC: I'll show you some identification. (*produces a small card*) My name is LiDuc. Father LiDuc.

He hands the CORPORAL *the card.*

CORPORAL: You're a goddamn chink! Goddamn—

He falls all over LIDUC.

Fever.

LIDUC: Oh my God. I mean. Oh. That is. This is. Oh.

He frees himself from the CORPORAL*'s grasp.*

OLGA: Here Father. Some coffee.

LIDUC: Yes. Thank you. (*takes it. Trembling*)

OLGA: Please excuse the Corporal. He suffers from several viruses.

LIDUC *nods. Hands coffee to the* CORPORAL.

Oh. How nice. Won't you sit down.

LIDUC: Yes. Thank you. (*sits somewhere*) Thank you.

OLGA: (*to* ROCCO) Breakfast is a disaster. I should have expected it. Actually I did expect it. But I was hoping to be surprised.

ROCCO: (*to* LIDUC) Difficult journey? (*no response*) The mud! On your clothes!

LIDUC: Yes. I stepped into a quagmire. I'm a bit myopic, you see. And I lost my glasses in a brief encounter with a wild pig.

ROCCO: People don't usually get out of quicksand once they're in.

LIDUC: No. Well, I wouldn't have either, I suspect. I spent two entire days clinging to a vine. And then this native gentleman came along and pulled me out.

OLGA: You must be very hungry.

LIDUC: No, the native gentleman took me to his home and fed me.

ROCCO: Did you talk to him.

LIDUC *stands. Turns towards the* CORPORAL.

LIDUC: I would like an apology from you. I think it is only fair.

The CORPORAL *waves stupidly.*

ROCCO: I said, did you talk to him.

LIDUC *turns slowly back towards* ROCCO.

LIDUC: Yes. Not much though. He was a bit reticent.

ROCCO: What did he tell you.

LIDUC: I don't understand.

ROCCO: What do you know.

LIDUC: Oh. I know that Father Ricci is dead. I was to have been his assistant, you see. And I know that he is a policeman. And that you are a doctor. He made no mention of the lady, though.

OLGA: I keep a low profile.

ROCCO: My wife, Olga.

OLGA: My husband, Enrico Rocco, M.D.

LIDUC: Good. Introductions. (*shaking everyone's hand*) I am Father LiDuc. Until they send Father Ricci's replacement I will be in charge of the mission.

OLGA *grabs* ROCCO*'s sleeve. Directs his attention outward.*

ROCCO: (*smiles*) Oh, I'm afraid not.

LIDUC: What's that.

ROCCO: (*points*) Look.

They are all staring off towards the audience.

LIDUC: A fire.

The CORPORAL *has recovered sufficiently to express delight.*

CORPORAL: (*chuckling*) Ah. Too bad.

OLGA: (*to* LIDUC) Your mission.

CORPORAL: Well, I guess I better get over there. (*chuckles again*)

LIDUC: I'll come too. Doctor?

ROCCO: What.

LIDUC: Are you coming. Someone might be injured.

ROCCO: Impossible. No one ever goes near the place anymore.

LIDUC *starts out towards us.*

CORPORAL: Not that way. Too dangerous. Follow me.

The CORPORAL *is deciding which is the longest, most pleasant route. Finally he slaps* LIDUC *jovially on the back. Gestures for him to follow and starts off.*

LIDUC: (*backing off*) It was nice meeting you.

OLGA: Yes. Come again soon. And you can look at my original Renoir. It's superb. Like a dove in orgasm.

OLGA *waves. The* CORPORAL *and* LIDUC *are gone.*

He seems so innocent.

ROCCO: Eh. Sure.

OLGA: Enrico. Who set that fire.

ROCCO: I don't know. Honestly.

OLGA: Thank goodness for that at least.

ROCCO: (*chuckles*) You're still standing guard over my soul, woman.

OLGA: Habit. I'm going in for a nap.

ROCCO: Send Tomas out to me.

OLGA: If I can wake him up.

ROCCO: The secret is to apply pressure to his head. At the point where the blood stain is the brightest.

OLGA *nods. Goes inside.* ROCCO *produces a notebook and pen. Writes something.*

Who'd expect to find so many social obligations in the midst of such desolation.

A scream from the house.

Tomas!

Muttering from the house.

Tomas! Get out here!

TOMAS *rushes out of the house, wearing an oversized lab coat, rubbing his bandaged head. There is more blood showing.* ROCCO *hands him a piece of paper and his knife.*

I need what is written on that paper by tonight.

TOMAS: O'Ponokéfalos.

ROCCO: That's Greek. You're regressing.

TOMAS: Yais. My haid.

ROCCO: What.

TOMAS: O'Ponokéfalos.

ROCCO: Headache?

TOMAS: Yais. My brain. Kséhasis. Forget. I forget.

ROCCO: Of course you do. But stop worrying. You're lucky to be alive. You had a severe wound in your brain. You understand?

TOMAS: Sometimes.

ROCCO: Almost totally destroyed. I have fixed. Maybe all. Maybe just some. A great miracle nevertheless. Don't worry. Here. Aspirin.

TOMAS: (*suspiciously*) Efharisto.

ROCCO: Now go about my business. You are not my only concern. Be careful. Get going!

> ROCCO *points to paper and knife. Gives* TOMAS *a push.* TOMAS *takes three or four quick paces, almost running. Grasps his head. Groans. Falls into a dead faint.*

Basta! Basta! No! You don't understand. No one understands. Existence is thrust. You get sick. You get cured. There is no room for relapse. Never mind.

> *He grabs the paper from* TOMAS' *hand.*

I'll do it myself

> *Takes off his coat. Produces a nylon stocking from his pants' pocket. Puts it over his head. Picks up his knife. Rushes off.* TOMAS *sits up. Looks around. Drops the aspirin on the ground. Muffled drums.*
>
> *Blackout.*

SCENE THREE

Evening

RITA *and* TOMAS *sitting on the steps. Both have their chins in their palms. A long silence.* RITA *blows down into her blouse.*

RITA: I'll never get used to this heat. It just whacks me out.

TOMAS *produces a small fold-out fan from inside his shirt. Fans* RITA *slowly.*

Ah, thanks. Hey. What's wrong with you anyway. Are you in a funk.

TOMAS: Funk. Sad.

RITA: I know. I know. It's not easy. Ah, you're bleeding again. (*she touches his wound. He groans*) I'm sorry.

TOMAS: Funk.

RITA: Yeah. Me too. I miss my man. Did I ever tell you about him. A winner. A six-foot smile. The only genuine winner I've ever known in my life.

TOMAS: Rub.

RITA: Sure thing.

She massages the back of his neck.

He's the guy who is going to make my movie. Not porn. I did porn in New York. This one is going to be a classic. It'll have sex. But it'll be sex with class. No pubics. That's what I'm doing here, you know. Research. I'm immersing myself in the place. Digging in. You know. So that when we make the movie I'll come across super real. I play a stupid slut who has always wanted to be an actress. It's a great script. It needs rewrites but basically it's a great script. I know I've told you all this before, but it's just that if I don't keep saying it I'll forget it's the truth.

TOMAS: Rub.

RITA: Yeah. Sure.

She continues his massage.

Anyway, the Doctor thinks it's a joke. You know, 'cause I've been here for years, one year, and Chad, that's my man's name, still hasn't shown up. The Doctor's an asshole sometimes. He has no idea how much dough you need to make a film. I mean as soon as Chad gets outta prison he's going to get right back to work on raising the money. God I miss him. He never was much of a letter writer.

Pause. She looks around.

This place has nice sunsets. You know that? Sometimes I just pour myself a stiff gin and lean against that big tree outside my tent and just let that sun sink slowly down into the ground while I shake the ice cubes around in the glass. And when I do that I get so deeply into Rita Hayworth I could just about die.

TOMAS *sighs as he slowly rubs his crotch.*

You and the Doctor are the only ones who know. I play the role for the rest of them. It's a defence mechanism. My mother taught me all about it. When you're dealing with men, do it like you got two balls and you'll be one up on most of them. (*laughs*) It works too. I've never been raped or exploited. And I couldn't stand either.

Voices from the jungle.

All right! All right! Cut the crap! I'm coming!

Silence.

(*to* TOMAS) See what I mean. Be right back.

She goes into the jungle. OLGA *comes out in her nightgown.*

OLGA: I heard voices. What was it.

TOMAS *just stares at her.*

I don't like the way you look at me. Some day I'm going to tell my husband.

She hands TOMAS *a letter.*

Mail that for me tomorrow. Don't forget. Someone somewhere might be contemplating suicide. And that letter could save a life.

OLGA *goes back in.* TOMAS *rips up the letter. Throws the pieces up in the air.* RITA *returns, adjusting her clothing.*

RITA: They're lunatics. I don't trust them. No way do I trust them. They drink too much and they're always wiped on this weird extract they get from the root of some fruit tree. But they've got money. And they pay me well.

TOMAS: Sex?

RITA: No. That's stupid gossip. Part of my false image. I smuggle for them. Just so I can help Chad get the money for our movie.

TOMAS: Poso?

RITA: You know I don't understand Greek. Listen. How'd you like to do me a favour.

TOMAS: Poso?

RITA: I want you to cross the border for me. I'd do it myself but I've been across too many times lately and my nerves are a little jangled. Whatya say.

TOMAS: Your eyes. I love them. Like sky at night above Athens. We live in Hilton. You pay. I am always horny. Get it?

RITA: Come on. We've been through this already. That gigolo stuff must be in your past or something. What's wrong, are you hallucinating.

TOMAS: Sick.

Drums, very quietly.

RITA: Bloody Doctor. Mucking around with your head. Do me a favour and I'll get him to lay off you.

She hands him an envelope.

Here's their money. Take it. Cross the border. Give it to the man waiting in the yellow Citroen. He'll take you to a warehouse and give you a large crate. Hire a truck and put the crate in the back under some sacks of flour. When you're driving back over the border wink at the guard and say, 'The lady from Illinois has legs.'

TOMAS: (*who has been repeating odd words*) Legs.

RITA: Then drive the truck to the ruins of the mission and leave it there.

TOMAS *is ogling the money in his hands.* RITA *stands. Helps* TOMAS *up. Kisses him on the forehead.*

Thanks, sweet baby.

TOMAS: Sex?

RITA: No. We did it once. Because I liked your smile. More than once is infidelity. And I could never look Chad in the eye. Besides we're friends. We've got the only real friendship around here. Let's not screw it up, eh.

TOMAS smiles. Kisses her on the cheek.

Thanks. Now shoo.

RITA gives TOMAS a little push. He leaves. She watches him go. Lights a cigarette. Takes a couple of puffs.

(*to the jungle*) Okay, boys. You can pick them up at the ruins of the mission. Anytime after midnight.

Voices from the jungle. RITA counts her money. The voices annoy her.

Is it worth it.

Silence. ROCCO comes on, a corpse over his shoulder. Sees RITA. Drops the corpse. Walks to her. Produces a wad of bills. Hands them to her.

ROCCO: This is for forgetting that you saw this. Put it away. It's a great deal of money.

She puts the money in her blouse. Snuffs out her cigarette.

Excuse me.

He is dragging the corpse around the back of the house.

I have to get to sleep. Tomorrow is clinic day and I am expecting many patients. The fever is with us again.

ROCCO starts to go around the back. RITA turns back towards the audience. Stares silently off for a moment. The CORPORAL is waiting for ROCCO. He snaps his fingers. ROCCO sighs. Gives the CORPORAL some money. Disappears. The CORPORAL is counting the money. RITA is smoking and thinking. Eventually the CORPORAL comes around the front, still counting. Sees RITA. Smiles. Puts the money in his pocket nonchalantly. Starts to circle RITA, sizing her up. Stops. Stands there making a rude clicking noise with his tongue. RITA looks at him, sizing him up. Circles him. Stops. Stomps out her cigarette. They stare at each other for a while. It is a late-evening, contemptuous conversation.

CORPORAL: I've got a problem.

RITA: I'm sure you do.

CORPORAL: I'm all alone.

RITA: I know.

CORPORAL: And I need a woman.

RITA: That's too bad.

CORPORAL: Lie down for me.

RITA: Not a chance.

CORPORAL: I'll pay the going rate.

RITA: There is no going rate, mister.

CORPORAL: You're a whore.

RITA: You're an asshole.

CORPORAL: I could force you.

RITA: No you couldn't.

> *Long pause.*

CORPORAL: I've just come into a lot of money.

RITA: I know. So have I.

CORPORAL: Enough to make your movie?

RITA: Not nearly.

CORPORAL: You could be charged as an accessory.

RITA: So could you.

CORPORAL: I'm immune.

RITA: So am I.

CORPORAL: How's that.

RITA: I talked to Father Ricci the night before he was killed.

CORPORAL: Me too.

RITA: What did he tell you.

CORPORAL: What did he tell you.

RITA: It's a secret.

CORPORAL: Then tell me the secret. I could force you.

RITA: No you couldn't!

CORPORAL: Is it why you killed him.

RITA: No, but it might be why you killed him.

> *Long pause.*

CORPORAL: Maybe it's why the Doctor killed him.

RITA: Maybe.

> *Pause.*

CORPORAL: Hot, isn't it.

RITA: I don't know. I never really notice it.

> *Pause. The* CORPORAL *takes out his money. Waves it at her.*

CORPORAL: Can you use this.

> RITA *takes out a card. Waves it at him.*

RITA: Can you use this.

CORPORAL: What is it.

RITA: A girl. Her name and where to find her.

CORPORAL: What are you. Her pimp or something.

RITA: Her agent.

CORPORAL: Same thing.

RITA: Yeah. I guess it is.

CORPORAL: Is she good.

RITA: She has one very intriguing asset.

CORPORAL: What is it.

RITA: She's only eleven years old.

CORPORAL: I'll take her. Give me that paper.

RITA: You first.

> *Slowly he hands her the wad of bills.*

(*counting*) Try to be gentle. She's a close friend.

CORPORAL: (*grabbing the paper*) Oh, sure. (*starts off. Stops*) I want you to forget this.

> *He leaves.*

RITA: I'll try.

> RITA *stuffs the money into her blouse. She looks out towards the audience.*

(*with style*) I'll try.

> *Five or six strong drum beats.*
> *Blackout.*

SCENE FOUR

Morning.

Bird noises. The odd very unusual one. LIDUC *is standing by the operating table. He appears to be blessing it.* ROCCO *comes on. Abruptly throws a pail of hot water on the table. Begins to scrub it down with a brush. He is just a bit drunk.* LIDUC *steps back a bit.*

ROCCO: Where did they go.

LIDUC: The native lady took her child to be buried.

ROCCO: It was hopeless. What are you doing.

LIDUC: Praying for your other patients.

ROCCO: Hopeless. The fever. That child is just one of many.

LIDUC: You would give them a better chance if you were sober.

ROCCO: If I was sober I couldn't even look at them.

Pause.

LIDUC: The mother left you that tire as payment.

ROCCO: (*chuckles*) That belongs to the Corporal's motorcycle. Look around. Tires. Old magazines. All this debris. The booty of my practice. Sad, eh.

LIDUC: Well, if they ever take your licence away you can open up a junkyard. (*smiles*)

ROCCO: European wit. Where did you pick it up. Never mind. Save it for my wife. She'll relish it.

LIDUC *goes to the porch. Sits on the steps, his Bible held to his chest.*

LIDUC: I'm sorry if my staying with you causes inconvenience.

ROCCO: Just don't get in the way of my work and you'll be tolerated.

LIDUC: Yes. What work is that.

ROCCO: My experiments. I'm searching for the cure for cancer.

LIDUC: Which one.

ROCCO: All of them.

LIDUC: It seems like an impossible goal.

ROCCO: That's why I chose it.

LIDUC closes his eyes. Sways gently back and forth. There is a bottle and a glass on the floor of the porch. ROCCO *picks them up. Pours himself long drink. Leans against the porch. Drinks.*

How can I love with such hell in my heart. And worse knowing that the hell is what keeps me going. Knowing that when I was of the age when men make those kinds of decisions I decided to steep myself in corruption. Because corruption was the only powerful force around. And now because the age of passion is dead there is no energy to reverse the decision. My baseness is my strength. The farther down I go the safer I am.

Pause. Drinks.

Ah. But how to explain that I cannot love. (*turns to* LIDUC) There is a tower growing in the jungle. It is the power of light and the shrewd mind of darkness. It is the culmination of all history and civilization. And it is turning my mind into soup.

They stare at each other. Long pause.

LIDUC: You need a psychiatrist.

ROCCO: There's no psychiatrist alive who could cope with me. I am the absence of God.

LIDUC: I feel obliged to answer that.

ROCCO: Ah, I'm not listening to you. Where was the Church when I needed her. I'll tell you. The world was being torn apart. Mothers walked around grinning foolishly at their children's graves. Compromise was ruining good men forever. Chronology and reason were being shot to hell. And the Church was locked up inside an old stone palace hiding under a gigantic mahogany desk with His Eminence. Do you drink.

LIDUC: I have a glass of wine each Christmas eve. A tradition.

ROCCO: A family tradition?

LIDUC: No. A tradition of my order.

ROCCO: Difficult things. Family traditions. Especially for a man in your situation. What do you do to keep the Chinese half of you loyal to tradition.

LIDUC: Nothing.

ROCCO: The Chinese are great gamblers. I knew one in medical school. He was killed in that Zeppelin crash. Do you ever gamble.

LIDUC: Never.

ROCCO: No. Well, Father LiDuc, I'm afraid this is the end of our relationship. I'm a busy man. I have to rely on first impressions. Obviously you have nothing to offer me.

LIDUC: I'm sorry. Perhaps your wife and I will find more in common.

ROCCO: Go easily with her. My wife is classically deluded. Are you familiar with 'The Three Sisters' by Chekhov.

LIDUC: Of course.

ROCCO: My wife believes that she is a character from that play. Her namesake. The eldest sister.

LIDUC: How does she reconcile this belief with reality.

ROCCO: Which reality.

LIDUC: I understand.

ROCCO: Do you.

LIDUC: No.

ROCCO: No. The only way to understand it is to become part of it. I write letters. I send them to a friend in London. He posts them for me. She thinks they're from her sister. That's a secret. Do you like secrets.

LIDUC: No. But sometimes they're necessary.

ROCCO: Wisdom. Glib wisdom. But it's better than nothing. Maybe you'll save us all in spite of the odds.

LIDUC: I'm too young.

ROCCO: And I'm drunk. Tell my wife not to wait up. I have to disappear for a while.

   ROCCO *starts off taking the bottle with him.*

LIDUC: May I ask where to.

ROCCO: No! Yes. I'm having an illicit affair with a leopard. Three trees due east of the quagmire. Beware the cobra. Ask for Zelda.

ROCCO leaves. LIDUC sits. Closes his eyes. Leans back. The sound of an approaching automobile. Screeches to a halt. Door opens. Door slams shut. Footsteps. Eventually RITA appears. She is wearing a decorated bathrobe.

RITA: The new priest.

LIDUC: Yes.

RITA: You don't look Chinese. They told me you were Chinese.

LIDUC: Who told you.

RITA: Them. The guys in the bushes.

LIDUC looks around nervously.

Don't worry. They're harmless. They just follow me around 'cause they haven't got anything better to do.

Muttering from the bushes. She turns.

You guys are getting pretty paranoid. You know that? Keep it down or you'll give yourselves a bad name.

Silence.

Well, are you or aren't you.

LIDUC: What.

RITA: Chinese.

LIDUC: Half.

RITA: No kiddin'. Why are you shaking.

LIDUC: Nerves. This is my first mission. I mean I have—

RITA: Stage fright. Yeah. Where's the Doctor.

LIDUC: He went for a walk.

RITA: I'll bet he did.

LIDUC: I don't like the innuendo. Say what you mean.

RITA: Forget it.

She hands LIDUC a wad of bills.

Here. Give him this for me, will ya. Tell him I don't need the action. Tell him he's worse than shit. Never mind. Just give him the money. I'll tell him he's worse than shit myself next time I see him.

LIDUC: All right.

RITA: Do you like my bathrobe. I painted it myself. Do you like the glitter.

LIDUC: It's very ...

RITA: Crass. Yeah. It's crass. But I had no choice. It was either do it up vulgar or blend in with the scenery. I mean everyone else is so weird you know. Well, I was the last one to get here and all the other styles were taken. So I got left with 'vulgar.'

LIDUC: That's too bad.

RITA: I'm getting used to it. Yeah. You know, I was thinking about that on the way over. I haven't got much to do while I'm waiting for Chad, so sometimes I just think. I was thinking how much I've come to like this place. It used to bore the bejesus outta me. But now, well, I guess it's just been a good change of pace for me. Like I'm on top of things. And back home it was always things being on top of me. Not that the money wasn't good. But the hours were lousy and my body was taking a real beating. And my flicks weren't good enough to be considered art so I was getting to feel kinda cheap. You know what this place is? I just thought of this. This place is my Virgin Father, Father. The one we all want.

LIDUC: I've never heard of anyone wanting a Virgin Father before. That's interesting.

RITA: Nah. It's hype. But at least it matches my clothes. Gotta run.

     Starts off.

LIDUC: Bye-bye.

RITA: Wait. (*stops*) You must have testicles. You know that? Staying here after what's happened. I mean Father Ricci was just a nosy son of a bitch and that one before him. Father what's-his-face.

LIDUC: Carson.

RITA: Yeah. He was a meddling mother too. But you seem different. You got testicles. And you look like the kinda man who'll mind his own business.

LIDUC: Is that a suggestion.

RITA: Could be. Gotta run. (*starts off. Stops*) Oh, tell the Doc I understand, but that maybe some other people won't.

LIDUC: And what does that mean.

RITA: Don't worry about what it means. Just tell him. Bye for now.

LIDUC: And who can I say was calling.

RITA: (*leaving*) Just tell him Rita was here.

Laughs. Leaves, humming 'Heat Wave.' LIDUC *waves. Notices that his hand is trembling. Produces an envelope from a pocket. Sits on the steps. Pours some powder from it on to the back of his hand. Sniffs it. Closes his eyes. Sways gently for a while.*

LIDUC: Personality is a dangerous illusion. (*falls back on the porch*)

Blackout.

And the sound of some strange people in the distance singing 'Stand up for Jesus.'

SCENE FIVE

Late evening paranoia.

We hear the CORPORAL *laughing. Lights come up. The* CORPORAL *is startled and frightened. He staggers back. Sits, staring at us in fear.* LIDUC *is sitting on the picnic table, underlining passages in his Bible.* OLGA *comes briskly through the door, fresh and bright, carrying a parasol and a book.*

OLGA: I've decided to make a comeback. First things first. I'm going for a walk.

She comes down the steps. Takes several confident steps straight ahead. Stops. Turns. A few paces to the left. Stops. Turns. Looks right.

It's all the same. Foreign. Uninviting. Blandness in one direction. Danger in the other. Why bother choosing.

She returns to her chair on the porch.

(*to no one in particular*) It's like this, I think. One cannot afford to be a romantic. In this time. At this place. It's just too dangerous. Emotion is apt to be mistaken for weakness and weakness as an invitation to manipulate.

Pause.

Yes. Good. I am thinking again. I'm going to be all right. (*sits*) Good morning.

LIDUC: Good morning.

CORPORAL: (*directly outward*) And further more! (*looks around. Whimpers*) Where was I.

LIDUC: You were describing the murders in all their gory detail.

CORPORAL: Yeah. Yeah, right. Are you feeling better. Not gonna vomit after all, eh.

LIDUC: No.

CORPORAL: Okay. Post scriptum to all that. (*with great emphasis and delight*) Both victims were found without clothing. Conclusion. The murderer has a fetish or two. Even Ricci's various pieces and parts were all found unclad. This brings into question sexual abuse, homosexuality, sodomy, obscene sexual abuse and necrophobia!

Falls to his knees.

OLGA: (*writhing from his descriptions*) Lunch!

LIDUC: Necrophilia.

CORPORAL: Yeah. Right.

OLGA: (*recovering*) Lunch?

LIDUC: I haven't had breakfast yet.

OLGA: Good idea. Neither have I. Tomas!

> LIDUC *begins to underline in his Bible again. The* CORPORAL *recovers. Closes in on* LIDUC.

CORPORAL: Do I have your undivided attention, Father.

LIDUC: Not really.

CORPORAL: Why not?!

LIDUC: (*nervously*) You see, Doctor and Mrs. Rocco are allowing me to give my lessons here. I've called the first one for this afternoon. And I'm not very well prepared. Perhaps we could talk later.

CORPORAL : Whatya mean later, man. You might not last the day.

OLGA: Tomas!

CORPORAL: Will you shut up!

OLGA: Shut up yourself, Lance! This is my house!

CORPORAL: So what!

> *The* CORPORAL *and* OLGA *stare at each other until* LIDUC *is overtaken by the silence.*

LIDUC: All right, Corporal. Out with it. All this talk was in order to frighten me into doing what.

CORPORAL: Nothing. Don't go anywhere. And don't do nothin'. just stay here where you're safe. I've got my hands full. There's rebellion in the air and we're surrounded by unpredictable primitives. And I don't need another dead priest.

> *He grabs* LIDUC*'s ears.*

Do you understand me.

LIDUC: Yes.

CORPORAL: (*shaking* LIDUC) I hope so. I hope so, mister. 'Cause if I catch you out running around unprotected I'm going to have to toss your ass in jail. And you know what that means. That means embarrassment. For both of us. Do you understand me.

LIDUC : (*crying*) I said yes.

CORPORAL: Okay. Okay. (*to* OLGA) Call me on the radio at the first sign of trouble.

OLGA: Of course.

CORPORAL: (*to* LIDUC. *Pointing a finger*) Okay.

> *The* CORPORAL *leaves.*

OLGA: He's worried about his job.

LIDUC: He's a fascist.

OLGA: Oh. You don't care much for fascists.

LIDUC: Who does.

OLGA: Other fascists, I suppose.

> *Pause.*

I mean they're still human beings, aren't they. Aren't they.

> TOMAS *comes out. Dressed in wonderful and fancy new clothes, strutting, smiling.*

Tomas. You are getting arrogant. In the future when I call you, come out immediately and humbly like the lackey you really are. Now go prepare tea and heat the croissants. We are breakfasting en retard upon the terrace.

TOMAS: Kali thiaskéthasi.

OLGA: Just get the tea.

> TOMAS *nods. Hands* OLGA *a letter. Goes back into the house.*

LIDUC: Where did he get the clothes.

OLGA: I don't know. He just came home one day wearing them. And he had an entire new wardrobe as well. I don't know where he got the money.

LIDUC: Why don't you ask him.

OLGA: Enrico doesn't allow me to say anything to him except to give him the simplest domestic commands. He says it might cause a hemorrhage. You see, we found him in the desert surrounded by a platoon of dead soldiers. He was wearing an apron. And he had a bullet in his brain. It was like a godsend to both of us. I needed a servant and Enrico needed someone on whom to test this new neurosurgical procedure.

LIDUC: Which procedure is this.

OLGA: I can't tell you. It's illegal.

LIDUC: I was afraid it might be.

OLGA: It's a secret. All right?

LIDUC: I'll have to think about it.

OLGA: Oh, no. I only told you because I thought I could trust you. If anyone finds out they'll send Enrico away and I'll have to go too. And I have a feeling I wouldn't much like it out there.

LIDUC: Out where.

OLGA: Anywhere.

LIDUC: All right. I won't tell anyone.

OLGA: Good.

LIDUC: I hope so.

> *Pause.*

OLGA: Another letter from Masha. My sister. A good creature with an unfortunate past.

LIDUC: I know.

OLGA: What's that.

LIDUC: Nothing. Your sister. Is she your only relative.

OLGA: No. I have another sister. But she's too young and happy to be of any importance. And I had a brother too. But that's a long story.

LIDUC: Olga.

> *He goes to her. Touches her shoulder.*

I think I can help you.

> *She reacts violently. Pushes him away.*

OLGA: What nonsense is that. I don't need any help. I gave myself to Christ back in Russia and he promised he would take care of me. But if you have any spare time on your hands, I mean when you're not teaching the native people, you might see what you can do for my husband. He's 'haunted.' And Lance. He's 'haunted' too.

LIDUC: The Corporal's 'haunted'? How do you know.

OLGA: We had a brief affair. Enrico said he wouldn't mind as long as I didn't enjoy it too much. It was in the middle of the monsoon season. I became restless. (*sighs*) It's all right. I confessed to Father Ricci and he beat me unconscious to help me repent. (*sighs again*) Anyway Lance talks in his sleep. I found out that he was drummed out of the RCMP for shooting a farmer's cows. It seems that the expression in their eyes made him feel they were in 'eternal misery.' He can't stand seeing 'eternal misery.' He calls it 'evil whining misery.' Under all that bravado, he's really just a frightened boy.

LIDUC: (*looks around. Sits*) Does he still kill things that he thinks are in eternal misery.

OLGA: I don't know. That's a good question. You should ask him. But be careful how you do it. Because he's 'haunted.' Why are you shaking.

LIDUC *takes out his envelope. Sniffs some of his powder.*

What's that.

LIDUC: A dangerous drug.

OLGA: (*backs away*) How nice. You know I wonder if our conversation has been good for me. It seems I decided to forget all these things a while ago. Of course I can't forget my family because Masha keeps writing me these damn letters. But I do try and forget about Lance. And especially my husband.

LIDUC: I'm sorry. I thought some information about everyone might help me adjust.

OLGA: Well. We're simple people, really.

TOMAS *brings out the tea and biscuits on a tray. Sets them down on a small table near* OLGA's *chair.*

Change your bandage, Tomas. You're bleeding on the croissants.

TOMAS *touches his head. Frowns. Goes back inside.*

Tell me about yourself. Tell me about your family. I just love hearing about families.

LIDUC: Well ...

OLGA: No. Please. It helps me. You said you wanted to help me.

LIDUC: You said you didn't need help.

OLGA: Well, I expected you to see that I was lying. Tell me. Please. Especially about your problems. Hearing about other people's problems somehow comforts me. (*a disturbing smile*) Please!

LIDUC *stands.*

LIDUC: My father was Chinese. My mother was a Jew. They were both incurably insane by the time I was ten. Some say they drove each other mad. Others say it was a bizarre game of one-upmanship. I was taken by the only relative I had. An uncle who was a convert to Catholicism. He was a fanatic. He died and I was put in the custody of the Church. That was twelve years ago. I just got out last month. I am a neurotic who is also like you say 'haunted.' And I developed several habits along the way through my education. Among them, a desire for the bodies of lean young men, and an attraction to the joys of several drugs. The more dangerous the better. I am a potential source of deep embarrassment to the Church. Which is why I was sent here. This is where priests like myself and Father Ricci, who was an infamous sadist by the way, are sent in the hope that they will never be heard of again. So far a perfect record. Why is your mouth hanging open.

OLGA: Would you like some tea.

LIDUC: (*only now does he become mobile*) But the strangest thing. In the middle of all that and even now, my occasional relapse into total catatonia notwithstanding, I still have a relationship with God. I love him. And I trust him. And until I am done away with I will endeavour to bring him and his word to others. All I need now is a congregation. Do you think they'll come. If I wait long enough they will. They must.

OLGA: Father. Would you like some tea.

LIDUC: (*smiles*) Yes. I feel good. Thank you for the opportunity to speak. Yes I will have some tea.

> *He goes to get himself some.*

And what about you. Has hearing all this helped you. God is a reality, you know. He's better than even the best illusions.

OLGA: Maybe. But he's not so accessible.

> ROCCO *comes out, in an undershirt. He is hung over.*

LIDUC: Good morning.

ROCCO: Liar. Don't you know that the sun is slowly dying. How can there be any good mornings? Where's your compassion. Ah, what a bunch of shit. Who wants to hear that shit. This isn't Italy. And I am no longer young enough to call out my reserves and hope for the best.

OLGA: Is your work going badly. (*to* LIDUC) His work is his life.

ROCCO: The freighter of my existence has struck a reef and all my chattels are getting wet.

> LIDUC *reaches into his pocket. Produces the money. Hands it to* ROCCO.

LIDUC: From the lady called Rita.

ROCCO: Excuse me. No. Don't. Who cares. (*starts back inside*)

OLGA: (*to* LIDUC) He's trying to forget. He spends a lot of time trying to forget.

ROCCO: (*turning around*) Shut up. Hear it?

OLGA: What. (*pulls a small pistol from her skirt*)

LIDUC: Why do you carry a gun.

OLGA: Self-protection. We're surrounded by unhealthy people. You and I are the only ones around here who aren't paranoid.

ROCCO: Shush. Hear it?

OLGA: What?!

ROCCO: Hear it now?

OLGA: No.

ROCCO: Hit the dirt!

They all duck. After a moment ROCCO *stands. Looks through the open door into the house. The other two join him.*

OLGA: What was it.

ROCCO *scratches his head. Looks around. Tucks in his undershirt. Makes a meaningless gesture. Looks around. Smiles. Scratches his head.*

ROCCO: Poison dart.

They all start slowly into the house, looking around cautiously. OLGA *and* ROCCO *go inside.* LIDUC *changes his mind. Comes back down the steps. Looks around. Opens up his arms.*

LIDUC: I have nothing to hide. In spite of everything I am still innocent. (*hears something. Whimpers. Puts his hands above his head*)

Blackout.

Drums, muffled and slow.

SCENE SIX

Evening.

The drums become gradually more distinct. Then they fade in and out throughout the scene.

LIDUC *is still waiting with open arms. He moves only his eyes, which dash about in reaction to various noises from the bushes. Talking. Muttering. Footsteps. Branches breaking. Muffled screams. Complaints. Garbage cans banging. Babies crying. Birds screeching. And every once in a while a shot. A moan. And an explosion or two in the distance. And the sound of grass burning. Through all this* LIDUC *waits, moving only his eyes. Finally ...*

OLGA: (*voice from inside the house*) No. Keep them out of my house.

ROCCO: (*voice from inside the house*) What are you doing.

OLGA: (*voice*) Keep away.

ROCCO: (*voice*) Give it back.

OLGA: (*voice*) Keep away.

ROCCO: (*voice*) Don't do it.

OLGA: (*voice*) Damn you! Damn you!

ROCCO: (*voice*) No! Don't!

The sound of a bottle crashing.

(*voice*) Oh my God. My work. My work.

OLGA: (*voice*) Out of my house.

She comes through the door hysterically, covered with blood, her hands full of human organs, intestines and things. LIDUC *turns away in disgust, starts to wander aimlessly around.* OLGA *throws them down on the ground. Picks them up. Throws them towards the audience. They don't go very far so she kicks them some more, closer to the audience, then closer.* ROCCO *comes out, in a rage, carrying a piece of intestine.*

ROCCO: Stupid woman. Goddamn lunatic. You've ruined my work. No brains, woman. You've got mush for brains.

OLGA: You brought them into my house. You put them on my dresser.

ROCCO: Jesus. Simple Jesus. It wasn't me. It must have been Tomas.

OLGA: I don't care. I saw them. I never wanted to see them. You're sick and evil and you let me see them. Damn you anyway. Damn you.

ROCCO: Shut up. (*looks at his piece of intestine*) What did you do with the rest.

OLGA: Into the swamp. Threw it away. Threw it away.

ROCCO: That was Old Peter. You threw away Old Peter. This is all that's left.

OLGA: Oh my God.

ROCCO: I taught that man how to play chess. It took me two years. Because he was a dumb native. Two wasted years reclaimed for my experiments. And you've thrown him into the bushes to rot away uselessly.

OLGA: You're a butcher.

ROCCO: I'm a scientist.

OLGA: Scientists experiment with pigs.

ROCCO: What a bunch of shit. Even a child could tell you that you don't experiment with pigs to find out what's wrong with people.

OLGA: You've lost your mind. It's for nothing. They'll look up your war record and put you in prison forever. It's all for nothing.

ROCCO: It's for my work. I will find the cure to end all cures. No matter what it is. Or even that I do not know what it is. And even if I never find it, I'm safe. Safe. Safe. In the bowels of the earth. Because there's something about committing crimes against humanity that puts you in touch with the purpose of the universe.

LIDUC: That is the most intellectually obscene comment I have ever heard.

OLGA: (*hears something inside the house*) What's that.

She starts to go inside in a daze muttering 'Oh no, oh no.'

LIDUC: God have mercy on the feeble, the diseased and the deluded.

ROCCO: Woman! You will mean nothing to me in the end. I am a scientist. And you are just a diversion. (*to the intestines*) I'm sorry, Old Peter. This is the truth. Just between you and me. It's not glory I'm after. It's redemption.

LIDUC *utters a sentence in Chinese directed at the Doctor's condition.*

Nonsense. I am safe. I am sinking with confidence into the mire. It's all out in the open and I'm safer than ever. I have finally destroyed that fucking tower and now there are only three forces in the world. God. Ignorance. And me.

OLGA *screams inside the house. More a cry of anguish than a scream, actually.*

LIDUC: Doctor, your soul is in serious trouble.

OLGA *runs out of the house carrying a picture frame.*

OLGA: We've been robbed. They've taken my Renoir. In retribution for your crimes. You've capsized me.

ROCCO: My notebooks!

He runs into the house.

OLGA: My Renoir. My Renoir. My sanity.

LIDUC: (*takes out his cocaine*) Have some of this.

OLGA: No.

LIDUC: Please. A touch of oblivion will settle you down.

OLGA: No. I prefer to have a dream. Yes. I'm going to go inside. Lie down. And have a dream. A very vivid one. About the Victoria and Albert Museum. Yes. (*stands*) Masha will meet me at the station. (*starts inside*) Sloan Square. South Kensington. Gloucester Road.

She disappears into the house.

LIDUC: (*sits. Sniffs some powder. Looks up*) I don't like the odds. (*sniffs some more*) But I will not give up.

ROCCO *comes out.*

ROCCO: My notebooks. My experiments. Gone. All gone. My safety is on the way. Now only to wait for the cataclysm.

ROCCO *lies down on the operating table. The drums get a bit louder.* LIDUC *looks around. Looks at* ROCCO. *Chuckles. Goes and sits on the picnic table.* TOMAS *comes out of the bushes counting money, wearing a new suit, smoking a cigar. Sees the Doctor. Pulls a knife. Sneaks up towards him. His head is larger and more blood is showing on his bandage.*

LIDUC: Be careful, Doctor. Behind you.

ROCCO sits up. TOMAS puts on a look of surprise.

ROCCO: What were you doing.

TOMAS: Mistake.

ROCCO: Go inside. Have a bath. Have two baths. Then crawl into bed with my wife. She's a bit frustrated. She needs sex. And I have other things on my mind. Inside. My wife. Sex. Understand?

TOMAS: Yais. Sex. You come too.

ROCCO: (*looks at him oddly*) No. (*lies down again*)

TOMAS starts inside. Stops. Goes to LIDUC. Sizes him up. Musses his hair.

TOMAS: You come too.

LIDUC: Maybe later.

TOMAS laughs. Goes inside. LIDUC looks out at us.

Clever. Clever. (*shaking a finger*) But I'm not going to be led into temptation. You naughty God you. (*laughs*)

We hear RITA approaching through the jungle, cursing to herself. LIDUC produces a bottle of pills from his coat pocket. Pops a couple. Laughs. RITA comes on, her bathrobe torn, black underwear beneath it, her face a bit soiled, muttering, walking oddly.

RITA: Those fuckers. Those mothers. Those lousy scumbags. Jesus. It's a double cross. Screwed on all sides. Where's Tomas.

ROCCO: Busy. Come back later.

RITA: He's done me in. He took their money and bought himself clothes. Fucking suits and ties and shoes. Clothes.

LIDUC: What was he supposed to buy.

RITA: Guns.

LIDUC: What for.

RITA: I don't know what for. For some stupid uprising, I guess. I don't know. And I don't care. I needed the money. The money.

LIDUC: I'm sorry for you.

RITA: What's that.

LIDUC: I'm sorry for you.

RITA: Oh, you are. Why.

LIDUC: Because you're dumb. Because you've been exploited. Exploited by people who you were trying to exploit. And that's sad. Jesus doesn't mind losers but he has no patience for idiots.

RITA: They raped me.

LIDUC: Did you enjoy it.

RITA: Hey, come on. Even Father Ricci never asked questions like that. You're weird.

LIDUC: True.

> RITA *sits down on the steps. Pause.*

RITA: I was caught off guard. Leaning against my tree. Sipping Southern Comfort. Looking north towards the high grass. Thinking everything was fine. Counting money in my head. Figuring we had enough for a month's shooting. Thinking how sorry Chad was every time he beat me up and how sorry I was for calling the police that, last time. And how sincere Chad looked when he came into my hospital room with those cops. Leaning against that tree with the flies in my ears. Getting really very deeply into Susan Hayward in 'The Snows of Kilimanjaro.'

> *Drums start. Louder.*

And then they were on me with their funny talk and their wiped out eyes and their hands smeared with elephant fat. Sticking their long dry dongs in me. And all the time asking where their money was and telling me how they'd had to get that money by cashing in empty soda bottles and stealing hub caps and costume jewellery from all the white trash and that they were really pissed off that they didn't have any guns to blow everyone's head off and set up a new republic dedicated to socialistic democracy and put the white European honky trash in little boxes with bars on them and feed them gruel and hit their hands with long sticks.

Drums stop. Pause.

But through all that I was fine. I was all right . Because I kept telling myself it wasn't real. Nobody rapes me. Nobody ever raped Susan Hayward or Rita Hayworth. And nobody rapes me. But, Jesus, they said that if they didn't get their money or their guns pretty damn soon they were gonna do it again. Only this time torture me and take pictures of my mutilated body and send them to all those cheap tabloids back home. That's when I passed out. Because the idea of being on the front cover of one of those things lying there like a matted rug just ran like vomit all through my body and my mind. And I passed out.

A scream from the house. TOMAS *runs out. Putting on his undershorts.*

(*to* TOMAS) And it's your fault, you mother.

She steps towards TOMAS. *He runs away. Before he disappears into the bushes,* RITA *produces a pistol from her bathrobe and points it at* TOMAS' *back. But does not shoot.* TOMAS *is gone.* RITA *drops the gun.*

I couldn't. He's still my only friend.

A gunshot from inside the house. ROCCO *sits up.*

ROCCO: She's shot herself.

ROCCO and LIDUC *rush towards the door.* ROCCO *goes in.* LIDUC *stops. Returns for his Bible. Gets it. Runs in.*

RITA: Sometimes I just feel like giving up.

Pause. TOMAS *comes running on. Disappears into the bushes on the other side of the house. The* CORPORAL *comes running on. He is delirious and sweating profusely.*

CORPORAL: Did you see him.

RITA: A total blur.

CORPORAL: A subversive. One of many. They're all over the place. Getting ready to attack. I've got an informant. He tells me they've got a new leader and a real sharpy he's supposed to be too. He's organized them and they're ready to move.

RITA: You're sweating like a pig.

CORPORAL: Fever. Malaria.

Drums start again.

(producing a nylon stocking. Turning around feverishly) Here we go. They followed me. It's all over.

He approaches RITA *slowly.*

Listen I know you're in with them. Use your influence. It's me they want. They know I've been doing you-know-what with all their eleven-year-old daughters. Old Joseph's eleven-year-old daughter in particular. It was good. We both liked it. But she went funny. Stole my pistol and tried to shoot off my you-know-what. I liked that too. But then she started to cry and her eyes got all spongy and I knew she was in 'misery.' 'Evil whining misery.'

RITA: You killed that little girl!

CORPORAL: Shut up. It's a secret.

The CORPORAL *puts the stocking around* RITA*'s neck.* RITA *is gagging. The* CORPORAL *is squeezing.* LIDUC *comes out.*

LIDUC: Olga has shot herself in the chest. Can we divert ourselves for a moment to pray for her.

The CORPORAL *drops* RITA. *Turns on* LIDUC.

CORPORAL: Shut up. You smell. I saw what you've got written on the inside cover of your Bible. 'Prophecy is an escape from memory.' Now what in the hell does that mean.

He raises the stocking and lunges at LIDUC. LIDUC *ducks. Runs back inside.* RITA *has crawled to a chair. The* CORPORAL *is strangling himself.*

It means misery! Misery in the mind. Everyone's got it and everyone has to be put out of it. (*thinks. Drops the stocking*) But not me. I gotta live.

He grabs RITA. *Lifts her in a bear hug.*

Help me.

RITA: No.

CORPORAL: I gotta live. Gotta overcome the disgrace of being drummed outta the Mounties. My father was a policeman.

RITA: Cut the crap. And let me go.

CORPORAL: My father was a bull. Deep murky brown eyes. Lips like pancakes. We called him Sarge.

RITA: Let me go, you goddamn oaf.

Drums stop. The CORPORAL *drops* RITA. *Looks around in a panic.*

CORPORAL: What's going on here.

RITA: It's a power struggle.

Pause.

CORPORAL: Yeah. That's it. Between who.

RITA: You and me.

CORPORAL: Yeah. Who's winning.

RITA: I am.

He slaps her.

CORPORAL: Who's winning now.

RITA: I am.

He slaps her.

CORPORAL: And who's winning now.

She knees him in the groin. He falls to his knees.

RITA: I am.

CORPORAL: Don't look at me like that, eh. I know what you're thinking.

RITA: I'm thinking how silly you look. Just like my man looked when I hit him with my cast in that hospital room.

The CORPORAL *is crawling away from her.*

CORPORAL: You're passing judgement on me. In times of crisis there are only two kinds of people. People who behave badly and people who pass judgement on the people who behave badly. And you're one of them. Just like my father. He's dead. But he never lets me forget.

The CORPORAL *collapses. Face down.* LIDUC *comes out carrying his valise.*

LIDUC: What's wrong with him.

RITA: He's delirious.

Suddenly the CORPORAL *gets to his knees. Draws his gun.*

CORPORAL: I know what they want. I know what they all want. They want to be put outta their misery. And maybe they want a little sexual abuse too. Oh, and I'm just the man to give it to them. (*gets to his feet*) All right. All right.

The CORPORAL *staggers off.* ROCCO *comes out of the house.*

ROCCO: I've decided that I want to live. (*talking to the audience*) I'll do anything you want. Just let me get on with my work. My work is my penance. And my penance is everything. (*to* LIDUC) You. Priest. Go see if you can make them understand.

But LIDUC *has taken the materials of a heroin user out of his valise. And is in the process of shooting up.*

LIDUC: Okay. Sure. But first I have to get closer to God. I have the feeling we've been out of touch.

RITA: Don't let them take any pictures of my mutilated body.

ROCCO: Be quiet. I'm preparing myself to beg.

OLGA *comes out of the house. Carrying her picture frame. Her chest is wrapped in bandages.*

OLGA: Oh, hello Shirley.

RITA: The name's Rita.

OLGA: Your name is Shirley Morgan. But not to worry. Our secret. (*groans*) Enrico. I have a complaint to make about that animal you sent into my bed. His erection was monumental but his manner was disgusting. He took me in the rectum. Good taste died immediately. And I have decided to follow.

Pause.

To die. On my way to Moscow. Finally leaving. Finally getting there. Finally. Moscow. (*giggles*) Ah. What a bad joke it really is.

A scream from the jungle.

Bravo.

She dies, leaning against a post on the porch.

RITA: Is she dead.

ROCCO: I guess so.

LIDUC: I can cope. No. I can't cope.

RITA: Well, if it's gonna happen I wanna look my best. Or else everyone will just look at my picture and say, 'She was a cheap porno queen and she died looking like one.' And no one will ever believe that I had what I had beneath all this shit. And the world won't be able to remember me with love.

She takes a small compact and lipstick from her pocket. Begins to apply the lipstick. The CORPORAL *comes on. Minus one arm. Blood dripping. A note attached to his sleeve. The note is plainly visible. A child's handwriting. It reads, 'Entertain us.'*

Your arm.

CORPORAL: Where is it.

RITA: I don't know.

CORPORAL: Then it's gone. They really took it off. Failed again. (*looks up*) Sorry, Sarge.

ROCCO: That note on his sleeve.

LIDUC: (*chuckles. Looks up*) Amazing. I don't understand how you make all this violence seem so gratuitous.

ROCCO: What's it say. I'll do anything it says.

RITA: (*reads*) 'Entertain us.'

Pause. They all look around. And from this moment there is a distinct tendency for everyone to play outward.

ROCCO: (*pacing*) Entertain them? Entertain them.

RITA: How.

ROCCO: I'm thinking.

CORPORAL: I'm bleeding to death! (*begins to cry*)

ROCCO: Then do it quietly. I'm thinking.

RITA: (*beginning to disrobe*) I won't do anything disgusting. I'll entertain but I won't be cheap.

ROCCO: You'll do what I tell you. Or I'll slit your throat.

RITA: Hey. We're friends.

She crumples onto the steps.

ROCCO: I want to live.

LIDUC: Excuse me. But what for.

ROCCO: You give me a reason.

LIDUC: To save humanity.

> *He whistles in self-approval.*

ROCCO: Corporal. Shut up. You're whining.

> *The* CORPORAL *has been writhing on the ground.*

CORPORAL: Whining? (*sits up*) Oh my God. I'm whining. Evil whining?

> *He wraps his one arm around* ROCCO*'s leg.*

Oh Doctor, you gotta put me outta my misery.

> ROCCO *shakes him loose.*

ROCCO: No. You'll live. Till I'm safe. You'll bleed till I'm safe. All of you. We'll all entertain together. No one gets safe before me.

LIDUC: (*points to* OLGA) Except her.

> ROCCO *grabs* RITA*'s lipstick. Goes to* OLGA.

ROCCO: No. Not even her.

> *The* CORPORAL *is crawling towards us. Looking along the ground. Smiling insanely.*

CORPORAL: Ants. Huge red ants. They've smelled my blood. And they've come to nibble on my stump.

> ROCCO *is using the lipstick to paint* OLGA*'s face two tears and a huge obscene smile.* TOMAS *comes out of the jungle wearing priest's clothes, two crosses around his neck, carrying a spear and an enormous wad of money.*

LIDUC: (*giddily*) Look at him. Where'd you get those clothes.

TOMAS: God.

LIDUC: Where'd you get those two crucifixes.

TOMAS: God.

> LIDUC *has one moment of unbridled passion in this play. He stands. And projects.*

LIDUC: Liar!

> TOMAS *attacks him. Pushes him down. Leans over. Massages his crotch. Whispers something terrible in his ear.*

(*trembling*) It's true. Oh my God. It's true.

TOMAS *laughs maniacally. Screams. Throws the money up and all over the ground.*

ROCCO: I've got it! Hum. (*goes to* RITA) Everyone hum!

RITA: (*singing*) 'We're having a heat wave ...'

ROCCO: No. Something Russian.

ROCCO *starts to hum 'Swan Lake.'* RITA *joins in.* ROCCO *goes to* LIDUC. *Drags him up. Gets* LIDUC *to join in. The* CORPORAL *is hearing humming noises.*

CORPORAL: Locusts! Enormous pecking locusts!

ROCCO *is now standing over the* CORPORAL. *Pulling his hair.*

ROCCO: Hum!

Everyone is humming and singing 'Swan Lake,' staring hard at us and singing with increasing concern, getting louder and louder. ROCCO *goes to* OLGA. *Drags her to a chair. Puts her on his knee. Sticks his hand up the back of her dress to her throat. And as 'Swan Lake' approaches a crescendo it is interrupted by a bizarre scream from* OLGA's *throat. Silence.* ROCCO *is manipulating* OLGA's *vocal chords, her head flopping lifelessly around until his is able to position her properly. He clears his throat. Moves* OLGA's *jaw. And the following speech comes from* OLGA, *in her own voice, but distorted and unbearably erratic.* ROCCO *silently mouths the words of* OLGA's *final speech.*

OLGA: 'The music is so gay, so confident. And one longs for life! Oh my God! Time will pass, and we shall go away forever, and we shall be forgotten, our faces will be forgotten, our voices and how many there were of us. But our sufferings will pass into joy for those who will live after us, happiness and peace will be established upon earth and they will remember kindly and bless those who have lived before. Oh dear sisters, our life is not ended yet. We shall live! The music is so gay, so joyful, and it seems as though a little more and we shall know what we are living for, why we are suffering ... Oh. If only we could know. If only we could know?!'

And OLGA's *mouth is still moving as if there were more to say. But all we hear are groans and muttering.* ROCCO *is smiling at the audience obsequiously. The others are staring in disbelief at* OLGA. TOMAS *looks at them. At us. Raises his arm and beckons. The drums explode.*

Sudden violence and activity from the bushes, getting closer and louder. Everyone on their feet now, edging towards the door of the house, looking at the audience in confusion and growing anxiety—backing up slowly.

Blackout.

End.

Zastrozzi: The Master Of Discipline

Zastrozzi was first produced at Toronto Free Theatre on
November 2, 1977 with the following cast:

ZASTROZZI Stephen Markle
BERNARDO George Buza
VEREZZI Geoffrey Bowes
VICTOR David Bolt
MATILDA Diane D'Aquila
JULIA Valerie Warburton

Director: William Lane
Designer: Doug Robinson
Lighting Designer: Gerry Brown
Sound Designer: Wes Wraggett
Fights arranged by: Patrick Crean

Persons
ZASTROZZI, a master criminal, German
BERNARDO, his friend
VEREZZI, an Italian, an artist, a dreamer
VICTOR, his tutor
MATILDA, a gypsy, a raven-haired beauty
JULIA, an aristocrat, a fair-haired beauty

Place
Europe, probably Italy.

Time
The 1890s.

Set
It should combine a simplified version of a Piranesi prison drawing with the ruins of an ancient city. There are interesting and varied chambers within and the walls are crumbling. The tops of several trees are visible and weeds are growing out of the stones.

Note
This play is not an adaptation of Shelley's *Zastrozzi*. The playwright read a brief description of this novella in a biography of Shelley and that provided the inspiration for *Zastrozzi: The Master of Discipline*, something quite different from Shelley's work.

Zastrozzi: The Master Of Discipline

Just before the storm.
BERNARDO *is looking up at the sky.*

BERNARDO: It is not a passion. Passion will eventually reward the soul. It is not an obsession. Obsession will sustain you for a lifetime. It is not an idea. An idea is the product of an ordinary mind. It is not an emotion. It cannot be purged. It is not greed or lust or hate or fear. It is none of those things. It is worse. The sky is swelling. And all those with timid natures had better go hide. It will conspire with the sky, and the air will explode, and the world will break apart and get thrown around like dust. But it is not the end of the world. It is easily worse. It is revenge.

Blackout followed by a loud sustained volley of thunder. Deadly calm. ZASTROZZI *lights an oil lamp and stands rigidly. His face is twisted with hatred.*

ZASTROZZI: You are looking at Zastrozzi. But that means very little. What means much more is that Zastrozzi is looking at you. Don't make a sound. Breathe quietly. He is easily annoyed. And when he is annoyed he strikes. Look at his right arm. (*holding it up*) It wields the sword that has killed two hundred men. Watch the right arm constantly. Be very careful not to let it catch you unprepared. But while watching the right arm (*suddenly producing a dagger with his left hand*) do not forget the left arm. Because this man Zastrozzi has no weaknesses. No weakness at all. Remember that. Or he will have you. He will have you any way he wants you.

Lightning. A long pause. ZASTROZZI'S *face and body relax. He looks around almost peacefully. He smiles.*

I am Zastrozzi. The master criminal of all Europe. This is not
a boast. It is information. I am to be feared for countless
reasons. The obvious ones of strength and skill with any
weapon. The less obvious ones because of the quality of my
mind. It is superb. It works in unique ways. And it is always
working because I do not sleep. I do not sleep because if I do
I have nightmares and when you have a mind like mine you
have nightmares that could petrify the devil. Sometimes
because my mind is so powerful I even have nightmares
when I am awake and because my mind is so powerful I am
able to split my consciousness in two and observe myself
having my nightmare. This is not a trick. It is a phenomenon.
I am having one now. I have this one often. In it, I am what I
am. The force of darkness. The clear, sane voice of negative
spirituality. Making everyone answerable to the only constant
truth I understand. Mankind is weak. The world is ugly. The
only way to save them from each other is to destroy them
both. In this nightmare I am accomplishing this with great
efficiency. I am destroying cities. I am destroying countries. I
am disturbing social patterns and upsetting established
cultures. I am causing people such unspeakable misery that
many of them are actually saving me the trouble by doing
away with themselves. And, even better, I am actually making
them understand that this is, in fact, the way things should
proceed. I am at the height of my power. I am lucid, calm,
organized and energetic. Then it happens. A group of
people come out of the darkness with sickly smiles on their
faces. They walk up to me and tell me they have discovered
my weakness, a flaw in my power, and that I am finished as a
force to be reckoned with. Then one of them reaches out
and tickles me affectionately under my chin. I am furious. I
pick him up and crack his spine on my knee then throw him
to the ground. He dies immediately. And after he dies he
turns his head to me and says, 'Misery loves chaos. And
chaos loves company.' I look at him and even though I know
that the dead cannot speak, let alone make sense, I feel my
brain turn to burning ashes and all my control run out of my
body like mud and I scream at him like a maniac,
(*whispering*) 'What does that mean.'

   Blackout

A vicious series of lightning bolts flash, illuminating the entire stage. A bed chamber. ZASTROZZI *is reeling about violently.*

ZASTROZZI: Where is the Italian Verezzi. Tell him I have come to send him to hell. Tell him that Zastrozzi is here. Tell him I am waiting. He can hide no more. He can run no farther. I am here. And I am staying. (*grabbing a flask of wine and drinking*) Ah, Jesus, this wine tastes like it was made by amateurs. I hate amateurs. Death to all of them. Remember that.

BERNARDO *bursts into the chamber.* ZASTROZZI *throws a sabre at him like a spear.* BERNARDO *ducks. The two men look at each other.*

BERNARDO: It's Bernardo.

ZASTROZZI: Step closer. The light is tricky.

BERNARDO: It is Bernardo, sit.

ZASTROZZI: Ah, Jesus! (*turning and violently ripping all the coverings from the bed*) I thought I saw an Italian to be killed.

BERNARDO: Not this one I hope. Please be more careful.

ZASTROZZI: Don't worry, Bernardo. Of all the Italians worthy of killing I am interested in only one. (*sitting on the bed*) But my mind is becoming clearer by the minute and unless I get some satisfaction I may come to the inevitable conclusion that all Italians are worthy of killing for one reason or another.

BERNARDO: Yes, I like your threats. They keep me alert.

ZASTROZZI: Learn to smile when you are being ironic. It might save your life some day.

BERNARDO: (*smiling*) The best advice is that of the best advised.

ZASTROZZI: Remind me to order you to say that again when I'm not preoccupied.

BERNARDO: It doesn't—

ZASTROZZI: Have you found him.

BERNARDO: He is here.

ZASTROZZI: Where.

BERNARDO: At least he was here. He has gone off into the countryside. But he is expected back.

ZASTROZZI: How soon.

BERNARDO: Eventually.

> ZASTROZZI *advances on* BERNARDO.

That is what I was told. And that is what I am reporting.

ZASTROZZI: Told by whom.

BERNARDO: The innkeeper where he stays.

ZASTROZZI: Then you were at his rooms?

BERNARDO: Yes.

ZASTROZZI: How do they smell. What do they look like. Describe them to me. No, wait, first, are you sure it is the same man. Verezzi the poet.

BERNARDO: Now Verezzi the painter.

ZASTROZZI: Yes, yes. And before that Verezzi the dramatist. And before that Verezzi the dancer. His vocation makes no difference. Always changing. Always pleasantly artistic. But the man himself, Bernardo. A description.

BERNARDO: The innkeeper described the same man.

ZASTROZZI: Even so. Possibly a coincidence. But the important things.

BERNARDO: Those as well.

ZASTROZZI: A religious man?

BERNARDO: Very.

ZASTROZZI: Always praying?

BERNARDO: Before and after every meal. Often during the meal. Occasionally throughout the meal.

ZASTROZZI: And the ladies. Does he have a way with them.

BERNARDO: Many ladies have visited him in his room. Most come back again.

ZASTROZZI: What about the smile. The smile that I see clearly in my head even though I have never met the man who wears it. That smile is an unnatural thing, Bernardo. Empty.

BERNARDO: 'He smiles an annoying much of the time.' I quote the innkeeper directly.

ZASTROZZI: Then it is him. It is Verezzi the artiste. The Christian. The great lover. The optimist. I will have him soon. Are you happy for me, my friend.

BERNARDO: I have watched you wanting him for a long time. I have grown fond of the force behind the search for revenge. I think I'll miss it.

ZASTROZZI: At first I wanted him just for myself. For what he did to my mother. But what I have learned of this man, Verezzi, makes me want him for another reason. That smile, Bernardo, I will remove it from the earth. It is a dangerous thing. It raises a bigger issue than revenge. (*repeating this last sentence in German*)

BERNARDO: Is this a new development.

ZASTROZZI: Actually, it is still revenge. But in a larger sense. In fact it is revenge in its true and original meaning. And, therefore, some other word is probably necessary. It is 1893 and language, like everything else, has become pleasantly vague.

BERNARDO: I'm not sure I understand.

ZASTROZZI: Naturally. Because if you did then there would be two of us and there is only need for one. No. Call it revenge, Bernardo. Tell everyone else to call it revenge. If it will make you happy I'll even call it revenge.

Blackout.

SCENE TWO

The countryside, a light rain is falling. VEREZZI *is sitting behind an easel, paintbrush in hand.* VICTOR *holds an umbrella over* VEREZZI's *head and examines the painting in silence for a while.*

VICTOR: Always tell the truth. Except when under pressure.

VEREZZI: What does that mean.

VICTOR: How can you paint a German landscape when you have never been to Germany.

VEREZZI: My father was in Germany. He told me all about it.

VICTOR: That's silly. You present a false image.

VEREZZI: Perhaps. But my heart is in the right place.

VICTOR: Unsuspecting people will look at your art and think they see the truth.

VEREZZI: Perhaps my Germany is the real Germany. And if not, then perhaps it is what the real Germany should be.

VICTOR: What is that supposed to mean.

VEREZZI: I'm not quite sure. Yes, I am. Perhaps Germany is ugly. Or perhaps Germany is bland. What is the point of creating bland or ugly art.

VICTOR: To illustrate the truth.

VEREZZI: Art has nothing to do with truth.

VICTOR: Then what is its purpose.

VEREZZI: To enlighten.

VICTOR: How can you enlighten if you don't serve the truth.

VEREZZI: You enlighten by serving God.

VICTOR: Then God is not serving the truth.

VEREZZI: Is that a question or a statement.

VICTOR: Both.

VEREZZI: Then you are a heretic.

VICTOR: And you are a liar.

VEREZZI: A dreamer, Victor. A dreamer.

VICTOR: The same thing.

VEREZZI: Enough. I don't even remember asking your opinion.

VICTOR: If I waited to be asked you would never receive my criticism and, therefore, no education.

VEREZZI: You weren't hired as a tutor. You were hired as a servant.

VICTOR: That was before either of us realized how monumentally ignorant you are.

VEREZZI: Enough. What colours do you mix to make ochre.

VICTOR: Ochre is unnecessary.

VEREZZI: That hill should be shaded with ochre.

VICTOR: On some other planet perhaps. On earth it's green.

VEREZZI: Earth is boring.

VICTOR: Why don't you ask God to move you.

VEREZZI: Don't make fun of God.

VICTOR: I was making fun of Verezzi.

VEREZZI: The two are interchangeable.

VICTOR: That sounds slightly narcissistic to me.

VEREZZI: *I* am His messenger on earth.

VICTOR: What.

VEREZZI: (*a revelation*) I *am* His messenger on earth.

VICTOR: This is a new development. Until recently you were His servant.

VEREZZI: Through devotion and regular prayer, I have attained a new position.

VICTOR: Then God encourages linear growth.

VEREZZI: I beg your pardon.

VICTOR: When will you be made Messiah.

VEREZZI: Atheist. How do you sleep without fear.

VICTOR: A secret. Besides, I am not an atheist. I just have a more pragmatic relationship with God than you do.

VEREZZI: What is it.

VICTOR: It is based on reality, Verezzi. You wouldn't comprehend it.

VEREZZI: I should dismiss you. I think you mean to corrupt me.

VICTOR: Can I ask you a question.

VEREZZI: No.

VICTOR: Not even a sincere one?

VEREZZI: In all the time I've known you, you've never once been sincere on the subject of my religious experiences.

VICTOR: Be patient. At least I don't laugh in your face anymore.

VEREZZI: Ask your question.

VICTOR: How do you reconcile being God's messenger on earth with the fact that you find earth boring.

VEREZZI: That is my cross. I bear it.

VICTOR: (*sadly*) Yes. Of course you do. You probably do.

VEREZZI: Besides, I am an artist. Even if I was not a religious artist I would be dissatisfied. That is the nature of an artist.

VICTOR: That is the opinion of a very silly man.

VEREZZI: Enough. I have to finish.

VICTOR: When are we going back to the village.

VEREZZI: When I have completed my painting.

VICTOR: And what will you do with the painting.

VEREZZI: It contains His message. I'll give it to someone.

VICTOR: Not sell it?

VEREZZI: His message should not be sold. It's a gift. Besides I have no need of money.

VICTOR: That's because your father was very rich.

VEREZZI: Yes. So what.

VICTOR: I was just wondering how a messenger of God would get by if he weren't independently wealthy.

VEREZZI: You are a subversive.

VICTOR: And you are a saint.

VEREZZI: Oh. Thank you.

VICTOR: No. It wasn't a compliment.

  Blackout

SCENE THREE

A dining chamber. Occasional thunder, lightning, and rain outside. MATILDA *and* ZASTROZZI *are some distance apart preparing to fight. They cut the air with their sabres. On the table are the remnants of a meal.* BERNARDO *sits in a chair, munching a chicken leg, his legs on the table. He describes* VEREZZI*'s room.*

BERNARDO: The room smelled of lilacs, incense and mint tea. This Verezzi is an orderly fellow for sure. Nothing about the room was haphazard. Everything was neat and clean. In fact, the place appeared to have been arranged by a geometrist, for all objects were placed at perfectly right angles to each other. And between the two halves of the room—one used for work and the other for play—there was a perfect symmetry.

ZASTROZZI: Then he has someone with him. A man like Verezzi is not capable of symmetry.

Pause

Balance. A dangerous opponent in regulated combat. But get him in an alley or a dark street and you have him disoriented. Nevertheless, out of respect for his inclination, I'll cut him up into thirty-two pieces of equal size. Are you ready, Matilda.

MATILDA: First I want to make one thing clear. I do not suffer from rapier envy. I just like to fight.

MATILDA *and* ZASTROZZI *cross swords and begin to fight. As they progress it becomes clear that* MATILDA *is very good even though* ZASTROZZI *is not trying very hard.*

BERNARDO: There were several of his paintings in the room. For the most part he is a mediocre artist but occasionally he exhibits a certain flair. It's naive but it's there. One painting in particular caught my eye. An informal unrecognizable series of swirls and circles in white, off-white and beige. He seems very fond of it himself. He has given it a title.

ZASTROZZI: What does he call it then.

BERNARDO: God's Stomach.

MATILDA: The man is a fool.

BERNARDO: I would tend to agree.

ZASTROZZI: Then how has he evaded us for three years.

BERNARDO: I've been thinking about that.

ZASTROZZI: Thinking?

BERNARDO: Perhaps he doesn't know we've been chasing him.

ZASTROZZI: Nonsense. He's a clever man.

BERNARDO: But surely there are none more clever than the guileless.

ZASTROZZI: Stop thinking, Bernardo. It causes you to have absurd poetic fantasies. I am clever. I am the most accomplished criminal in Europe. Matilda is clever. She is the most accomplished seductress in Europe. Do either of us seem guileless to you.

BERNARDO: No. But you, sir, are motivated by a strange and powerful external force and Matilda has certain physical assets which allow her activities a certain ease.

MATILDA: I also have a first-class mind, Bernardo, and it gives me self-confidence. But if I didn't and I heard that patronizing comment about my body I would take off your head.

BERNARDO: If I ever have my head taken off I hope you'll be the one who does it. But not with your sword. I would like you to use your teeth.

MATILDA: Are comments like that what you use to show sexual interest in someone.

BERNARDO: Excuse me. (*standing and starting off*)

MATILDA: Don't be shy, Bernardo. Are you being shy, Bernardo.

BERNARDO: If you wish.

MATILDA: Actually all I wish is that men in general could perform with the same intensity that they lust with.

BERNARDO: I might surprise you.

MATILDA: You might. But I think we both doubt that.

BERNARDO: Excuse me. I think I'll go visit the inn again. (*starting off again*) Oh, I forgot. Here is one of his drawings. I took it from his room.

ZASTROZZI: You stole it.

BERNARDO: Yes.

ZASTROZZI: Why.

BERNARDO: Zastrozzi asks why someone steals something. Zastrozzi, who has stolen more than any man alive.

ZASTROZZI: Put it back.

BERNARDO: Why.

ZASTROZZI: We are not thieves anymore.

BERNARDO: Then what are we.

ZASTROZZI: We are not thieves.

BERNARDO *leaves.*

MATILDA: I don't want to do this anymore. (*throwing down her sabre*) Let's make love.

ZASTROZZI: I'm preoccupied.

MATILDA: With what.

ZASTROZZI: The image of Verezzi's painting.

MATILDA: You didn't even look at it.

ZASTROZZI: I saw it in my head. It is a colourful pastoral. An impression of a landscape. Impressionism. Distortion.

MATILDA: Very interesting. Great material for preoccupation, I'm sure. But you were preoccupied the last time I came to you. And the time before that as well. We haven't made love in over a year.

ZASTROZZI: Then go somewhere else. Making love is not an accurate description of what we do anyway.

MATILDA: I realize that. I know what we do. We ravage each other. Nevertheless I miss it. Don't you?

ZASTROZZI: No.

MATILDA: Zastrozzi is hollow. I have come three hundred miles just to be reminded once again that Zastrozzi is hollow.

ZASTROZZI: Drink. (*picking up a flask and drinking*)

MATILDA: Don't you ever get physically aroused anymore.

ZASTROZZI: No. All sexual desire left me the moment I realized I had a purpose in life.

MATILDA: So now you have a purpose. I thought you just wanted to make people suffer.

ZASTROZZI: Can't that be a purpose.

MATILDA: I don't know. But I do know it can't stop you from desiring me. There's something you're not telling me.

ZASTROZZI: Very well. I swore a vow of chastity.

MATILDA: To whom.

ZASTROZZI: The Emperor of Spain's mistress.

MATILDA: Nonsense. When would you have met her.

ZASTROZZI: When I robbed the Emperor's country estate. His mistress was there alone. One thing led to another and I raped her. Just as I was leaving she looked up and said, 'I can live with this if you vow never to be intimate with another woman.' I shrugged my shoulders, said 'all right,' and left.

MATILDA *laughs.*

I knew you would understand.

MATILDA: I'm the only woman alive who could. We belong together. It would be delicious while it lasted. There's no one alive we couldn't victimize in one way or another. And when we're finally caught we can go to hell together.

ZASTROZZI: No, not hell. Some place less specific. Atheists don't go to hell. They don't know where it is. The Christians invented it and the only decent thing they've done is to keep its whereabouts a secret to outsiders.

MATILDA: Then forget hell. Let's go to Africa instead.

ZASTROZZI: Later. I have things to do.

MATILDA: Ah, yes. This search for revenge on some God-obsessed Italian. You are letting it change your personality.

ZASTROZZI: He murdered my mother.

MATILDA: So find him. Then kill him. It's a simple matter. It should not be your purpose in life. Revenge is an interesting obsession but it isn't worthy of the powers of Zastrozzi.

ZASTROZZI: I know. But Verezzi represents something which must be destroyed. He gives people gifts and tells them they are from God. Do you realize the damage that someone like that can do.

MATILDA: Damage to what.

ZASTROZZI *makes a dismissive gesture.*

I don't understand.

ZASTROZZI: I don't need your understanding.

MATILDA: Yes. I know that. I haven't been coming to you all these years because I think you need anything from me. It's that I need something from you.

ZASTROZZI: Really. What.

MATILDA: The whore sleeps with the devil so she can feel like a virgin?

ZASTROZZI: Something like that. Yes. What a comfortable little solution to guilt. Except that your devil is unpredictable. (*hits* MATILDA *and knocks her down*) Get out.

MATILDA: Let me stay.

ZASTROZZI: Get out. Or your devil might slit your throat just to show the flaw in your argument.

MATILDA: If I crawl across to you and beg, will you let me stay.

ZASTROZZI: (*looks at her silently for a moment*) First, let's see how you crawl.

> MATILDA *crawls slowly over to him, wraps her arms around his legs and rests her head on his boot.*

MATILDA: Let me stay. Do what you have to. Go send this Italian Verezzi to hell and then let me stay forever.

ZASTROZZI: Shush. (*thinking, breaking away from her and pacing slowly*) Send this Verezzi to hell. (*chuckling*) Yes.

> ZASTROZZI *paces some more, stops and looks at* MATILDA.

I will. He is a Christian. He can go to hell. Or at least he thinks he can. And the pain. Such excruciating pain. Much, much more than if I were to merely kill him. He must be made to send himself in his mind to hell. By killing himself. The most direct route to hell is by suicide. Over a woman. The most desirable woman in the world. She will entrap him then destroy him. And his destruction will be exquisitely painful and it will appear to everyone to have happened naturally as if it were meant to be.

> *Pause.*

You will do this for me, won't you, Matilda.

> MATILDA *looks at him. Stands. Straightens her clothes.*

MATILDA: First, let's see how you crawl.

They stare at each other. Finally ZASTROZZI *gets down and slowly crawls over to her. He wraps his arms around her legs.*

ZASTROZZI: Entrap him. Then destroy him.

BERNARDO *walks in, sees them, smiles.*

BERNARDO: He's back.

Blackout.

SCENE FOUR

Street scene. A light rain is falling. JULIA *is sitting on some steps, holding an umbrella above her head.* VEREZZI *is standing centre stage, looking up, smiling, hitting himself on the head with both his hands and moving about delicately.*

VEREZZI: I'm so happy. Life has once again given me the giggles. What a surprise. In the ruins of an ancient city, on a foul, damp day in spring, the soggy young artist, walking aimlessly about in search of something to draw, meets the most beautiful and sensitive woman alive.

JULIA: You are kind. But you flatter me.

VEREZZI: Not yet. But I will. I am growing silly with delight. (*reeling around a few times*)

JULIA: Good heavens. What's wrong with you. Why can't you just come sit down and have a pleasant conversation.

VEREZZI: You want me to be sober.

JULIA: If you'd just stay still for a moment. We only met a minute ago. All we said to each other was hello. And you started prancing about and giggling.

VEREZZI: Yes. A less perceptive person would think I was insane.

JULIA: Well, you might be insane for all I know. Can't you even introduce yourself.

VEREZZI *sobers.*

VEREZZI: Yes. Of course. (*walking over*) I am Verezzi.

JULIA: My name is Julia.

VEREZZI: (*spinning around*) Of course it is! Could it be anything else. You are spectacular and your name is a song.

JULIA: Sir. You will sit down. You will stop talking like a frenzied poetic moron and will make rational conversation. It can be pleasant conversation. It can even be romantic conversation. But it will be rational or I am leaving.

VEREZZI: (*sitting*) I am Verezzi.

JULIA: Yes, you've said that.

VEREZZI: And you are Julia.

JULIA: And I have said that.

VEREZZI: Will you marry me.

JULIA: No.

VEREZZI: I am depressed.

JULIA: How old are you.

VEREZZI: Twenty-five.

JULIA: You have the emotions of a ten-year-old.

VEREZZI: That is often the case with a visionary.

JULIA: So you have visions.

VEREZZI: (*a revelation*) I am a visionary.

JULIA: So you ... have visions.

VEREZZI: Yes. But don't tell anyone. I'm not ready to meet my followers yet.

JULIA: Visions of what nature.

VEREZZI: Religious.

JULIA: Visions of God?

VEREZZI: Of God. By God. For God. Through God.

> VEREZZI *smiles.* JULIA *just stares silently at him for a while.*

JULIA: You are the first visionary I have met. At least the first one who has told me that he was one.

VEREZZI: I hope you're not thinking I'm bragging.

JULIA: No, that's not what I'm thinking.

VEREZZI: Good. Because I worked hard to be what I am. At first I was just a person, then a religious person, then a servant of God, then a messenger of God.

JULIA: And now a visionary.

VEREZZI: Yes.

JULIA: When did you have your first vision.

VEREZZI: I haven't had one yet.

JULIA: I don't understand.

VEREZZI: Neither do I. I suppose I'll just have to be patient.

> *Pause.*

JULIA: But you told me you had visions. Of God. By God. For God etcetera.

VEREZZI: Yes. I was speaking hypothetically.

JULIA: I'm sorry. But I don't think that makes any sense.

VEREZZI: No. Then I was speaking metaphorically.

JULIA: That neither.

VEREZZI: Symbolically.

JULIA: No.

VEREZZI: Will you marry me.

JULIA: No. (*standing*)

VEREZZI: Where are you going.

JULIA: Home.

VEREZZI: May I call on you.

JULIA: No. (*exiting*)

VEREZZI: I love her. She is just the right kind of woman for me. She has no imagination and she takes her religion very seriously. God is creating a balance.

> VICTOR *enters.*

VICTOR: Who was that woman.

VEREZZI: Her name is Julia. She lives here. She is very bright. She is an aristocrat. She thinks I'm insane. I gave her that impression intentionally by making fun of religious states of mind. It was a test. She passed. I'm going to marry her.

VICTOR: Shut up.

VEREZZI: I won't shut up. You are my servant. You shut up.

VICTOR: You're getting worse daily. You're almost insensate. There is danger here and you can't appreciate it.

VEREZZI: There is no danger here. There is only love here.

VICTOR: You are insane.

VEREZZI: Who says so.

VICTOR: I do.

VEREZZI: You are my servant. You are not to say I am insane. I say you are insane. Yes, Victor, you are insane. So there.

VICTOR: Shut up.

VEREZZI: You shut up.

> VICTOR *grabs* VEREZZI *by the throat and shakes him.*

VICTOR: Shut up, shut up, shut up.

> VEREZZI *raises a hand and* VICTOR *lets him go.*

Now are you ready to listen to me.

VEREZZI: You hurt me.

VICTOR: I'm sorry. You were in a daze.

VEREZZI: I was?

VICTOR: Yes. How do you feel now.

VEREZZI: My throat hurts.

VICTOR: But are you sensible.

VEREZZI: Of course.

VICTOR: I found out from the innkeeper that someone has been making enquiries about you. Do you know what that means.

VEREZZI: Yes. My followers are beginning to gather.

VICTOR: Shut up. You don't have any followers.

VEREZZI: As of last count my followers numbered 454. I can describe each of them to you in detail.

VICTOR: You've hallucinated every one of them. The man making enquiries about you was probably a friend of that man Zastrozzi.

VEREZZI: Zastrozzi. Zastrozzi, the German? The master criminal? The man who seeks revenge upon me?

VICTOR: Yes.

VEREZZI: He does not exist! He is a phantom of your mind. For three years you have been telling me I have been hunted by Zastrozzi and yet I have never seen him.

VICTOR: Because I have kept us ahead of him. I have evaded him.

VEREZZI: As only you could. Because he is a phantom of your mind.

VICTOR: He was making enquiries about you.

VEREZZI: That was one of my followers.

VICTOR: Your followers do not exist. It was Zastrozzi.

VEREZZI: Zastrozzi does not exist! I have 454 followers. Follower number one is short and bald. Follower number two is tall with a beard. Follower number three is ...

VICTOR: Shut up. You are insane. And you grow worse every day. But I promised your father I would take care of you so I will.

VEREZZI: You didn't know my father. I hired you. As a servant. You must be feverish in your brain. But I will save you. You are a challenge.

VICTOR: Very well. But let's move on. You can save me at some other place.

VEREZZI: I can't. The birds are here.

VICTOR: I beg your pardon.

VEREZZI: Look up. What do you see.

VICTOR: A flock of birds.

VEREZZI: Yes. They are the sign.

VICTOR: What sign.

VEREZZI: The one my followers will be able to see in order to know where I am.

VICTOR: I don't believe this.

VEREZZI: Try. Please.

VICTOR: I will not.

VEREZZI: Very well. But when my followers arrive you're going to feel very out of place. They all believe it.

> VICTOR *gestures in disgust and leaves.* VEREZZI *drifts off in his mind.*

Follower number 54 is of medium height but he limps. Follower number 101 is blind. Follower number 262 is ... a Persian immigrant.

> BERNARDO *comes on dragging* MATILDA *by the hair. He is carrying a whip.*

BERNARDO: Here's a nice quiet place for a beating. Strip to the waist.

MATILDA: No, sit. Please forgive me. I won't do it again.

BERNARDO: For sure you won't. Not after this.

> MATILDA *tries to run away. He intercepts and throws her down.*

VEREZZI *raises his hand.*

VEREZZI: Excuse me.

BERNARDO: What do you want.

VEREZZI: A little human kindness, sir.

BERNARDO: Mind your own business.

BERNARDO *raises the whip.* VEREZZI *approaches them.*

VEREZZI: Leave her alone.

BERNARDO: You have been warned. (*drawing his sabre*) Defend yourself.

VEREZZI: Do I look like an angel of God, sir.

BERNARDO: No.

VEREZZI: Then you are in for a big surprise.

VEREZZI *draws his sabre. Swishes it about. Trying to impress* BERNARDO *with his style.* BERNARDO *laughs. They fight.* BERNARDO *allows himself to be disarmed.* VEREZZI *has his sabre at* BERNARDO's *chest. Suddenly* VEREZZI *drifts off in his mind.*

No. This is violence, isn't it. I shouldn't be doing this. This is wrong. I am an artist. I am in touch with Him.

BERNARDO *slips away.* MATILDA *goes to* VEREZZI *and seductively runs her fingers through his hair.*

MATILDA: Thank you.

VEREZZI *looks up.*

VEREZZI: You're welcome.

MATILDA: No. Thank you very, very much.

MATILDA *smiles.* VEREZZI *smiles.*

Blackout.

SCENE FIVE

Evening.

A secluded place. ZASTROZZI *is sitting inert.* JULIA *comes on with a picnic basket.*

JULIA: Excuse me, sir. But do you mind if I sit here.

ZASTROZZI slowly turns towards her and looks at her impassively for a moment.

ZASTROZZI: It would be best if you did not.

JULIA: But I always come here at this time on this particular day of the week to have my picnic.

ZASTROZZI: Without fail?

JULIA: Yes.

ZASTROZZI: Well, today you have been broken of a very silly habit. Move on.

JULIA: Why should I.

ZASTROZZI: I want to be alone.

JULIA: Then you move on.

ZASTROZZI: I want to be alone. And I want to be alone exactly where I am.

JULIA: Well, today you are not going to get what you want. I am sitting and I am eating.

JULIA eats and ZASTROZZI watches her for a moment.

ZASTROZZI: You are an only child from a very wealthy family.

JULIA: Perhaps.

ZASTROZZI: You don't have a worry in the world.

JULIA: Perhaps not.

ZASTROZZI: You don't have a thought in your head.

JULIA: I have one or two.

ZASTROZZI: And you are a virgin.

Pause.

Well, are you or are you not a virgin.

JULIA: Why. Are you looking for one.

ZASTROZZI: Go away.

JULIA: In good time. Perhaps when I'm finished eating this piece of cheese. Perhaps after I eat my apple. In good time.

    Pause.

ZASTROZZI: Do you know who I am.

JULIA: No. Who are you.

ZASTROZZI: I am the man who is going to take away your virginity.

JULIA: Many have tried. All have failed. It will never be taken away. It will be given. In good time.

ZASTROZZI: Yes. Before you eat your apple to be exact.

JULIA: I'll scream.

ZASTROZZI: If you scream it will be the last sound you ever hear.

JULIA: Then I'll go limp. You won't enjoy it.

ZASTROZZI: It's not important that I enjoy it. It's important that you enjoy it.

JULIA: Impossible.

ZASTROZZI: Look at me.

JULIA: No. I don't think I will.

ZASTROZZI: Why not. Don't you find me attractive.

JULIA: That's not the point. You've threatened to rape me.

ZASTROZZI: Surely you knew I was joking.

JULIA: You didn't sound like you were joking.

ZASTROZZI: I was only trying to hide the embarrassing truth.

JULIA: And what might that be.

ZASTROZZI: That, like so many other men, I have admired you from a distance and could never gather the courage to approach you.

JULIA: So you waited here knowing I was coming on this particular day.

ZASTROZZI: Yes.

JULIA: And you adopted an aggressive attitude to disguise your true and romantic feelings for me.

ZASTROZZI: Yes.

JULIA: Yes. I can believe that. Men have done sillier things for me. Do you still want me to look at you.

ZASTROZZI: No. I'm too embarrassed.

JULIA: I understand.

ZASTROZZI: Just look ahead.

JULIA: If you wish.

> *Pause.*

ZASTROZZI: I hope you don't mind that I'm doing this.

JULIA: What.

ZASTROZZI: Running my hand through your hair.

> ZASTROZZI *does nothing. He will do nothing.*

JULIA: Oh. I don't feel anything.

ZASTROZZI: I am running my hand through your hair. Very softly.

JULIA: Well, I guess it's all right.

ZASTROZZI: You have a very soft neck.

JULIA: Are you touching my neck. (*looking at him*)

ZASTROZZI: Please just look ahead. (*looking at her*) Please.

JULIA: All right. (*turning away*)

ZASTROZZI: Very soft neck. Very soft shoulders too. And if I may just lower my hand a little.

JULIA: Please, sir.

ZASTROZZI: I'm sorry you spoke too late. Yes, your breast is also soft. But firm.

JULIA: Please. No one has ever—

ZASTROZZI: Both breasts so wonderfully firm. And my face so nice against your neck. If I could just reach down.

JULIA: No, sir—

ZASTROZZI: You should have said so earlier. Your stomach. My God. This is such a wonderful feeling, isn't it.

JULIA: I'm not quite—

ZASTROZZI: That's it. Lean back a little.

JULIA: I shouldn't be doing this.

JULIA *does nothing. She will do nothing.*

ZASTROZZI: Back a little farther. Lie down.

JULIA: All the way?

ZASTROZZI: Yes.

JULIA: But—

ZASTROZZI: Lie down.

JULIA: Like this?

ZASTROZZI: Yes.

JULIA: What are you doing now.

ZASTROZZI: Kissing you on your mouth.

> *Pause.*

JULIA: Yes. And now?

> *Pause.*

ZASTROZZI: Your breasts.

> *Pause.*

JULIA: Yes. And now?

> *Pause.*

ZASTROZZI: Relax.

> *Pause.*

JULIA: Yes.

> *Blackout.*

SCENE SIX

The sky is rumbling again. ZASTROZZI *is drunk. He is at the doorway of his bed chamber. He drinks the last of the wine in his flask and throws it on the floor.*

ZASTROZZI: Where is my wine. I called for that wine an hour ago. I warn you it is in your best interest to keep me drunk. I am at my mellowest when drunk. Innkeeper!

A VOICE: Coming, sir.

ZASTROZZI grunts. He goes and sits in a chair near the bed, picks up a book, reads, grunts, grunts louder, throws the book across the room.

ZASTROZZI: Liar! (*standing, pacing*) They're all liars. Why do I read books. What is this new age of optimism they're all talking about. It's a lie sponsored by the Church and the government to give the people false hope. The people. I care less about the people than I do about the Church or the government. Then what do you care about sin. I care that I should not ask myself questions like that. I care to be dumb and without care. I care that I should not ask myself questions like that ever again. (*sitting, pausing*) Sad. (*standing*) Wine! (*sitting*) Sad.

VICTOR comes in with the wine.

Who are you.

VICTOR: I own this inn.

ZASTROZZI: No. I've met the owner.

VICTOR: The former owner. I won it from him in a card game last night.

ZASTROZZI: Congratulations. Put the wine down and get out.

VICTOR puts the wine down.

VICTOR: You are the Great Zastrozzi, aren't you.

ZASTROZZI: I am a lodger in your inn.

VICTOR: Are you ashamed of being Zastrozzi.

ZASTROZZI: If you were to die in the near future would many people attend your funeral.

VICTOR: No.

ZASTROZZI: Then save yourself the embarrassment. Get out.

VICTOR: I heard that Zastrozzi once passed through Paris like the plague. Leaving the aristocracy nearly bankrupt, their daughters all defiled and diseased, the police in chaos and the museums ransacked. And all because, it is said, he took a dislike to the popular French taste in art.

ZASTROZZI: A slight exaggeration. He took a dislike to a certain aristocratic artist who happened to have a very willing daughter and one painting in one museum.

VICTOR: And did Zastrozzi kill the artist, rape his daughter and destroy the painting.

ZASTROZZI: The daughter was not touched. She had syphilis. Probably given to her by the father. The painting was not worth destroying. It was just removed from the illustrious company it had no right to be with. (*taking a drink*)

VICTOR: But the artist was killed.

ZASTROZZI: Yes. Certainly.

VICTOR: Why.

ZASTROZZI: To prove that even artists must answer to somebody.

VICTOR: And what has Zastrozzi come to this obscure place to prove.

ZASTROZZI: Zastrozzi is starting some new endeavour. He is going to murder only innkeepers for a year.

VICTOR: I am not afraid of you.

ZASTROZZI: Then you are stupid.

> *Pause.*

And you are not an innkeeper.

VICTOR: They say that all Europe has no more cause to fear Zastrozzi. They say that for three years he has been single-minded in a search for revenge on one man and that all the rest of Europe has been untouched.

ZASTROZZI: They think and say only what Zastrozzi wants them to think and say.

VICTOR: They also say that any man can cross him, that any woman can use him. Because the master criminal, the Great Zastrozzi, is in a trance.

ZASTROZZI: Ah. But then there are trances …

He draws his sword and does four or five amazing things with it.

… and there are trances.

He puts the sword to VICTOR*'s throat.*

Now, who are you.

VICTOR *steps back. Afraid.*

VICTOR: Your revenge upon Verezzi will be empty.

ZASTROZZI: Who is he to you.

VICTOR: I'm his tutor.

ZASTROZZI: His what.

VICTOR: Tutor. I teach him things.

ZASTROZZI: Is that so. And what, for example, do you teach him.

VICTOR: How to evade the man who wants to destroy him.

ZASTROZZI: You are the one responsible for stretching my search to three years.

VICTOR: Yes.

ZASTROZZI: Interesting. You don't look capable of having done it. You look ordinary.

VICTOR: I am.

ZASTROZZI: No. In your case the look might actually be deceiving. But we'll soon find out. Where is your weapon.

VICTOR: I don't have one.

ZASTROZZI: Then why the innkeeper disguise. You must be here to intervene for your student.

VICTOR: Intervention doesn't have to be violent.

ZASTROZZI: I'm afraid it does. Haven't you been reading the latest books. The world is in desperate need of action. The most decisive action is always violent. (*repeating this last sentence in German*)

VICTOR: Interesting. But all I'm saying is that I didn't think killing you would necessarily have to be the only way to stop you. I thought I could try common sense with you.

ZASTROZZI: You were wrong. Try something else.

VICTOR: Verezzi is insane.

ZASTROZZI: I don't care.

VICTOR: But revenge on an insane man can't mean anything.

ZASTROZZI: Wrong. I don't share the belief that the insane have left this world. They're still here. They're just hiding.

VICTOR: But he thinks he is a visionary.

ZASTROZZI: Well, perhaps he is. I don't care about that either. That's between him and his God. This matter is between him and me.

> *Pause.*

VICTOR: I know why you seek revenge on Verezzi.

ZASTROZZI: No one knows!

VICTOR: I know of the crime that he and his father committed upon your mother.

ZASTROZZI: Ah, yes. The crime. What version have you heard.

VICTOR: The real one.

ZASTROZZI: Is that so.

VICTOR: I was a friend of his father. I was away studying. Hadn't seen him for years. Had never even met his son. A letter arrived. He said he was dying. And asked if I would protect his son who would probably be in danger.

ZASTROZZI: And the letter described what they had done?

VICTOR: Yes.

ZASTROZZI: What did you think.

VICTOR: It was horrible, of course.

ZASTROZZI: Describe exactly what you mean by horrible.

VICTOR: Bloody. Vicious. Unforgivable.

ZASTROZZI: Wrong. Not even close. Horrible is when things proceed unnaturally. When people remain unanswerable for their actions.

VICTOR: But the letter also told me why they had done it. This woman's son had killed my friend's daughter. Verezzi's sister.

ZASTROZZI: No. It wasn't me.

VICTOR: Then who was it.

ZASTROZZI: Never mind. But even if I had killed her then the quarrel would be with me. Not my mother. That is usually the way with revenge, isn't it.

VICTOR: You couldn't be found.

ZASTROZZI: I was away. Studying. I was called back to examine my mother's corpse. And the father's letter actually did describe what they had done to her?

VICTOR: Yes.

ZASTROZZI: Imagine that. How could he bring himself to tell anyone. I thought he was a Christian.

VICTOR: It was a confession, I think.

ZASTROZZI: Are you a priest.

VICTOR: I was at the time.

ZASTROZZI: And you left the Church just to protect Verezzi?

VICTOR: It doesn't matter why I left the Church.

ZASTROZZI: Yes. That's correct. Only two things should matter to you. That Verezzi killed my mother in a horrible manner. And that I, her son, have a legitimate claim to vengeance.

VICTOR: But he has no memory of the crime. He never has had. He must have blocked it out almost immediately.

ZASTROZZI: I don't care. I seek revenge. Revenge is a simple matter. You shouldn't have turned it into such an issue by hiding him from me for all this time.

VICTOR: But there's something else, isn't there.

ZASTROZZI: I beg your pardon.

VICTOR: I think there's another reason altogether why you want to destroy Verezzi.

ZASTROZZI: What is your name.

VICTOR: Victor.

ZASTROZZI: No. You are not an ordinary man, Victor. But you would be wise to become one within the next few hours.

VICTOR: When are you coming to take him.

ZASTROZZI: I am here now. Are you going to run off again.

VICTOR: No. He won't leave. He's waiting for his followers. Listen. I don't care much for violence. But to get to him you will have to go around me.

ZASTROZZI: I have already done that. And I didn't even know you existed.

VICTOR: How.

ZASTROZZI: Never mind. Concern yourself with this. If what I plan doesn't work I will not be going around you or anyone or anything else. I will be coming directly at him. And if you are in the way you will be killed. Now go away. I'm tired. Tired of the chase. The explanation of the chase. Of everything. Of you specifically at this moment.

> ZASTROZZI *turns around.* VICTOR *pulls a knife from inside his shirt, raises it to* ZASTROZZI*'s back, and holds it there. Finally* VICTOR *lowers it.*

Go away.

> VICTOR *exits, passing* BERNARDO *coming in.*

BERNARDO: He had a knife about six inches away from your back.

ZASTROZZI: Why didn't you stop him. He could have killed me.

BERNARDO: I doubt it.

ZASTROZZI: Did you arrange for the introduction.

BERNARDO: Yes.

ZASTROZZI: I wonder now if it is a good enough plan.

BERNARDO: Probably not. (*starting off*)

ZASTROZZI: It doesn't matter. It's almost over. I sense it. One way or the other I have him. This way would be less violent but more satisfying. Where are you going.

BERNARDO: A young woman in the village smiled at me. She's very pretty. And obviously well-off. I think I'll seduce her and rob her blind.

ZASTROZZI: You know, Bernardo, that you don't have to do these things just to impress me.

BERNARDO: Thank you.

ZASTROZZI: You could try to become the nice young man you were before your one little mistake.

BERNARDO: And what was that.

ZASTROZZI: You murdered Verezzi's sister. Don't tell me you had forgotten.

BERNARDO: Yes, I had. I've murdered so many others since then.

ZASTROZZI: You really are a seedy little butcher, aren't you.

BERNARDO: Once you make your one little mistake, sir, you must continue or be destroyed. The insulation of evil is the only thing that makes you survive. I learned that from watching you.

ZASTROZZI: But sometimes your crimes are heartless enough to shock even me. Who is the dark personality here after all.

BERNARDO: You, sir. But I strive hard to be your shadow.

ZASTROZZI: Good. That man with the knife to my back. His name is Victor. He is Verezzi's tutor. He looks harmless, doesn't he.

BERNARDO: Yes.

ZASTROZZI: He isn't. I give him to you. He'll probably present a challenge.

BERNARDO: Thank you. (*starting off*)

ZASTROZZI: Oh, Bernardo.

BERNARDO: Yes.

ZASTROZZI: I don't expect you to understand why you are killing him. But I do expect you to do it with some imagination!

BERNARDO *leaves.* ZASTROZZI *takes a long drink.*

Blackout.

Intermission.

VEREZZI's *room.* VEREZZI *and* MATILDA *are making love. He is delirious. We know they are finished when he makes an absurdly loud and sustained groaning sound.* MATILDA *gets out of bed and looks at him in disbelief. She is clothed. He is naked.*

VEREZZI: I am in love.

MATILDA: So soon?

VEREZZI: I am enthralled. You were wonderful. What a new treat. Usually I am the one who is wonderful and the women are enthralled. Where did you get this strange power.

MATILDA: It's something I was born with.

VEREZZI: How do you know.

MATILDA: What else could it be. It's not something you get from practice. I'm not a whore.

VEREZZI: No. But you're not a saint either. I'd know if you were. Because … (*a revelation*) I'm a saint.

MATILDA: Of course you are.

VEREZZI: Don't be intimidated. Saints are human.

MATILDA: Why should I be intimidated. Saint or no saint. You are the one who loves me.

VEREZZI: You mean you don't love me?

MATILDA: No. Of course not.

VEREZZI: I don't understand. Explain. But be kind about it.

MATILDA: I love someone else.

VEREZZI: Who.

MATILDA: You saw him earlier.

VEREZZI: That man who was going to beat you?

MATILDA: Yes. Bernardo.

VEREZZI: That's disgusting. How can you love someone who beats you.

MATILDA: It's not that he beats me. It's how he beats me.

VEREZZI: I don't understand. Explain. But be kind.

MATILDA: He beats me like he could kill me. And I love him for that.

VEREZZI: You should love me instead. I'm gentle. I'm an artist. I'm a saint. And I love you.

MATILDA: Could you kill me. If you could kill me I might love you.

VEREZZI: You're very strange. And you're very exciting. But I don't think you're very healthy. That's a challenge. I can help you. Stay with me.

MATILDA: I can't! I love someone else.

VEREZZI: Then why did you make love to me.

MATILDA: A part of me is gentle. It wanted to thank you. But a larger part of me is something else. It wants to be beaten. (*starting off*)

VEREZZI: Stay. I could beat you. A little.

MATILDA: If you really loved me you could do better.

VEREZZI: But I'm a saint. I love things. I can't hurt things. How could I face my followers. They're coming soon. Some of them are very vulnerable. Some of them are swans. Some of them are tiny little caterpillars who have been crawling for weeks to get here. I can't disappoint them. How can I preach love and human kindness to all my followers then go into the privacy of my bedroom and beat a woman unconscious.

MATILDA: If you are a saint you can take certain liberties. People will understand.

VEREZZI: But will the caterpillars. They are dumb. I love them. Honestly I do. But they are dumb. Crawl, crawl. That's all they do. Crawl. Life's dilemmas are multiplied for a saint. He has to deal with too many things at once. One of my followers is a Turk. I don't even speak his language. When he comes, how am I going to give him the message. I keep waiting for the gift of tongues but it never comes. God is handicapping me. And now you want me to beat you. I abhor violence. It makes me retch. But I love you. I'll die if you leave me.

MATILDA *starts off,* VEREZZI *crawls out of the bed and over to her.*

Please don't go. I know. You can beat me instead.

MATILDA: That just won't do.

VEREZZI: But won't you even try.

> VICTOR *comes in.*

VICTOR: What's this. Get up.

> VEREZZI *stands.*

(*to* MATILDA) Who are you.

VEREZZI: She is the woman I love.

VICTOR: And why were you grovelling on the floor.

VEREZZI: Because she doesn't love me. What can I do, Victor. She's breaking my heart.

VICTOR: It seems to me that I met the woman you love earlier. That virgin God sent for you.

> VICTOR *starts to pack.*

VEREZZI: Yes. Julia. That's right. I love her. I'd forgotten. Oh, thank God. For a moment there I didn't know what I was going to do. It's all right, Matilda. You can go now.

MATILDA: So you don't love me after all.

VEREZZI: But I do. It's just that I also love Julia. And she's less of a challenge. She just thinks I'm insane. I can deal with that. But I don't know if I can ever deal with you, Matilda. You want me to want to kill you. That's unique. But it's not healthy. But I do love you. And if it weren't for Julia I would probably destroy myself over you. Or something to that effect.

MATILDA: (*with clenched teeth*) Or something to that effect. (*starting off*)

VEREZZI: Oh. Say hello to Bernardo for me. I think he likes me.

> MATILDA *looks at him oddly, shakes her head and leaves.*

VICTOR: What was that all about.

VEREZZI: One of the tests of sainthood, I imagine.

VICTOR: Did you pass.

VEREZZI: I don't know. Tell me, Victor, how do you suppose I can find out.

VICTOR: Oh, shut up. Get packed. We're leaving.

VEREZZI: Why.

VICTOR: Zastrozzi is here.

VEREZZI: Who.

VICTOR: Zastrozzi. Zastrozzi!

VEREZZI: Oh, yes. The phantom of your brain. You've dreamt him up again have you.

VICTOR: I've seen him. I was at his rooms.

VEREZZI: Oh, really. And what does he look like. Does he have fangs. Does he have horns. Does he have eyes dripping blood.

VICTOR: No. He's a man. Just a man. Calm. Purposeful. And very, experienced. Just a man. But a very dangerous one.

VEREZZI: Well then, bring him along and I'll deal with him. A little human understanding should get him to leave you alone.

VICTOR: You're no match for him.

VEREZZI: Why not.

VICTOR: Because he's perfectly sane. And you're a delirious lunatic.

VEREZZI: And if I am, is it good and right for you to be telling me so. Would it not be more good and more right for you to be more understanding. That's an hypothesis of a religious nature. I have decided that your degeneration has gone far enough. And I am commencing spiritual guidance with you immediately. (*sitting on the bed*) Now come sit at my feet.

VICTOR: Get packed.

VEREZZI: Lesson number one. When the Messiah speaks, listen.

VICTOR: When did you become the Messiah.

VEREZZI: Did I say Messiah. No.

VICTOR: I heard you.

VEREZZI: No. Not me. God. God said Messiah.

VICTOR: I don't understand. Are you God or are you the Messiah.

VEREZZI: I am Verezzi. I am whoever He wants me to be.

VICTOR: You are exploring new dimensions of the human mind, Verezzi. But I don't think the world is ready for you yet. Get packed. We're leaving.

VEREZZI: No.

VICTOR: Please! I promised your father. It's the only promise in my life I've ever kept. It keeps me sane. Please get packed!

VEREZZI: No. I have to go find Julia. I have to tell her that God is talking to me. I know she'll marry me now.

VICTOR: Let me try to explain it to you in a way you will understand.

>   VICTOR *drops to his knees.*

VEREZZI: Don't patronize me, Victor. I am not a moron. I am just a good and lovely man.

VICTOR: Well, that could be a matter of opinion. But let us suppose you are in fact just a good man.

VEREZZI: And lovely.

VICTOR: Yes.

VEREZZI: And very tidy as well.

VICTOR: Yes. All those things. A good lovely tidy man. Who is gentle to all things living and dead, etcetera, and wishes only to carry about the positive uplifting spirit of God. Then doesn't it make sense that in order to do that you should become aware of the obstacles that lie naturally in your path. The forces of evil that wish to stop you. In effect, doesn't it make sense that a good man should also be a cunning man.

VEREZZI: No.

>   VEREZZI *leaves.* VICTOR *sits on the bed. Shakes his head.*

VICTOR: I give up. Zastrozzi will get his revenge on the lunatic Verezzi. After three years he will finally destroy a vegetable. I don't know who to pity more. Zastrozzi, the poor vegetable, or whatever it was that created them both. Sad. (*shrugging*) No. I can't give up. I promised. I must save him. Even if I must hurt him a little.

>   VICTOR *stands and searches the room for something heavy. He finds something, takes it, and runs out.*
>
>   *Blackout.*

SCENE EIGHT

A lull in the storm. VICTOR *is walking through a dark alley. Suddenly a torch is lit. It is held by* BERNARDO. *He is standing with sword drawn in* VICTOR's *way.*

VICTOR: Excuse me. Did a man pass by here recently. A young man.

BERNARDO: Forget him. His time is almost here. You have business with me.

VICTOR: What do you want.

BERNARDO: I am from Zastrozzi.

VICTOR: And what does Zastrozzi want from me.

BERNARDO: Your life.

VICTOR: A bizarre request. Do you understand the reason for it.

BERNARDO: No. I am a more simple man than Zastrozzi. I can only understand simple reasons for killing a man. And very simple ways of going about it.

VICTOR: Interesting. What, for example, are the simple reasons for killing a man.

BERNARDO: To get his money.

VICTOR: I have none.

BERNARDO: If he has done some wrong to me.

VICTOR: I don't even know you.

BERNARDO: Or if he presents some kind of threat.

VICTOR: Surely you can tell just by looking at me that I'm harmless.

BERNARDO: Zastrozzi says you are not.

VICTOR: Zastrozzi flatters me.

BERNARDO: Zastrozzi sees things that others cannot.

VICTOR: Perhaps that is because he is insane.

BERNARDO: He is not the least bit insane.

VICTOR: Are you absolutely sure of that.

BERNARDO: Yes.

VICTOR: Oh.

BERNARDO: In fact, he is the sanest man I have ever met. He is also the most perverse. The combination makes him very dangerous. You do not upset a man like this. When he tells you to kill someone, you do it. Even though you personally have nothing to gain from it. When he tells you to do it with imagination you try to do so. Even though you do not know why or even how to go about it.

VICTOR: Poor fellow. You're in quite a fix.

BERNARDO: While you on the other hand are not, is that it.

VICTOR: I am probably going to die. That I can understand. You are going to spend the rest of your life fulfilling someone else's wishes that you do not understand. That, sir, is a state of mental chaos usually associated with purgatory. I pity you.

BERNARDO: Shut up.

VICTOR: I pity you like I would a diseased dog.

BERNARDO: I said shut up.

VICTOR: You are out of your element. Zastrozzi is the master of evil and you are just a thug.

BERNARDO: I am more than that, I know.

VICTOR: A thug. And a murderer. You cannot think of an imaginative way to kill me because you have no imagination. You stand there with a sword and threaten a man who is unarmed. That is the posture of a cheap murderer.

BERNARDO: I could use my hands. Would you feel better about that.

VICTOR: I am only thinking of you.

BERNARDO: (*throwing down the sword*) It will take a little longer this way.

> He approaches VICTOR.

I'm going to have to strangle you.

VICTOR: Well, it's not exactly inspired. But it's better than just cutting me down with a sword. Congratulations.

BERNARDO: Thank you.

VICTOR: But before you start, I have a confession to make.

VICTOR *quickly takes out the heavy object he has taken from the room in the previous scene and hits* BERNARDO *over the head.* BERNARDO *falls unconscious to the ground.*

I lied about not being armed.

VEREZZI *comes on, in a daze.*

VEREZZI: Victor. I'm glad you're here. I can't find any of my followers. They must have gotten lost.

VICTOR: (*pointing off*) No. There's one now.

VEREZZI *turns and* VICTOR *hits him over the head with his object.* VEREZZI *falls unconscious.* VICTOR *picks him up under the arms.*

A place to hide. Some place quiet. I have to think about what is happening to me. That vacant prison I saw this morning. (*dragging* VEREZZI *away*) What's this. He's smiling. Even in pain he smiles.

Blackout.

SCENE NINE

> ZASTROZZI's *room.* ZASTROZZI *is standing in the middle of the room, a blanket wrapped around him, shivering.*

ZASTROZZI: I am having a nightmare. It involves the final battle over control of the world between the forces of good and evil. It is the most terrifying nightmare I have ever had. Something so extremely unusual has happened that my mind in all its power cannot even begin to comprehend it. I am in charge of the forces of good. And I am winning. I think there is just the slightest possibility that there might be something wrong with my mind after all. The nightmare continues. I lead the forces of good with their toothy, God-obsessed smiles into the fortress of the commander of the forces of evil. We easily overcome the fortress and become gracious victors—not raping or murdering or even taking prisoners. We just smile and wish goodness and mercy to rain down on everyone. And I am smiling and wishing out loud for goodness and mercy as well except that inside I am deeply ill and feel like throwing up. And then we are taken to meet the commander of the forces of evil and he walks through a large wooden door and I see that he looks familiar. And he should. Because it is Zastrozzi. And even though I know that I am Zastrozzi I cannot help but feel extremely confused. And he reinforces this confusion when he opens his mouth and says, 'I am Zastrozzi.' At which point I feel myself smile even wider, so wide that I feel my skin tighten and I know that my face will become stuck forever like this in the widest, stupidest, most merciful and good smile ever worn by a human being. Then I die. But before I die I remember thinking—they are going to make me a saint. They are going to make me a Christian saint. The patron saint of smiles. The nightmare ends. I need a drink. I need to sit down. I need more than anything to stop having nightmares. They're getting worse every day. There might be something wrong with my mind. (*shivering*) The nightmare continues. Again. (*smiling*)

> MATILDA *comes on dragging a whip along the floor. She is furious.*

MATILDA: Zastrozzi! (*swinging the whip around above her head, cracking it*) Zastrozzi! I'm going to whip you. I'm going to whip you for making a fool out of me. For sending me to entrap a man who is an idiot and feels nothing except idiotic things.

Pause.

The nightmares. (*sighing and starting off, seeing him shaking*) No. (*turning back*) Zastrozzi, I have failed. Whip me.

ZASTROZZI: I can't be bothered. (*turning to her, smiling stupidly*)

MATILDA: Zastrozzi, you have a stupid empty smile on your face. Just like the one the idiot wears. You are standing there shivering under a blanket like a sick old man. You don't look like Zastrozzi. You look like an ass.

ZASTROZZI: (*trying to concentrate*) And now.

MATILDA: You are still shivering.

ZASTROZZI: (*closing his eyes and concentrating*) And now.

MATILDA: You are still smiling like an idiot.

ZASTROZZI: (*closing his eyes and concentrating*) Now? (*approaching her slowly*) Now?!

MATILDA: Now I feel like whipping you for threatening me.

MATILDA *begins to whip him. He doesn't move.*

Don't ever make a fool of me again. Don't ever threaten me again. Who do you think I am. I am not one of those who quiver when they hear your name. I am your match, sir. I am every bit your match.

MATILDA *throws the whip down.*

ZASTROZZI: Are you.

MATILDA: In every way.

ZASTROZZI: In every way?

MATILDA: Yes.

ZASTROZZI: Ah, well. You must know. And if you know then I must agree. Correct?

MATILDA: Yes. So you will let me stay? We'll be together?

ZASTROZZI: I'm afraid that's impossible.

MATILDA: Why.

ZASTROZZI: We're too much alike. You've just said so. I am in love with someone else.

MATILDA: Impossible.

ZASTROZZI: Life is strange, isn't it. I met her just a short while ago. She is quite different from me. That is probably why I love her. She is pure and innocent and possesses a marvellous gentle sensuality that I have never experienced before. In fact, just thinking about her arouses me. I am thinking about her now and I am getting aroused now.

> ZASTROZZI *grabs* MATILDA.

MATILDA: What are you doing.

ZASTROZZI: I am going to make love to you. Haven't you wanted me to for a long time.

MATILDA: Not while you are thinking about another woman.

ZASTROZZI: I'm sorry. But that is the way it must be.

MATILDA: I couldn't bear it.

ZASTROZZI: But you are a match for me in all ways. And I could bear it. I could even enjoy it. In fact that is the way people like us should enjoy it. Try to enjoy it.

MATILDA: I can't.

ZASTROZZI: Try.

MATILDA: No.

ZASTROZZI: Are you crying.

MATILDA: No.

ZASTROZZI: You are crying, aren't you.

MATILDA: No.

ZASTROZZI: Are you sure.

MATILDA: Yes.

ZASTROZZI: Are you crying.

MATILDA: Yes.

> ZASTROZZI *hits her and she is propelled across the room and falls.*

What are you doing.

ZASTROZZI: Making a point.

MATILDA: You treat me this way because I am a woman.

ZASTROZZI: Nonsense. Women, men, children, goats. I treat them all the same. I ask them to be answerable.

BERNARDO *walks on, his head bandaged.*

(*to* MATILDA) Here. I'll show you what I mean.

ZASTROZZI *walks over to* BERNARDO.

I take it from your wound that you have failed.

BERNARDO: Yes, I'm sorry.

ZASTROZZI: That's not necessary. I don't want you to feel sorry. I don't want you to feel anything. Do you understand.

BERNARDO: I think so.

ZASTROZZI: Try to understand. Try to feel nothing. Are you feeling nothing now.

BERNARDO: I'm not sure.

ZASTROZZI: Try. Feel nothing. Are you feeling nothing.

BERNARDO: Yes.

ZASTROZZI: Good.

ZASTROZZI *hits* BERNARDO*'s face viciously with the back of his hand.* BERNARDO *staggers back, but doesn't fall.*

Fall down when I hit you, Bernardo.

BERNARDO: Why.

ZASTROZZI: Because it makes it appear that you are resisting when you don't. And you have nothing to gain from resisting.

ZASTROZZI *hits* BERNARDO *again.* BERNARDO *staggers back but doesn't fall. He looks at* ZASTROZZI *and drops to his knees.*

Some advice for both of you. Get to know your limitations. Then remember that as you go through life there are only two things worth knowing. The first is too complex for you to understand. The second is that life is a series of totally arbitrary and often meaningless events and the only way to make sense of life is to forget that you know that. In other words, occupy yourselves. Matilda, go seduce Verezzi and if he is preoccupied remove his preoccupations. The plan to drive him to suicide is not the most inspired I have ever thought of but it will do to keep us occupied for a while. After you have done that, come looking for me and if I am in the mood we can play your silly whipping games. And as for you, Bernardo, go do something you at least understand.

Commit some foul, meaningless crime. That village girl you
mentioned earlier. Go abuse her and steal everything she
values. And enjoy it as much as possible because eventually
you will be made accountable. And now if you will excuse
me, I am going to visit the local prison. It hasn't been used in
years. But I'm sure it is still full of wondrous sensations. I do
some of my best thinking in prisons. Did you know that.

MATILDA: Yes.

BERNARDO: No.

ZASTROZZI: It's true though. I've visited some of the best prisons
in Europe. I find it invigorating. It helps to confirm my
sanity. Only a sane person could function in those places as
well as I do. Does that make sense.

BERNARDO: Yes.

MATILDA: No.

ZASTROZZI: You see I must visit these prisons. It is the only way
to make myself answerable. I have never been apprehended
and I never will be. So I have to voluntarily submit to a prison
in order to make myself experience judgement. When I have
experienced enough, I escape. Do you understand.

BERNARDO: Yes.

MATILDA: Yes.

ZASTROZZI: No, you don't.

ZASTROZZI *smiles and leaves.*

BERNARDO: He is crazy.

MATILDA: Of course he is. He has always been crazy.

BERNARDO: Not always.

MATILDA: How would you know. You are crazy yourself. For that
matter so am I. For wanting him the way I do. I should find a
more simple man.

BERNARDO *stands and goes to* MATILDA.

BERNARDO: I am a more simple man.

MATILDA: That's the problem. It is men like you who make me
want men like him.

BERNARDO: I could surprise you.

MATILDA: You would have to.

BERNARDO: I would like to make love to you.

MATILDA: I know.

BERNARDO: May I.

MATILDA: I will be thinking of Zastrozzi.

BERNARDO: I might surprise you.

MATILDA: Well, you can try at least.

> BERNARDO *grabs her and kisses her.*

Harder.

> *She grabs him savagely and kisses him.*
>
> *Blackout.*

SCENE TEN

For the first time the focus is on the full set. Stripped of all furnishings, it should appear like an old dungeon. BERNARDO *comes on pulling* JULIA, *whom he has chained at the wrists. He takes her into one of the chambers.*

JULIA: What are you doing this for.

BERNARDO: You smiled at me.

JULIA: It was just an invitation for polite conversation.

BERNARDO: What would that mean to me. What was I supposed to do after the conversation. Marry you? Settle into a wonderful, lawful, domestic life?

JULIA: I really had no plans beyond conversation, sir.

BERNARDO: You wouldn't. You spend too much time with civilized men. This will teach you never to smile at strangers.

JULIA: Have I offended you.

BERNARDO: No. I'm just accepting your invitation and using it in the only way I can.

JULIA: What are you going to do with me.

BERNARDO: Anything I please.

JULIA: What is this place. I've never been here.

BERNARDO: No, you wouldn't have. It's an old prison. It used to house the criminally deranged but now it's vacant. More or less. A friend of mine found it. He has a way of finding places like these. What do you think of it.

JULIA: It's horrible.

BERNARDO: Yes. It is, isn't it. It will do very nicely.

JULIA: For what.

BERNARDO: For whatever I please.

JULIA: You're going to rape me, aren't you. You're going to rape me and murder me.

BERNARDO: Not necessarily in that order, though.

JULIA: You appeared to be such a nice young man.

BERNARDO *grabs her hair.*

BERNARDO: Nice? What would I do if I was nice. If a pretty woman smiled at me and we had a polite conversation could I marry her and be lawful and decent? No, I wouldn't do that now. My mind would explode. Yet I am a man. When a woman smiles, I must do something. So I do what I am doing.

JULIA: You don't have to do this. Let me go. We'll start again from the beginning. We'll meet in the fresh air on a sunny day. Talk about healthy things. Develop a respectful attitude towards each other. Eventually fall in love on just the right terms.

BERNARDO: Impossible. You're not the woman I could be in love with.

JULIA: I could try.

BERNARDO: Impossible. I can tell from your smile. There is a woman I love, though, who could love me on the right terms. But she loves someone else. His name is Zastrozzi. Have you heard of him.

JULIA: I ... I think so.

BERNARDO: He is the one they talk about in whispers in your circles. I am the one who follows him around like a dog. (*starting off*)

JULIA: Where are you going.

BERNARDO: Back to your house. To rob it of everything of any value at all. And to kill your parents.

JULIA: Please don't.

BERNARDO: Why not. And give me a reason I can understand.

JULIA: They're dreadful people. You would only be putting them out of their misery.

BERNARDO: Not bad. That's interesting. So there is something else behind that civilized smile. I'll be back.

JULIA: If you leave me alone I'll scream until someone finds me.

BERNARDO: (*walking to her*) You shouldn't have said that. That was a mistake.

> BERNARDO *hits* JULIA. *She falls, unconscious. He unlocks the chain.*

She doesn't need these now. And I might have to use them. (*sadly*) I might want to use them. I might love to use them.

He leaves. In another corner of the set VICTOR *comes on carrying the unconscious* VEREZZI *on his shoulders. He takes him into a chamber, puts him down and examines his head.*

VICTOR: Perhaps I hit you too hard. You're barely breathing. Well, you were doomed anyway. At least this way you have a chance. (*looking around*) This place is horrible. But he'll be safe here I suppose. (*sitting*) Now what am I to do. The only way I can get him to run is to keep him unconscious and that's just not practical. I could leave him here and forget the whole matter. That's practical. Leave him here! Forget the whole matter! That's practical! But I did make that promise. And it's the only promise I've ever kept. I certainly didn't keep my promise to God. But I don't feel so bad about that, having met this Zastrozzi. If he is one of God's creatures then God must be used to disappointment. On the other hand, I just don't like the man. Everything he does, everything he represents unsettles me to the bone. Zastrozzi decides that an artist must be judged by someone so he kills him. Zastrozzi is to blame for his own mother's death in a crime of passion but hounds a poor lunatic because he cannot accept the blame himself. Zastrozzi steals, violates and murders on a regular basis, and remains perfectly sane. Verezzi commits one crime of passion then goes on a binge of mindless religious love and becomes moronic. Something is wrong. Something is unbalanced. I abhor violence. But I also abhor a lack of balance. It shows that the truth is missing somewhere. And it makes me feel very, very uneasy. Uneasy in a way I have not felt since I was … Yes, Verezzi, I will restore a truth to your lunatic mind and your lunatic world. (*taking* VEREZZI*'s sword*) Zastrozzi.

> VICTOR *exits.* JULIA *groans, she slowly regains consciousness and gets up. She makes her way around the dungeon, sees* VEREZZI *and goes to him. She kneels down and takes his pulse.*

JULIA: What's happening to me. I go for a series of walks in the street. Smile at two young men. One of them tells me he is a visionary. The other one abducts me and tells me he is going to rape and murder me, not necessarily in that order. Then he hits me like he would a man and knocks me unconscious. I wake up and find the young man who thinks he is a visionary lying on the ground bleeding to death from a head wound. What's happening to me.

MATILDA *enters.*

MATILDA: You must be the virgin. The one with the marvellous, gentle sensuality.

JULIA: Who are you.

MATILDA: My name is Matilda. I am your competition. I have a sensuality which is not the least bit gentle.

JULIA: Really. What do you want.

MATILDA: I want to kill all the virgins in the world.

JULIA: Oh no. What's happening to me.

MATILDA: Unfortunately for you, we are both in love with the same man.

JULIA: (*pointing to* VEREZZI) Him? I don't love him. I don't even like him.

MATILDA: Not him. Zastrozzi.

JULIA: I've heard of him. He's the one who is whispered about in polite society.

MATILDA: He is the evil genius of all Europe. A criminal. And I am a criminal too. We belong together. So we must fight and I must kill you.

JULIA: Why can't I just leave.

MATILDA: That won't do. Besides, I will enjoy killing you. It is women like you who make me look like a tart.

JULIA: Nonsense. It's the way you dress.

MATILDA: Stand up, you mindless virgin.

JULIA: (*standing*) Madame, I am neither mindless nor a virgin. I am merely a victim of bizarre circumstance. A product of healthy civilization thrown into a jungle of the deranged.

MATILDA: Yes, get angry. You are better when you are angry. If I were a man I would seduce you on the spot.

JULIA: That's perverse!

MATILDA *takes a knife from under her skirts.*

MATILDA: Yes, get indignant. You are quite provocative when you are upset. Take off your clothes.

JULIA: Why.

MATILDA: We are going to make love.

JULIA: Oh no, we are not.

MATILDA: Yes, get confused. You are quite ridiculous when you are confused. And it is exactly the way someone like you should die. (*advances*)

JULIA: What are you doing.

MATILDA: We are going to fight. And we are only going to stop fighting when one of us is dead.

JULIA: I would rather not. I would rather discuss some other possibility. I'm only seventeen years old. People tell me I have so much to live for.

MATILDA: Oh. Name something worth living for and I might spare your life.

JULIA: But how could I. A woman like you could never appreciate what I think is worth living for. No offence. But take your dress for example. I would live to dress much better than that.

MATILDA: You mindless, coy, disgusting virgin!

> MATILDA *attacks and they struggle. The knife falls and* JULIA *scrambles after it.* MATILDA *leaps on her and somehow* MATILDA *is stabbed. She falls over dead.* JULIA *feels her pulse.*

JULIA: Dead. Oh my God. (*standing*) What is happening to me. First a victim. Now a murderer! And I don't even know her. This is grossly unfair. I'm young. I've had the proper education. My future was a pleasant rosy colour. I could see it in my head. It was a rosy colour. Very pretty. This is truly grossly unfair.

> BERNARDO *comes in. He sees* MATILDA*'s body and rushes to it.*

BERNARDO: You killed her.

JULIA: I had no choice. She attacked me.

BERNARDO: She was the only woman I could have been in love with on the right terms. You have blocked out my future.

JULIA: I'm sorry. But she didn't love you anyway. She loved that Zastrozzi.

BERNARDO: You have closed off my life from my brain. It is exploding!

JULIA: Well, if you'll pardon me expressing an opinion, I think she was not entirely a rational person. Not at all the kind of person you need. You are not a rational person either and you would be better off with someone who could tame your tendency towards violence. If you'll pardon my opinion, I mean.

> BERNARDO *approaches her.*

What are you going to do.

BERNARDO: Stay still.

JULIA: (*backing away*) No. This isn't fair. I shouldn't be involved in any of this. I didn't love him. I didn't hate her. I've only a strange and vague recollection of this Zastrozzi. And all I did was smile at you.

BERNARDO: Stay very still.

JULIA: Please.

> BERNARDO *strangles her.* ZASTROZZI *appears out of the darkness.*

ZASTROZZI: Bernardo.

> BERNARDO *drops* JULIA, *who falls to the floor lifeless. He turns to face* ZASTROZZI.

Another victim, Bernardo?

BERNARDO: She murdered Matilda.

ZASTROZZI: She was merely defending herself.

BERNARDO: You saw?

ZASTROZZI: I have been here for hours.

BERNARDO: Why didn't you do something.

ZASTROZZI: I was preoccupied.

BERNARDO: Matilda is dead.

ZASTROZZI: I didn't know you had such deep feelings for her.

BERNARDO: It wouldn't have mattered to you. You only have one thought. Well, there he is. Verezzi the Italian. Take him. I am going to bury Matilda.

ZASTROZZI: Verezzi will wait. You are not going anywhere. You have to face your judgement.

BERNARDO: It will come.

ZASTROZZI: It has.

BERNARDO: From you?

ZASTROZZI: Is there anyone better at it.

BERNARDO: Judgement for what exactly.

ZASTROZZI: For all your crimes. All the people you have murdered have spoken to me in my nightmares and asked that you be made answerable.

BERNARDO: I am just a student to the master.

ZASTROZZI: And only the master is qualified to judge. Draw your sword, Bernardo. Let us have the formality of a contest. But know now that you are dead.

BERNARDO: Sir. Let me go.

ZASTROZZI: No.

> ZASTROZZI *draws his sword.* BERNARDO *draws his. They fight. Viciously. Expertly.* BERNARDO *is good.* ZASTROZZI *is the master though, and eventually he pierces* BERNARDO*'s chest.* BERNARDO *drops to his knees.*

BERNARDO: Sir.

ZASTROZZI: You are dead.

> ZASTROZZI *knocks* BERNARDO *over with his foot.* BERNARDO *is dead.* ZASTROZZI *walks over to* VEREZZI *and stands silently looking down at him for a while, then sits down and cradles* VEREZZI*'s head.*

Verezzi. Finally. Not dying at all. It's just a flesh wound. Your breathing becomes stronger. Soon you will wake up. I want you to be awake for this. It would have been more satisfying to have you destroy yourself. But you are too clever for that. Everyone thinks you are out of your mind. But I know you have just been hiding. Hiding from your crimes, Verezzi. Hiding from the crime of telling people you are giving them gifts from God. The crime of letting them think there is happiness in that stupid smile of yours. The crime of making language pleasantly vague and painting with distorted imagination. The crime of disturbing the natural condition in which the dark side prevails. Wake up, Verezzi. Zastrozzi is here to prove that you must be judged. You can hide no more.

A VOICE : And what is Zastrozzi hiding from.

> ZASTROZZI *stands.*

ZASTROZZI: What do you want.

> VICTOR *comes out of the darkness carrying* VEREZZI*'s sabre.*

VICTOR: Sir. Tell me. What is this about. (*looking around*) All this death.

ZASTROZZI: It is a continuing process of simplification. I am simplifying my life. These people came here to be judged.

VICTOR: By you?

ZASTROZZI: Is there anyone better at it.

VICTOR: Apparently not. Well then, I too want to be judged by Zastrozzi, who judges for a profession.

ZASTROZZI: Then step closer.

VICTOR: Is there a fee.

ZASTROZZI: Yes. But I take it from you quickly. You'll never even know it's gone.

VICTOR: I have another idea. I think a man who enjoys his profession as much as you should be the one to pay the fee.

ZASTROZZI: Perhaps. But I have never met anyone who would collect from me.

VICTOR: You have now, sit.

ZASTROZZI: I doubt it very much. You don't even hold your weapon properly.

VICTOR: I have an unorthodox style. But it serves.

ZASTROZZI: Let's see.

> *He draws his sword.* VICTOR *begins a short prayer in Latin which* ZASTROZZI *finishes for him.* VICTOR *looks at* ZASTROZZI. *Pause.*

(*in German*) Did you not know that I could see into your heart.

VICTOR: (*in any Romance language*) Yes. But I can see into your heart as well.

ZASTROZZI: (*in the same Romance language*) Then it will be an interesting battle.

> *Pause.*

VICTOR: So.

ZASTROZZI: So.

> *They approach each other, cross swords and begin to fight. The fight will continue and move across the entire stage at least once.*

ZASTROZZI tests VICTOR. He responds well but his moves are very unusual. VICTOR will gradually get better by observing ZASTROZZI's moves.

What are all these strange things you are doing designed for.

VICTOR: To keep me alive.

ZASTROZZI: Eventually I will find a way to penetrate your unorthodox style.

VICTOR: That might be difficult. Since I am making it up as I go along.

ZASTROZZI: You look silly.

VICTOR: But I am alive.

ZASTROZZI: Perhaps more alive than you have ever been. That is sometimes the way a person faces death.

VICTOR: I intend to live.

ZASTROZZI: Then you should have taken my advice and become an ordinary man.

VICTOR: Sir. The point is that I am an ordinary man.

ZASTROZZI: An ordinary man does not challenge Zastrozzi.

ZASTROZZI attacks him viciously. VICTOR defends himself well.

VICTOR: I am still alive. I am still waiting to be judged.

ZASTROZZI: And growing arrogant as well.

VICTOR: You talk about arrogance. The man who kills on a whim. Who kills an artist simply because he is mediocre. Who commits crimes against people because he believes he is the thing to which they must be answerable.

ZASTROZZI: They must be answerable to something.

VICTOR: There is always God, you know.

ZASTROZZI: I am an atheist. If a man who is an atheist believes that people must be answerable, he has a duty to make them answerable to something.

VICTOR: Answerable to your own demented personality.

ZASTROZZI: I am what they are. They answer to themselves.

VICTOR: All right, forget God. A man is responsible to humanity.

ZASTROZZI: And I am part of humanity.

VICTOR: The irresponsible part.

ZASTROZZI: No. It is my responsibility to spread out like a disease and purge. And by destroying everything make everything safe.

VICTOR: Explain exactly what you mean by safe.

ZASTROZZI: Alive. Untouched by expectation. Free of history. Free of religion. Free of everything. And soon to be free of you.

> ZASTROZZI *attacks and* VICTOR *defends himself very well.*

VICTOR: I am still alive.

ZASTROZZI: But you are totally on the defensive.

VICTOR: I don't have to kill you. I only have to survive. By merely surviving I neutralize you.

ZASTROZZI: You cannot neutralize something you do not understand.

VICTOR: We are approaching a new century, and with it a new world. There will be no place in it for your attitude, your behaviour.

ZASTROZZI: This new world, what do you suppose it will be like.

VICTOR: Better.

ZASTROZZI: Describe what you mean by better.

VICTOR: More humane. More civilized.

ZASTROZZI: Wrong. Better is when the truth is understood. Understanding the truth is understanding that the force of darkness is constant.

VICTOR: No, it is not. Your time is over.

ZASTROZZI: Wrong again.

> ZASTROZZI *attacks him viciously.* VICTOR *defends himself and is ebullient.*

VICTOR: I am alive! Everything I said was true. You are neutralized. I am the emissary of goodness in the battle between good and evil. I have found God again.

> VICTOR *lunges forward wildly.*

> ZASTROZZI *plunges his sabre through* VICTOR*'s heart.*

I am alive.

VICTOR *falls down and dies.*

ZASTROZZI: Ah, Victor. You understood what was in your heart. But you did not know your limitations.

> ZASTROZZI *throws down his sabre.* VEREZZI *groans and slowly wakes up. He sits, then stands, while* ZASTROZZI *watches him.* VEREZZI *staggers around looking at the bodies and slowly regaining his equilibrium.*

VEREZZI: Look at all these dead people. What happened.

ZASTROZZI: A series of unfortunate accidents.

VEREZZI: Who are you.

ZASTROZZI: Zastrozzi.

> VEREZZI *freezes.*

VEREZZI: I thought you didn't exist.

ZASTROZZI: Nonsense. You know me well.

VEREZZI: Are you responsible for all these dead people.

ZASTROZZI: No. You are.

VEREZZI: That's quite impossible. I am a servant of God.

ZASTROZZI: You are dead.

> ZASTROZZI *has drawn a knife.*

VEREZZI: What are you going to do.

ZASTROZZI: Cut open your stomach.

VEREZZI: You can't. I'm immune. I am in touch with Him. Protected by Him. Loved by Him.

> VEREZZI *closes his eyes.* ZASTROZZI *approaches him.*

You can't hurt me. I'll just wait here. Nothing will happen.

ZASTROZZI: Do you feel anything.

VEREZZI: Yes.

ZASTROZZI: Do you feel fear.

VEREZZI: Yes.

ZASTROZZI: Now who am I.

VEREZZI: Zastrozzi.

ZASTROZZI: And what is Zastrozzi.

VEREZZI: The devil.

ZASTROZZI: Nonsense. What is he.

VEREZZI: A man.

ZASTROZZI: What kind of man.

VEREZZI: I don't know.

ZASTROZZI: A sane man. What kind of man.

VEREZZI: A sane man.

ZASTROZZI: And what kind of man are you.

VEREZZI: I don't know.

ZASTROZZI: You feel fear when you are about to be murdered. And you are no longer smiling. You are a sane man too. From this moment on and forever. Do you understand. Perfectly sane and very, very afraid.

VEREZZI: Yes.

ZASTROZZI: Now get going.

VEREZZI: Where.

ZASTROZZI: You have to hide. I am giving you a day and I am coming after you. And do you know why I am coming after you.

VEREZZI: No.

ZASTROZZI: Because it will keep me preoccupied. Now leave. And hide well. I wish to be preoccupied for a long time.

> VEREZZI *slowly leaves.* ZASTROZZI *looks at all the corpses.*

(*smiling*) I like it here. Sad. No. I like it here. (*He takes a cape off one of the corpses and wraps himself with it*) I think I'll visit here again. It will help me stay sane.

> *Pause.*

Yes. I like it here.

> *Blackout.*

> *End.*

Theatre of the Film Noir

Theatre of the Film Noir was first produced by the Factory Theatre for Onstage '81, Toronto's International Festival, in 1981 with following cast:

INSPECTOR CLAIR   Steven Bush
BERNARD   David Bolt
LILLIANE   Susan Purdy
ERIC   Jim Henshaw
HANK   Peter Blais

Director: George F. Walker
Set Designer: Jim Plaxton
Costumes and Set Decor: Peter Blais
Music composed by: John Roby
Stage Manager: Renee Shouten

Persons
INSPECTOR CLAIR, a police detective
BERNARD, a civilian clerk
LILLIANE, a former shop girl
ERIC, a German soldier
HANK, an American soldier

Place
Paris.

Time
1944.

Theatre of the Film Noir

SCENE ONE

Under a street lamp, INSPECTOR CLAIR. *His hands deep in the pockets of his coat.*

INSPECTOR: The war is over. For us. But the evidence of war is everywhere. Some of the wounded are walking around. Pretending to function. Behaviour has no recognizable pattern. Morality is a question of circumstance. And guilt a matter of degree. For a police detective like myself this is not an easy time. I am used to a precise definition of my job. I am used to a pattern of behaviour, a clear consensus of morality and a belief in absolute guilt. For over five years I have been doing my job in a kind of fog. It's time I made it go away. It's time I stopped pretending to function. (*lights a cigarette*) On the night of the very day the liberation army marched into this city a young man was killed on a back street not too far from here. He was brutally murdered under the fog of recent circumstance. While thousands of people were celebrating freedom he fell down with a bullet in his stomach and bled to death. It's an interesting case. It could go any number of ways. It's supposed to be a case which cannot be solved. That's why they gave it to me. I specialize in difficult mysteries. I think I'm going to begin specializing in just making things clear. (*looks around*) Paris. The fall of 1944.

Blackout.

SCENE TWO

Graveyard. BERNARD *is on his hands and knees searching for something on the ground. Muttering to himself.*

BERNARD: I've lost it. Jesus Christ, come help me. I've lost it.

He mumbles, groans, whines. Suddenly something on the ground catches his eye.

What's that.

He whines, groans, whimpers. He crawls quickly along the ground. Stops. Picks up a small coin. Sighs, giggles.

Where have you been. I was sick with worry. Now go back where you belong. (*puts the coin in his pocket*) And never try to escape again. Is my life cheap to you.

There is an open grave a few feet away from him. A wooden casket on the ground beside it. He walks over to it. Addresses the casket.

I found it. I'll be all right now.

Sits on the casket, lights a cigarette.

I know you'd be laughing. And I know what you'd be saying. 'Bernard, you're a superstitious fool.' (*takes a drag on the cigarette*) Ah well, what of it. I found that coin the day the Nazis invaded. God whispered strangely in my ear. Here's a little two-headed coin for you, Bernard. A little token of my affection that will see you through the dark times ahead. It was one of those rare moments when God chose subtlety instead of outright terror. Nevertheless the point was well taken and I have kept this with me at all times. I know you'd be laughing, Jean. But I have been shot at with pistols, rifles, machine guns and cannons and I am still alive. True, I am a coward. But I am alive. (*crushes his cigarette, stands*) And you are dead. You should have let God whisper in your ear. You should have let him give you a coin. You should have learned to run and hide like me.

He opens the casket, takes out a bottle of wine, takes a long drink, puts the bottle back in the casket, closes the lid.

Blackout.

SCENE THREE

LILLIANE*'s apartment.* LILLIANE *is sitting.* INSPECTOR CLAIR *is standing.*

INSPECTOR: You don't mind if I ask you a few questions?

LILLIANE: No. But I've already told several other policemen everything I know.

INSPECTOR: Of course. But this is such an unusual case … I'm sorry I didn't notice, you have your coat on. Were you on your way out. I mean you did get the message that I was coming.

LILLIANE: Actually I just got in.

INSPECTOR: Really. I must have missed you.

LILLIANE: What was that.

INSPECTOR: On my way into your building I met an old friend. He kept me in conversation for almost an hour.

LILLIANE: I came in the back way.

INSPECTOR: Of course. You have a back entrance. That must have been very helpful over the past little while.

LILLIANE: What do you mean.

INSPECTOR: Well the war, the occupation made everyone so tense. So suspicious. It was difficult for an attractive young person … to go about her business.

LILLIANE: I've never paid any attention to other people's opinions of me.

INSPECTOR: Good for you. And you have no political activity.

LILLIANE: No. Unless you consider the business of survival a political activity.

INSPECTOR: Under the circumstances, perhaps.

LILLIANE: It would be easy to say I was in the resistance. So many people are saying that now, I know. But I was scared. Scared of starvation.

INSPECTOR: Well no matter what we did or did not do for whatever reason, I suppose we must all begin again somehow.

LILLIANE: If we can.

INSPECTOR: Yes. Which unfortunately brings us back to your brother's death.

LILLIANE: The Communists killed him.

INSPECTOR: So you said in your statement. Because they suspected he was a spy, is that right.

LILLIANE: Yes.

INSPECTOR: But you didn't say why they suspected that.

LILLIANE: Because I didn't know. Jean didn't tell me.

INSPECTOR: He just told you that he was suspected.

LILLIANE: He said they were giving him a rough time. He was afraid of them.

INSPECTOR: That's all he told you. What I'm saying is, did he actually tell you they suspected him of spying on them.

LILLIANE: That's what they fear most. That's what they always assume. I know how they are.

INSPECTOR: You've had personal experience with them.

LILLIANE: I have friends who were with Communists.

INSPECTOR: You do?

LILLIANE: Friends of friends. I gave the names already.

INSPECTOR: Yes. None of them were helpful. By the time we reached them none of them were even Communists. Affiliations change so rapidly these days. One of these former Communists was also a known collaborator with the Nazis. He is now very friendly with the Americans. Ah, well. I suppose he too is just trying to survive.

LILLIANE: I survived without affiliations.

INSPECTOR: Good for you. On the night Jean was killed, he visited here. Correct?

LILLIANE: We had dinner. We talked.

INSPECTOR: Yes. Your apartment is so cozy. So safe. It was a nice relaxing evening?

LILLIANE: He was tense. He was going to that rally.

INSPECTOR: He expected trouble.

LILLIANE: There was always trouble. The Communists attracted it like flies.

INSPECTOR: But this time Jean wouldn't know which side his trouble would be coming from. Did he go to the meeting alone.

LILLIANE: Someone picked him up.

INSPECTOR: Who.

LILLIANE: I don't know. There was a knock on the door. Jean answered it. Grabbed his coat and left. I didn't see who it was.

INSPECTOR: None of this was in your statement.

LILLIANE: None of these questions were asked.

INSPECTOR: Of course. Well, even the police department is in the process of rebuilding.

LILLIANE: But you are not new at this.

INSPECTOR: Oh, no. No, I'm not new. I still make mistakes, though. Is that chocolate in your pocket.

LILLIANE: Yes. Would you like a piece.

INSPECTOR: Please.

She hands it to him. He breaks off a piece.

American chocolate.

LILLIANE: English.

INSPECTOR: I thought only American soldiers had this.

LILLIANE: English chocolate, Inspector. From a Free French soldier. They give it out freely. They give it to anyone. They give it to old women, young men, children. They just laugh and give it to you for no reason.

INSPECTOR: Good for them. Well. The problem is we've talked to the Communists. They say they liked Jean. They say he had just been elected to a responsible position in the party. Their position does not make things easy.

LILLIANE: They're lying.

INSPECTOR: Perhaps. But they lie so well. In any event, it does not make things easy.

LILLIANE: Did you expect they would be.

INSPECTOR: No.

He hands her the rest of the chocolate.

Can I visit you again. I might have more questions.

LILLIANE: Any time.

She offers the chocolate to him. He smiles. Takes it.

INSPECTOR: Thank you. In the meantime good luck. What are your plans.

LILLIANE: I'm not going anywhere.

INSPECTOR: I meant for work.

LILLIANE: I have a friend who knows an American soldier who makes films. I would like to be an actress.

INSPECTOR: Be careful of that kind of American film.

LILLIANE: I love American films.

INSPECTOR: Yes, but … Never mind. You would be very good in films, I'm sure. I hope you get the chance.

LILLIANE: I will. I've made my mind up.

INSPECTOR: I'll show myself out.

LILLIANE: Be careful. The stairway is very dark.

INSPECTOR: In that case, perhaps I should let myself out the back.

LILLIANE: No.

Blackout.

SCENE FOUR

Graveyard. BERNARD *is sitting on the coffin. Tossing his coin.*

BERNARD: Heads I stay. Tails I don't go. (*flips the coin, looks, frowns*) Tails I stay. Heads I don't go. (*flips it*)

LILLIANE *appears. Some distance away.*

LILLIANE: Bernard.

BERNARD: Over here.

LILLIANE: Why can't you come here.

BERNARD: I'm not moving. I'm standing guard.

LILLIANE *hesitates then starts slowly toward him.*

LILLIANE: You scared me on the telephone.

BERNARD: I didn't say anything.

LILLIANE: That's what scared me. So mysterious.

BERNARD: I was drunk. I got carried away.

LILLIANE *stops when she sees the casket.*

LILLIANE: What's that.

BERNARD: Coffin.

LILLIANE: That's Jean's coffin, Bernard. What are you doing with it.

BERNARD: I dug it up.

LILLIANE: Why.

BERNARD: Jean's still inside it. I checked. So that part of it's all right. No mistake there.

LILLIANE: I don't understand.

BERNARD: Well, they sometimes forget to put the body inside. And when that happens and they find it in the back room they just throw it in the Seine.

LILLIANE: That's ridiculous.

BERNARD: The truth is the dead are very light. Four or five kilos at the most.

LILLIANE: You're still drunk, aren't you.

BERNARD: Extremely. (*grins*)

LILLIANE: I don't think it's funny.

BERNARD: Neither do I.

LILLIANE: Then why are you smiling.

BERNARD: I'm drunk.

LILLIANE: Why did you dig up my brother's body.

BERNARD: His funeral was obscene.

LILLIANE: I beg your pardon.

BERNARD: When the priest was delivering the eulogy I got a hard-on.

LILLIANE: You're degenerate.

BERNARD: That's what I thought at first. Then I looked around. Everyone had a hard-on. The priest. The pallbearers. The choirboys. The concierge. And do you know who had the biggest hard-on of all. Your mother. I didn't even know your mother had a cock.

LILLIANE: What in the hell are you talking about.

BERNARD: The funeral was obscene and it made me hallucinate. I want another chance to pay my respects properly. I want another funeral.

LILLIANE: That's impossible.

BERNARD: You're right. That's not why I dug him up. I did it because I was lonely.

LILLIANE: I know. Do you want to come home with me for a while.

BERNARD: Don't look at me like that. That's not why either. The truth is this. I want an autopsy.

LILLIANE: You're not making any sense. You're just upset. I understand—

BERNARD: I want a fucking autopsy!

LILLIANE: I'm going home. (*starts off*)

BERNARD: No, don't go. Please listen. There's something wrong.

LILLIANE: (*stops*) Go ahead.

BERNARD: (*looks around*) The ghouls are out tonight. I can sense them. I must be mad to be out with the ghouls. They might not know that I'm a helpless coward. They might think I'm looking for trouble. Listen ghouls, leave me alone, I'm harmless. Lilliane, is that pity in your eyes.

LILLIANE: Jean used to say you'd be lost without him.

BERNARD: Jean had confidence. It was sometimes annoying. Do you suppose that's why they killed him.

LILLIANE: Who.

BERNARD: Standing on top of that barricade. His clothes so tight against his body. His head above the smoke. His clothes so tight. His trousers especially. That's why I got a hard-on at the funeral. I could imagine the way he was filling out his trousers when he was killed. Jean had the best body in the Communist Party. There was a Free French radio operator who had an even better body. But Jean had the best of the Communists. As for his mind, well, it was all right. Your average nineteen-year-old. With idealism and a touch of stupidity mixed together. But we have to find out why they killed him in memory of his body.

LILLIANE: You think the Party killed him, don't you.

BERNARD: They wanted to make him a martyr. They knew he was too stupid to be of any other use to them.

LILLIANE: He wasn't stupid.

BERNARD: Did you love him.

LILLIANE: Yes, of course.

BERNARD: What did you love about him.

LILLIANE: He was my brother.

BERNARD: That's what you loved about him? That's just loving yourself.

LILLIANE: I don't want to listen to your drunken philosophy.

BERNARD: Then why did you come here. Does a sober man invite a person to a graveyard at midnight.

LILLIANE: You made it sound important.

BERNARD: Did you sleep with Jean.

LILLIANE: No.

BERNARD: He told me you did. I believed him.

LILLIANE: He was lying.

BERNARD: I still believe him. But what's that mean. I'm so stupid. Almost as stupid as Jean.

LILLIANE: He wasn't stupid! He had a wonderful mind.

BERNARD: It's disgusting and ridiculous that you could love his mind, that you could miss his mind and not miss his body. I loved his mouth, his thighs and his ass, and we both loved his cock.

LILLIANE: If it's none of my business how you loved him it's none of yours how I loved him.

BERNARD: My only contact with the outside was your brother. Now that he's gone it's just a matter of time before I slip back in to my hole. I've been hiding in basements for years learning how to speak English so I could ingratiate myself with the liberation army. I've seen the Americans and they scare me as much as the Nazis. I know they hate queers. I can tell by the way they chew their gum when I walk by. The truth is I thought … (*he mumbles something*)

LILLIANE: What was that.

BERNARD: I thought that you and I could get married and live a life of convenience.

> *She smiles.*

Well give it some thought. I'd get a certain respectability from you. And you could take eternal satisfaction from being around the only other person Jean was intimate with.

LILLIANE: You're joking.

BERNARD: I don't think the Communists killed Jean. They didn't want him to be a martyr. Martyrs are no longer considered useful. I don't want an autopsy. That wouldn't be useful.

LILLIANE: Then what do you want.

BERNARD: For you to marry me. And someday love me.

LILLIANE: And that's why you dug Jean's body up.

BERNARD: Oh no. Well, I'm not behaving rationally. The truth is I wanted to kiss him. You see dead people don't turn cold. You see, when I kissed his lips they were warm. Even a bit wet.

LILLIANE: Well, whatever. Even if you've gone insane I suppose you deserve an answer. I won't marry you of course. And now you should bury my brother. (*starts off*)

BERNARD: But I have other things to say to you. The Communists didn't kill Jean. I don't want an autopsy. You won't marry me. I am a weak and cowardly man. There it is so clear and simple. But I still have other things to say to you.

LILLIANE: (*circling him in the darkness*) Maybe we'll talk again sometime.

BERNARD: But why did you come in the first place. Have you forgotten.

LILLIANE: Because you said it was important.

BERNARD: Yes. We've been through that. Because I was Jean's closest friend. And now you're leaving. Aren't I still Jean's closest friend.

LILLIANE: Jean's dead, Bernard.

BERNARD: And wasn't he dead when I talked to you on the phone.

LILLIANE: Goodbye.

BERNARD: Yes, he was. How silly. And yet you're leaving. Didn't you hear me. Just before I hung up. You weren't sure what I said, were you. And since I didn't bring it up you assumed I never really said it. But I did say it, Lilliane. I said—'Eric.' (*She stops. He goes to the casket. Takes out the bottle*) What are you doing out there in the darkness. If I were you I'd be scared half to death. All those ghouls out there and this drunken irrational fool over here. What a choice. (*She is walking back toward him*) Paris had just been liberated. Jean and I had stayed up the whole night celebrating. Making love and drinking. There was a certain potential for happiness that evening. Suddenly he turned to me and said, 'My sister has a lover. He's a German soldier. She's hiding him in her apartment.'

LILLIANE: I understand that you're lonely and that you don't know what to do with yourself. I know you don't have any money. I have a little that I could give you. It's not much.

BERNARD: No, it's not.

LILLIANE: What do you intend to do. Report me?

BERNARD: Well, I'm duty-bound of course. A patriotic Frenchman, a friend of the liberators, disgusted and shocked that a French lady of apparent taste and active conscience has taken in an enemy of all mankind. Taken him inside her night after night and hidden him from the forces of justice.

LILLIANE: You're vermin. The biggest coward in Europe. Pissing in a private hole since the war began. Protecting your own skin and nothing more. Save your disgust for yourself. You have no right to judge me.

BERNARD: Certainly true. However, it's the ideal that's important. Realistically I'm a self-serving mouse but ideally I am an enemy of fascism and a supporter of freedom. We are in a temporary state of peace. In times of peace, self-serving idealists surface and do well.

LILLIANE: But you don't know him. Eric is not like the rest. He's a good man.

BERNARD: And a terrific lover.

LILLIANE: You're obsessive. Your mind is disturbed. Even before I met you I wondered what Jean could see in you. After I met you I wondered even more. If he had to sleep with a man he could have done better without much effort.

BERNARD: I wondered about you as well. Jean talked about you. 'She lives an abstract life. Very introspective.' From the little he told me I tried to imagine what you looked like. What your apartment looked like. When I met you I wasn't surprised. But when I saw your apartment it seemed all wrong. Too big. It seemed like you were waiting for someone to share it with you. When Jean told me about Eric I would imagine how well he fit in your apartment. I saw him sitting in that big chair in the corner with his long legs stretched out in front of him. I saw him in your bed beside you, snuggling up against you. His legs wrapped around you. I imagined in incredible detail with colours and sounds and odours. I used to get very excited thinking about you and your apartment and Eric. I don't know why. The notion of a man and woman making love does not usually arouse me. I suppose it's because I knew Jean had made love to you and that he wanted to make love to Eric. Jean was such a ridiculous bastard. No discipline. No control over all those ridiculous adolescent cravings. Fucking an aging neurotic and his own sister and wanting to fuck his sister's Nazi lover. Such a fine ridiculous boy.

He approaches her.

We have to find out who killed him, Lilliane. Who put that sickening hole in his head and made his body crumple like garbage.

LILLIANE: Stay away from me, Bernard—

BERNARD *stops.*

BERNARD: Was I scaring you.

LILLIANE: No.

BERNARD: Oh. (*turns around*) How kind of you to stay with me when I'm drunk. Jean was right. You're very abstract and introspective.

LILLIANE: Are you going to report me and Eric.

BERNARD: I take that back. You're not at all abstract and introspective. You're brutal and realistic. Why are you talking about that. Why aren't you talking about your brother.

LILLIANE: He's dead!

BERNARD: But only for a week. His lips are almost wet. Even I know that to mourn properly you mourn longer than a week. Until the lips become dry. I read somewhere that that takes a month. Promise me you'll swear off everything for at least a month, Lilliane. Show us that you really loved him. Stop acting like a whore. Well, at least buy a black handkerchief for God's sake.

LILLIANE: I owe you no explanations. Jean was a dear and lovely boy. I loved him in many ways. Eric and I met by accident and became fond of each other by accident.

BERNARD: Yes. Tell me about Eric.

LILLIANE: No. It's none of your business.

BERNARD: Jean fought against the Germans.

LILLIANE: But could have been killed by the Communists.

BERNARD: But could have been killed by the Comm—! But fought against the Germans! There's a moral issue involved here.

LILLIANE: Jean knew. He said nothing.

BERNARD: Because he wanted to fuck Eric!

LILLIANE: You're disgusting!

BERNARD: Now he couldn't fuck—fuck Eric if Eric was locked up somewhere could he!

LILLIANE: You're disgusting, Bernard!

BERNARD: I am the moral conscience of the day.

LILLIANE: Oh?

BERNARD: Moral conscience! I am seeking justice. I will report you and your pretty German lover in his long tight trousers. I will go as a patriotic Frenchman and a friend of the liberators fluent in their language disguising my queerness as I walk past them chewing gum like they do and I will report your dangerous evil life with the German enemy of all mankind in incredible detail including colours, sounds and odours!

LILLIANE *turns away.*

Blackout.

A bistro. HANK, *a young American soldier, is sitting on a stool. Playing an old guitar. Singing a blues song. He is drunk.* ERIC *sits at a table. His head is bowed. The collar of his overcoat up. His hands cupped around a drink on the table.*

HANK: (*sings*)   Black and blue
                     Black
                     And blue
                     Empty house
                     Nothing to do
                     Dead old friends
                     And besides
                     I'm black all over
                     And blue inside

                     Black and blue
                     Blue inside
                     Got no future
                     That's all right
                     Baby's gone
                     Outta my life
                     Mama's gone too
                     Black all over
                     Black and blue

ERIC *looks up sheepishly.* HANK *catches his eye.* ERIC *claps hands twice. Then a third time.*

HANK: Thanks.

     ERIC *looks down.*

Hey.

     ERIC *looks up.*

Thanks.

     ERIC *nods. Looks down.*

Hey.

     ERIC *looks up.*

Thanks.

     ERIC *looks down.*

Hey.

ERIC *looks up.*

Hi ...

HANK *falls off the stool.* ERIC *looks down.*

Ah, fuck. (*struggles to his feet*) Jesus. (*looks at* ERIC) You liked that song?

ERIC: (*quietly*) Very nice.

HANK: What.

ERIC: (*whispering*) Very nice.

HANK *moves toward* ERIC.

HANK: Why are you whispering.

ERIC *shrugs.*

You liked that song?

ERIC *nods.* HANK *sits down at* ERIC*'s table.*

You wanna whisper some more? It's all right. Don't let the uniform scare you. Why does this uniform scare so many people. It's American. It's supposed to make you happy. You like this uniform.

ERIC: (*whispering*) Very nice.

HANK: What.

ERIC: Yes.

HANK: Yeah? You want it? They're going to take it away soon anyway. You want it?

ERIC *shakes his head.*

Court martial coming up. Conduct detrimental. Don't tell anyone.

He grabs ERIC*'s hand.*

Don't tell anyone.

ERIC *shakes his head.*

In the meantime I'm hanging around. This is a lousy place to hang around. You wanna hang around some other place. Or maybe you like this place. Do you like this place.

ERIC: Very nice.

HANK: Very nice. (*laughs*) Jesus. No, it's not. Jesus!

LILLIANE comes in. ERIC *sees her.* HANK *follows* ERIC*'s eyes to*
LILLIANE. LILLIANE *goes to the table.* HANK *stands, knocking over his
chair. Picks it up. Looks at* LILLIANE *and* ERIC *who are looking at each
other.*

Excuse me.

HANK *goes back to his stool.* LILLIANE *sits down at the table.* HANK
begins to play the guitar. Softly. LILLIANE *looks at* HANK. *At* ERIC.

ERIC: It's all right.

LILLIANE: You should be more careful.

ERIC: I was.

LILLIANE: You can't go back to the apartment yet.

ERIC: The policeman is still there?

LILLIANE: Bernard knows about us.

ERIC: Are you sure.

LILLIANE: Jean told him.

ERIC: Of course. We should have taken steps earlier.

LILLIANE: Bernard is deranged, Eric. He's dug up Jean's body. I
can't understand why. He called me. I went to the graveyard.
It was so strange. Talking like his brain was exploding.

ERIC: What does he want.

LILLIANE: I don't know. He's deranged.

ERIC: Give him what he wants. We can always take it away later.

LILLIANE: I think he wants me.

ERIC *touches her arm.*

ERIC: Lilliane.

LILLIANE: No.

ERIC: Lilliane, it's a difficult life. You have hidden me. Broken
the law. We could pay a high price. Be separated. Make a
sacrifice. He could cause trouble. Where is he now.

LILLIANE: I said I would meet him at my apartment.

ERIC: Then you should go.

LILLIANE: Eric.

ERIC: You can always take it away later. When the time is right.
When it's safe.

LILLIANE: He scares me.

ERIC: I scared you once. (*Pause*)

You should go.

Pause.

Go.

Long pause. She gets up. Starts off. As she is passing HANK *he looks at her. Hands her a chocolate bar.* LILLIANE *smiles. She starts off.* ERIC *extends a hand.* LILLIANE *hands the chocolate to* ERIC. *She leaves.* HANK *looks at* ERIC. *Frowns.* ERIC *smiles.*

Blackout.

> LILLIANE's *apartment.* INSPECTOR CLAIR *sits in a chair. Legs outstretched. Reading a book.* BERNARD *comes in quickly. Looking around as he enters.*

BERNARD: Who are you. What are you doing here. I was to meet Lilliane here. She wanted to talk. This is her apartment isn't it. Yes, this is her apartment. I've seen it in my head. Who are you.

INSPECTOR: A friend of Lilliane.

BERNARD: You're no friend. You're a policeman. I can smell it.

INSPECTOR: Why don't you sit down, Bernard.

BERNARD: How do you know my name.

INSPECTOR: Lilliane told me. Why don't you sit.

BERNARD: No, I can't stay long. I left something unguarded. I have to get back. I only came here because I thought Lilliane wanted to talk. Do you know Lilliane. You're not romantically involved with her are you.

INSPECTOR: Lilliane thought we should talk. I'm investigating the murder of her brother. You knew him.

BERNARD: A long time ago.

INSPECTOR: What does that mean.

BERNARD: We'd grown apart. Recently we'd become like strangers. I know nothing about his death. Of course I have my suspicions. But don't we all.

INSPECTOR: What do you suspect.

BERNARD: I suspect that you are trying to implicate me. What did Lilliane tell you.

INSPECTOR: She just suggested that you might have some information.

BERNARD: Lilliane should be careful what she suggests. Have you established her innocence in this matter.

INSPECTOR: Do you have something to tell me about Lilliane.

BERNARD: Lilliane is a lovely girl. She can be very useful in times like these. She has a certain stability as you can tell from her apartment. Have you spent much time in her apartment.

INSPECTOR: Where were you the night of Jean's death.

BERNARD: In my room, of course. I never leave my room. Except in emergencies.

INSPECTOR: Is this an emergency.

BERNARD: Lilliane and I have to talk.

INSPECTOR: What was it you were guarding.

BERNARD: What did Lilliane tell you I was guarding.

INSPECTOR: Why do you answer my questions with questions.

BERNARD: What is that in your pocket.

INSPECTOR: Chocolate. Lilliane gave it to me.

BERNARD: German chocolate?

INSPECTOR: American.

BERNARD: American?

INSPECTOR: No, I'm sorry, English. Would you like a piece.

BERNARD: No.

INSPECTOR: You were a clerk at the ministry of public works, weren't you.

BERNARD: Can I see your identification.

INSPECTOR: Certainly. (*shows his card to* BERNARD)

BERNARD: You really are a policeman.

INSPECTOR: You had doubts?

BERNARD: I thought you were one of Lilliane's lovers.

INSPECTOR: She has many lovers?

BERNARD: How would I know. I just suspect. She has so much to offer. Her apartment. Chocolate. (*begins to look around the apartment*)

INSPECTOR: You haven't worked at the ministry for the past two years.

BERNARD: No. I had to quit.

INSPECTOR: Why.

BERNARD: I was too afraid.

INSPECTOR: Of what.

BERNARD: Getting there. It was difficult for me to get there. There were always people on the street who were hostile towards me.

INSPECTOR: So what did you do instead.

BERNARD: Stayed home.

INSPECTOR: That's all?

BERNARD: Well, it was difficult. Staying home was difficult. It was hard to make a living at home. And hard to make new friends.

INSPECTOR: How did you eat.

BERNARD: Friends brought me food.

INSPECTOR: New friends?

BERNARD: Old friends.

INSPECTOR: Jean.

BERNARD: Yes, he was one. People liked Jean. He had a way of getting things from people. I think it runs in the family.

INSPECTOR: And other friends? People you knew from your days with the Communists.

BERNARD: Are you investigating the Communists.

INSPECTOR: I'm investigating a murder.

BERNARD: It's just that it's hard to follow the pattern of your questions.

INSPECTOR: I'm just stumbling around.

BERNARD: I see. Well, I was never really a Communist. Oh, I read the books, but I didn't understand them when they talked. I was never officially one of them. I observed. Eventually they observed that I was just observing and asked me to leave … (*sits*) It's too bad. I used to enjoy the meetings. When everyone had finished shouting, we'd have tea. I used to enjoy that. Also, the fact that no one seemed afraid of being discovered by the Germans. Some of them were resistance of course. Not all. But some. Some just liked to come to meetings. But no one seemed afraid. That was nice. Sometimes with tea we had biscuits. English biscuits.

Michel, the custodian of arms, used to bring them from the countryside. He said the English dropped them by parachute. He went out looking for weapons but he said the English were only dropping biscuits. Good biscuits though. Good with tea ... But they weren't weapons, and Michel used this to arouse anti-English pro-Russian sentiment. The Communists were stupid. Not as stupid as the fascists because these things are relative. But stupid ... Even so, I enjoyed the meetings.

INSPECTOR: What did you think of the Germans. Besides that they were stupid.

BERNARD: Oh, I hated them of course.

INSPECTOR: Of course.

> BERNARD *stands. Moves about aimlessly.*

BERNARD: Are you investigating collaborators.

INSPECTOR: I'm investigating a murder.

BERNARD: You can believe me. I hated the Germans for my own reasons. Sexual reasons. They were particularly nasty to me.

INSPECTOR: Jean had the same problem?

BERNARD: I don't know.

INSPECTOR: Your friends in the Party suggest he did.

BERNARD: That should make you suspicious of them, shouldn't it.

INSPECTOR: Why.

BERNARD: Character assassination.

INSPECTOR: Are suggestions of sexual preference a sign of character assassination.

BERNARD: During certain times. Times like these.

INSPECTOR: When you and Jean ceased to be lovers did you remain friends.

BERNARD: He felt sorry for me. He brought me food. And cigarettes.

INSPECTOR: German?

BERNARD: Russian.

INSPECTOR: Not German?

BERNARD: Russian. Why.

INSPECTOR: Lilliane's apartment is full of German cigarettes.

BERNARD: You searched.

INSPECTOR: Not too much. It wasn't difficult. They're not hidden.

BERNARD: Lilliane has nothing to hide. She was just doing what so many others were doing.

INSPECTOR: Yes?

BERNARD: Getting by.

INSPECTOR: Why did Jean feel sorry for you.

BERNARD: Well, look at me. I'm pitiful.

INSPECTOR: You seem fine.

BERNARD: It's an act.

INSPECTOR: What are you really like then.

BERNARD: Afraid.

INSPECTOR: But harmless?

BERNARD: I think Jean's death was a political act. The Communists needed a martyr.

INSPECTOR: That is possible of course. I'm looking into it. I came to the case late. A veil of contradicting evidence has been allowed to surround matters. It will take time. But I am looking to remove it.

BERNARD: Can I go now.

INSPECTOR: Yes.

BERNARD: I have to go.

INSPECTOR: Go ahead.

BERNARD: I can go?

> *The* INSPECTOR *nods.*

Will I be seeing you again. Will your investigation involve me any further.

INSPECTOR: We'll see.

BERNARD: But I can go now?

INSPECTOR: Yes.

BERNARD: Thank you. (*starts off*)

INSPECTOR: Oh, Bernard.

> BERNARD *stops. The* INSPECTOR *holds up a small package.*

Cigarettes. Here.

> *He throws the package to* BERNARD.

BERNARD: Thank you.

> BERNARD *leaves.* INSPECTOR CLAIR *smiles weakly. Searches his pockets. Reaches under the cushion of the other chair. Takes out a pack of cigarettes. Takes one out. Lights it. Inhales. Frowns. Looks at the cigarette.*

INSPECTOR: American.

> *Blackout.*

SCENE SEVEN

> *Graveyard.* LILLIANE *waiting.* BERNARD *comes on.*

BERNARD: Get away from that coffin.

LILLIANE: I'd thought you'd finally gone away.

BERNARD: No chance.

LILLIANE: Do you have your senses back.

BERNARD: I met a policeman in your apartment.

LILLIANE: I know.

BERNARD: You arranged it?

LILLIANE: No. I came home. Heard you talking, and went away.

BERNARD: He liked me. He'd like to hear from me again. I might call him.

LILLIANE: About what.

BERNARD: You and Eric of course.

LILLIANE: That would not be wise.

BERNARD: I don't care.

> ERIC *has come slowly out of the darkness. A long wool coat on. The only sign of a uniform beneath it, his boots.*

ERIC: Go home, Lilliane.

BERNARD: My assassin. (*drops to his knees*)

LILLIANE: How did you know where I was.

ERIC: I followed you.

BERNARD: A wily devil. I'm a goner.

LILLIANE: Did you hear.

ERIC: Yes. I was listening from the beginning.

BERNARD: Trained by the Gestapo for sure. Are you going to torture me. I warn you now. I'll tell you everything I know and it won't make a bit of sense. Please excuse my glibness. In fact I am genuinely frightened.

ERIC: I just want to talk. Will you excuse us, Lilliane.

LILLIANE: I'm staying.

BERNARD: Yes, let her stay. She'll make me feel more secure.

LILLIANE: Odd that you should say that. I was just thinking of cutting your throat.

BERNARD: Oh. Well, how was I to know. I'm not a mind reader.

LILLIANE: There's no other way, Eric. He's demented.

BERNARD: But harmless.

ERIC: You threaten to report us.

BERNARD: You want to cut my throat too.

ERIC: I just want to talk.

BERNARD: Then why do you want her to leave. You didn't want her to see the criminal in you. You wanted to send her away carefree and then cut me open in private. You have a technique for such things. Oh God, I'm so scared. I think I'm going to piss my pants. How pitiful.

> BERNARD *crawls into the grave. Pause.* LILLIANE *and* ERIC *exchange a look. They walk to the grave. And stand over* BERNARD.

ERIC: Get off your knees.

BERNARD: I'm too scared to move.

ERIC: I'll help you up.

BERNARD: Stay away from me. Why are you reaching inside your coat. You have a pistol.

> ERIC *produces a tiny box.*

ERIC: Cigarette?

BERNARD: I don't smoke.

LILLIANE: He's lying.

BERNARD: She's right. But it wasn't an important lie. Certainly no reason to punish me for it.

ERIC: Certainly not. Do you mind if I smoke.

LILLIANE: It was an example of his lying. He can't be trusted.

ERIC: You're on edge. It would be better if you left.

LILLIANE: I'm staying. I can't leave with this over my head.

ERIC: I understand.

BERNARD: You're very compassionate. I'm beginning to see what Jean saw in you.

ERIC: Thank you. Will you have a cigarette now.

LILLIANE *begins to pace.*

BERNARD: Yes. Perhaps I will.

ERIC: Will you get off your knees now.

BERNARD: If you don't mind.

ERIC: I would like it very much

BERNARD *stands.* ERIC *gives him a cigarette. Lights it.*

BERNARD: Turkish?

ERIC: Dutch.

BERNARD: Of course. I'm such a cretin.

ERIC: Not at all. It's a stronger blend than the usual Dutch. It fools most people.

BERNARD: You're very kind.

ERIC: Thank you. Will you excuse me a moment.

BERNARD: Certainly.

ERIC *nods. Goes to* LILLIANE. *Whispers in her ear.* LILLIANE *shakes her head.* ERIC *grabs her. Whispers.* LILLIANE *nods. They kiss.* LILLIANE *goes to* BERNARD.

LILLIANE: Will you excuse me for a few minutes, Bernard.

BERNARD: Of course.

LILLIANE: Just a few minutes.

She smiles. Leaves.

ERIC: She is just going for a walk.

BERNARD: It's a nice evening for a walk. That is if the ghouls and their associates don't feel hostile towards you.

ERIC *laughs.*

Does that make sense to you.

ERIC: Very much.

BERNARD: Really. Then would you mind explaining it to me. I'm afraid it's just one of the many things I'm prone to saying that make no sense to me.

ERIC *walks slowly to* BERNARD. *Smiling.*

ERIC: That is often the case with a complex mind like yours.

BERNARD: Is it. Why are you reaching inside your coat again.

ERIC *produces a package. Hands it to* BERNARD. *As* BERNARD *undoes the package,* ERIC *removes his overcoat to reveal a German officer's uniform. The package contains an officer's hat and* BERNARD *stares at it. He turns to* ERIC *and gasps. Puts the hat on* ERIC*'s head. Whimpers and turns away as if offering the back of his head as a target for the assassin.* ERIC *smiles.*

Blackout.

> LILLIANE*'s apartment.* LILLIANE *is sitting in a chair.* HANK *stands beside her, emptying his pockets of chocolate bars and dropping them into her lap. Two from one pocket. Two from another. Five from another. Six. Seven. About fifty chocolate bars. All gently dropped. When he is finished, pause.* LILLIANE *looks up.*

LILLIANE: Thank you.

HANK: You're welcome.

> *She stands. The chocolate bars fall to the floor.* HANK *watches them.* LILLIANE *puts her arms around* HANK*'s neck.*

LILLIANE: Thank you.

> *She kisses his forehead.*

Thank you.

> *She kisses his cheek.*

Thank you. Thank you. Thank you.

HANK: You're … welcome.

> LILLIANE *turns.*

Are you crying.

LILLIANE: I'm sorry.

> HANK *hands her a handkerchief.*

Thank you. (*turns toward him*) Thank you. (*turns away*)

HANK: Are you crying.

LILLIANE: I'm so sad.

HANK: Don't be sad.

LILLIANE: I need … what do I need.

HANK: Cigarettes?

LILLIANE: No. (*turns toward him*) Thank you.

HANK: What do you need.

LILLIANE: Help.

HANK: I can help.

LILLIANE: Can you.

HANK: Can I … May I.

LILLIANE: It's politics. Everything is politics. I'm a victim of other people's beliefs. I'm a stranger in my own country. I don't understand these new influences. The radio plays American jazz. That's political. I'm just trying to survive. But the demands are frightening. One man in particular is frightening. He wants to destroy me for political reasons only. I try to explain that I am not responsible. But he won't listen.

HANK: Someone should make him listen. Maybe I could make him listen. Maybe I could try. If that's all right with you. If that's what you want. Is that what you want.

LILLIANE: Thank you.

She puts her arms around him.

Thank you very much.

Tentatively he puts his arms around her. Tentatively he smiles.

Blackout.

Graveyard. BERNARD *is lying on the coffin.* ERIC *is standing over him, his tunic undone. Smiling.*

BERNARD: Why are you reaching inside your new pocket.

ERIC: Would you care for a piece of chocolate.

BERNARD: What kind of chocolate.

ERIC: American.

BERNARD: Does it have nuts in it.

ERIC: No. I'm sorry.

BERNARD: Don't apologize. I prefer chocolate without nuts.

ERIC: Should I break off a piece for you.

BERNARD: Yes. Not too big a piece though.

ERIC: Is this about right.

BERNARD: Yes.

ERIC: Here.

BERNARD: Thank you. (*eats the chocolate*) Good. Where did you get this American chocolate.

ERIC: Lilliane got it for me.

BERNARD: And where did Lilliane get it.

ERIC: From the Americans.

BERNARD: She must be very cunning.

ERIC: She gets many things from the Americans for me.

BERNARD: She must love you very much.

ERIC: Yes.

BERNARD: You're very lucky.

ERIC: Yes, I am.

BERNARD: Lilliane and I have had our disagreements. But basically I admire her. Especially for her introspection.

ERIC: I too.

BERNARD: Well, it's a rare thing in a beautiful woman.

ERIC: And an even rarer thing in a beautiful man.

BERNARD: You refer of course to Jean.

ERIC: A beautiful young man.

BERNARD: But stupid.

ERIC: Yes.

BERNARD: Yes.

> *Pause.*

ERIC: More chocolate?

BERNARD: No, thank you.

ERIC: Here, take the rest.

> *He hands it to him.*

I insist.

BERNARD: All right. I'll save it for later. (*puts it in the coffin*) If it's not too presumptuous of me to think there will be a later for me.

ERIC: Not at all. I hope we both will lead a long healthy life.

BERNARD: But I'm a stranger to you.

ERIC: Jean spoke of you often.

BERNARD: Really. What else does Lilliane get you from the Americans.

ERIC: Many things. Even money.

BERNARD: She must be very cunning indeed. So you had a conversation with Jean.

ERIC: Yes. We got along very well.

BERNARD: He liked you?

ERIC: We got along very well.

BERNARD: And he would not want me to report you. Is that what you are trying to say.

ERIC: I believe he liked me. He didn't report me.

BERNARD: Well, I was very fond of Jean as you know. I was his lover, as you know. I am respectful of his memory, as you know. These things are all very important and must be considered when I decide whether to turn you in or not. That is the rational way to proceed. Am I not a rational man. We have been having a rational discussion have we not. A very polite discussion. You have offered cigarettes and chocolates and I have accepted and made complimentary remarks about your lover, and always in a controlled fashion, never once—never once—referring to the spectacle of Jean's fine muscular body upon that barricade and the hideous sickening bullet hole which made him crumple like garbage onto the ground or the fact that he fought Germans like you, the enemy of all mankind, that he left me alone below the surface to fight his stupid fight, or the agony of the obscene nature of his funeral when everyone there had a grotesque erection, or that suddenly out of the corner of my eye I saw you for the first time leaning against the door of the church with a smile on your face. No, I have not even mentioned that, the most obscene and vivid thing of all because I am rational. I am calm. I am intuitive. I sensed that you wished me to be this way and I obliged.

Pause.

But be careful. Because I am capable of regressing.

ERIC: (*smiles*) Perhaps I was smiling. I sometimes smile when I'm embarrassed.

BERNARD: Was Jean's funeral embarrassing you.

ERIC: Yes.

BERNARD: Why.

ERIC: I am Lilliane's lover.

BERNARD: Surely there must be more.

ERIC: I had also been intimate with Jean.

BERNARD: Oh, what a delicate way of putting it. No, I don't believe it. Yes, I do. What a stinking disappointment. I was sure I was the only one. But of course not. He was so undisciplined. No, it's stinking Nazi propaganda. You will not demoralize the degenerates, I warn you. Take it back or I'll suck out your intestines.

ERIC: I'm sorry.

BERNARD: Well what of it. Jean's dead. Look inside that coffin if you don't believe me. No. We must unite. We have a common goal now. We must find Jean's murderer and avenge the corruption of his body. But first we must strike a bargain. Are you agreeable.

ERIC: What is the bargain.

BERNARD: I agree not to turn you in.

ERIC: I knew you would see it my way.

BERNARD: And you agree to give me Lilliane.

ERIC: But we are in love.

BERNARD: She can be in love with me.

ERIC: It's not so easy.

BERNARD: Isn't it. Well, I wouldn't know. I've never been in love.

ERIC: You loved Jean.

BERNARD: That moron? I was fond of his skin. I want to be in love with Lilliane in a legitimate manner so that I can surface and have her bring me things from the Americans.

ERIC: You frighten me when you talk like this, Bernard.

BERNARD: Do I. How.

ERIC: I worry that you really might be demented and that I won't be able to reason with you. That I will have to use other means.

    He slaps BERNARD.

BERNARD: He reveals himself to me.

    ERIC *slaps him again.* BERNARD *drops to his knees.*

My assassin.

    ERIC *pushes him.* BERNARD *falls face down on the ground.*

Oh Jesus, I'm so scared.

    ERIC *puts his foot on* BERNARD*'s head.*

Jesus come here. I'm so fucking scared.

    ERIC *pulls a pistol from his coat. Kneels. Puts the pistol to* BERNARD*'s head.*

Don't. Please don't. I'm harmless.

ERIC: You are forcing me to be brutal with you. I don't like this at all. Bernard I'm sorry.

ERIC: I prefer polite conversation.

BERNARD: I'm sorry.

ERIC: I prefer peaceful negotiation.

BERNARD: Very, very sorry.

ERIC: I've seen enough violence. I've been forced to kill enough. I've done my share. I have vast experience with violence. My victims were of several nationalities.

BERNARD: You poor man.

ERIC: It caused me great turmoil. Basically I'm a tranquil individual. Just because I am German doesn't mean I am violent, rigid and heartless. That's a cliché!

BERNARD: Yes, it is.

ERIC: I hate clichés!

BERNARD: So do I.

ERIC: War is a cliché!

BERNARD: Be careful with that gun.

ERIC: Death is a cliché!

BERNARD: Don't let your finger slip.

ERIC: Peace is a cliché.

BERNARD: I'm going to piss.

ERIC: Peace is obscene! It's hypocritical. It puts war criminals on trial. It turns cowards into vengeance seekers. Where were the cowardly vengeance seekers when it mattered. Don't blame the criminals. Blame the victims. Without victims there wouldn't be criminals, would there. That makes sense, doesn't it. That *makes* sense, doesn't it. That makes *sense*, doesn't it. Das ist richtig, nicht vahr?!

BERNARD: I suppose.

ERIC: What.

BERNARD: Yes. Of course.

ERIC: What?!

BERNARD: Yes, yes. Of course. Of course.

   Pause.

ERIC: Yes. (*stands. Puts the gun away*) I owe you an apology. Please shake my hand.

   BERNARD *looks at him.*

Please.

   BERNARD *gets up slowly. Extends a hand. They shake.*

I frightened you.

BERNARD: I almost wet myself

ERIC: I'm sorry. But now you see why we must keep our conversation rational. Certainly we are both capable of becoming quite disturbed and incoherent but in the long run that course will only prove disastrous. Do you agree.

BERNARD: Yes.

ERIC: Now where were we.

BERNARD: I'm not quite sure.

ERIC: What have you done with your chocolate.

BERNARD: It's in my pocket.

> ERIC *looks at him oddly.*

No, it's in the coffin.

ERIC: Why don't you have a bite.

BERNARD: I'm not hungry.

ERIC: Then would you like a cigarette.

BERNARD: No.

> ERIC *grabs* BERNARD*'s jaw.*

ERIC: You're not being very agreeable. You should be more agreeable.

BERNARD: Yes. You're right. Would you like one of my cigarettes.

ERIC: Thank you very much.

> BERNARD *takes out package of cigarettes. Gives* ERIC *one. Takes one himself.*

I'll light them.

BERNARD: No, I'll do it.

ERIC: I insist.

BERNARD: Very well.

> ERIC *lights the cigarettes. They both inhale.*

ERIC: This is a very good cigarette. Turkish?

BERNARD: American.

ERIC: How stupid of me!

BERNARD: Not at all. It's difficult to tell.

ERIC: No. I should have known. I spent a year in America doing serious espionage work.

BERNARD: You should tell me about it sometime.

ERIC: It's a part of my life I would greatly like to forget.

BERNARD: I understand.

ERIC: Although I had an American lover there. I don't mind remembering him. He was eighteen years old.

BERNARD: Does Lilliane know this.

ERIC: Lilliane and I are in love.

BERNARD: A respectable love.

ERIC: But dangerous. We live constantly in fear. My nerves are very bad.

BERNARD: Did your lover wear his trousers as tightly as you do.

ERIC: Yes. Do you like the way my trousers fit.

BERNARD: It suits you.

ERIC: Thank you. But we should be careful where this conversation leads. We have both been living underground too long. We don't have all our faculties.

BERNARD: Mine come and go.

ERIC: I've noticed.

BERNARD: Sometimes I'm perfectly sane.

ERIC: In fact, you seem sane right now.

BERNARD: And so do you.

ERIC: And polite.

BERNARD: And so are you.

ERIC: But you could be just trying to manipulate me.

BERNARD: And you could be doing the same.

ERIC: And yet of course if that were the case it could lead to a confrontation in which I would be superior. If it led to a violent confrontation I could seize hold of your head and squeeze your brains out into my hands.

> BERNARD *puts his hands in his pockets. Walks over to the coffin. Sits on it. Bows his head.*

I've frightened you again. I'm sorry.

BERNARD: I'm so sad. Jean is dead. I'm nothing without him. You could crush my skull and you would be crushing the skull of a nothing.

>   *Pause.*

ERIC: Are you crying.

>   BERNARD *nods.* ERIC *walks over, sits next to him.*

You really are a poor pitiful person.

BERNARD: Yes, I am.

ERIC: I get genuinely moved by a person like you. You have no hope.

BERNARD: And yet if I could surface.

ERIC: How could you.

BERNARD: I could have Lilliane. She would be my respectability.

ERIC: Poor man. Lilliane loves me.

BERNARD: But you don't love her.

ERIC: She gets me many things from the Americans. She lets me sit in her big chair in the corner. She makes my life comfortable and dangerous at the same time.

BERNARD: You could get someone else.

ERIC: Lilliane was the best choice. I selected her carefully. When I occupied the city and knew eventually the liberators were coming and that I couldn't go home to be caught in the web, I looked for someone to hide me. I looked for a girl with special qualities. A girl who led a special life.

BERNARD: An abstract life.

ERIC: An introspective life.

BERNARD: But you could find someone else.

ERIC: I cannot surface to search.

BERNARD: Neither can I. I must have Lilliane.

ERIC: I could eat your ears off. And let you bleed to death.

>   BERNARD *has put his hand on* ERIC*'s leg and is running it slowly up and down.*

BERNARD: I could have Lilliane and forget about Jean and seeking revenge for the corruption of his body.

ERIC: I could stick my fist into your mouth and force it all the way into your stomach, destroying your insides.

> BERNARD *lays his head in* ERIC*'s lap.*

BERNARD: You could lead a dangerous life with someone else. You wear your trousers so tight you could meet someone so else easily.

ERIC: I think I should kill you now.

> ERIC *covers* BERNARD *with his overcoat.*

BERNARD: You would be killing nothing.

> BERNARD *is doing something under the overcoat.*

ERIC: I have killed many nothings.

BERNARD: You should wait a minute.

ERIC: (*suddenly smiling*) I should do it now?

BERNARD: Wait for just a minute.

ERIC: (*breathing heavily*) Now?

BERNARD: Soon.

ERIC: (*his eyes closed*) Now?

BERNARD: Soon.

ERIC: Why not now.

BERNARD: (*muffled*) Soon.

> *A gunshot.* ERIC *Slumps.* BERNARD *struggles out from beneath the overcoat.* ERIC *falls over.* BERNARD *walks cautiously to* ERIC*'s body. Bends down. Singing, off key.*

Deutschland, Deutschland, ha-ha, ha-ha-ha.

> *Pause.*

ERIC: (*opens his eyes. Struggles up onto his elbows*) That is in very bad taste. (*coughs*) It is also a cliché. (*coughs*) I hate clichés. (*coughs, dies*)

> BERNARD *grabs* ERIC*'s ankles and begins to drag him to the grave.*
>
> *Blackout.*

> *Graveyard.* LILLIANE *is standing some distance from the coffin. Hands in pockets.* BERNARD*'s head is peering up from behind the coffin.*

LILLIANE: Where's Eric.

BERNARD: Eric who.

LILLIANE: (*looking around*) Eric?!

BERNARD: Don't shout. Please don't shout. You know, out there, the G … H … O … U … L … S.

LILLIANE: Where is he.

BERNARD: (*standing*) He tried to kill me. He was very aggressive. He proceeded aggressively. With confidence. Too much confidence. His confidence became arrogant. Did he know he'd lost the war. Didn't you tell him. Didn't you bring him newspapers in your apartment. Didn't he ever look out the window.

LILLIANE: Where is he!

BERNARD: Dead. Over here. Come and look.

> *She walks over slowly. Looks down.*

LILLIANE: You did that?

BERNARD: He tried to kill me. You look upset. Why.

> LILLIANE *just shakes her head.*

Why.

LILLIANE: I loved him.

BERNARD: Ah. That's sad. Because he didn't love you. He told me he just used you.

LILLIANE: I used him as well. We had an understanding.

BERNARD: But you loved him.

LILLIANE: Yes!

BERNARD: Well, he's dead now. You can love me instead. He killed Jean, you know. He confessed. Honest. He was a murderer. A mass murderer. You made an awful mistake loving him. But I'll forgive you. As the years flow by I'll forgive you. As long as you keep me safe in your apartment. As long as you bring me things from the Americans. Or the Russians. Or whoever. Come here.

LILLIANE: No.

BERNARD: I scare you, don't I.

LILLIANE: Yes.

> HANK *is moving up behind* BERNARD. *Slowly. A nylon stocking stretched between his hands. He is wearing a plain overcoat.*

BERNARD: No. I don't scare you. I wonder why. I know. (*pointing back over his shoulder without turning*) Because of him.

> HANK *stops.* BERNARD *turns to him slowly.*

Well, look at this then. (*to* LILLIANE) A new friend? Is there no end to them. Is there no end to what they'll do for you. (*to* HANK) You should have met her brother. He had many of the same qualities.

HANK: You should be letting this lady alone.

BERNARD: You speak my language. But you have an accent. Would you mind taking off your coat.

HANK: You upset the lady.

BERNARD: (*producing a gun*) Would you mind taking off your coat.

> HANK *takes off the coat. Lets it drop.*

I recognize that uniform. I've looked at it many times over the collar of my coat. Like this. (*demonstrates, lifting his collar, his eyes peering out*) That uniform has made me behave strangely in public. And earned me many anxious moments. I don't like it. I don't like uniforms in general. They shouldn't be allowed. They always show up uninvited and cause anxiety. For example, who invited your uniform here tonight. Don't move. Please. You moved. Just a bit, I know. But you moved. Don't.

HANK: She said she needed my help.

BERNARD: Did she tell you you might be putting your life in danger.

HANK: I don't care.

BERNARD: Do you love her.

HANK: I don't care.

BERNARD: Does she love you.

HANK: I don't care.

BERNARD: (*to* LILLIANE) He has a very limited vocabulary. These are complex issues we're dealing with. How is he going to manage with so few words.

LILLIANE: Why don't you let him go.

BERNARD: He tried to kill me. He's under your spell. He'll try to kill me again. (*to* HANK) Won't you.

HANK: (*pounding his fists against his thighs*) I don't care!

BERNARD: (*to* LILLIANE) You know, I think this man has problems of his own. It would have been kind of you not to involve him in ours. But of course you had to, just in case Eric failed. Or perhaps he was brought here to kill Eric if he didn't fail. You're often difficult to figure out, Lilliane.

HANK: I don't care about nothin' anymore. You hear me?

BERNARD: (*to* HANK) I think I understand you.

HANK: I don't care!

BERNARD: I don't care either.

HANK: Jesus. Jesus. Jesus!

BERNARD: (*laughs*) I don't care.

HANK: Jesus I tell you. I don't care. Really. I don't.

BERNARD: (*laughing*) Me neither. Me neither.

HANK: Jesus!

> HANK *attacks* BERNARD. BERNARD *shoots him.* HANK *falls. Dead. Pause.*

BERNARD: I did understand him. I did. I saw into his brain. It was broken into little pieces. And the pieces were talking to each other. Just like mine. Exactly like mine.

> *Looks at* LILLIANE. *Smiles.*

In my darker moments, of course. You don't look well.

LILLIANE: I'm going to pass out.

BERNARD: Haven't eaten? Can I get you something. Chocolate? Biscuits? Some wine? A cigarette? Chocolate? Biscuits?

Nylons? Winter boots? Coffee? Furniture? Electric heaters? Trips to the country? A week in the Mediterranean? What is it you want, Lilliane. What is it you haven't got yet.

LILLIANE: I want you dead. Rotting in the ground. Off the world. Out of my mind.

BERNARD: Be careful or I'll report you.

LILLIANE: Be careful or I'll have you killed.

BERNARD: You already tried that. Twice. Which reminds me. Did I tell you how Eric died. A nasty wound to the groin. He was aiming for my head. I nudged the barrel away with my nose and repointed. Like this. (*demonstrates with a finger*) Disgusting image, isn't it.

> BERNARD *is in a daze. He walks over to* HANK's *corpse. And sings, off key*

O—O say can you see, ha-ha, ha-ha-ha.

He stares at HANK's *corpse. Turns to* LILLIANE.

Don't look like that. He killed your brother. And he was a fascist.

> LILLIANE *looks at the grave. At* HANK. *At the grave again.*

LILLIANE: Eric was with me the night Jean was killed.

BERNARD: (*pointing at* HANK) He was a fascist. No. (*pointing at the grave*) He was a fascist. Capable of dark magic. Perhaps he was in two places at once.

LILLIANE: The Communists killed Jean.

BERNARD: Perhaps Eric was capable of being in two places at once as two different people. (*points at* HANK *and the grave*) Perhaps he was where Jean was killed as a Communist.

> LILLIANE *starts off.*

Where are you going.

LILLIANE: Home. I'm tired.

BERNARD: Don't go. We have plans to make.

LILLIANE: (*leaving*) I'm tired!

BERNARD: If you go, I'll follow you. And when I'm through following you, I'll report you. I'll tell the story of Eric and his cigarettes.

LILLIANE: I don't care.

BERNARD: Stop!

> *She leaves.*

Good. It's good that you stopped. Now that you've stopped we can talk. Make plans. About our life together. Certainly there will be some expedience about it, but also great comfort. And safety. Don't move. You moved. That's better. (*reaches into his pocket. Produces a chocolate bar, bites off a piece*) Now where were we …

> INSPECTOR CLAIR *comes on.*

INSPECTOR: Bernard.

> *But* BERNARD *is just eating the chocolate. His eyes are glazed.*

Bernard.

> *Without thinking,* BERNARD *lifts his gun and points it in the general direction of the* INSPECTOR, *who anticipates this and has his own gun pointing at* BERNARD. *Pause.* BERNARD *is still in a daze. The* INSPECTOR *slowly lowers his gun. Stares at* BERNARD. BERNARD *looks at the* INSPECTOR. *Confused. The* INSPECTOR *looks at* BERNARD *for a long time. Suddenly he lifts his gun and fires.* BERNARD *falls. Dead.*
>
> *Blackout.*

SCENE ELEVEN

A bistro. LILLIANE *is sitting at a table, staring into her drink.* INSPECTOR CLAIR *comes on. They look at each other. Pause.*

INSPECTOR: May I join you.

LILLIANE: If you want.

INSPECTOR: (*sitting*) Thank you.

LILLIANE: Would you like a drink.

INSPECTOR: No. Thank you. How have you been keeping.

LILLIANE: I'm all right.

INSPECTOR: You don't look well.

LILLIANE *shrugs. Pause.*

Perhaps you're not getting enough sleep. Perhaps your neighbours are noisy and keep you up. If that's the case, I could pay them a visit.

LILLIANE: No. Thank you. I'm all right.

INSPECTOR: Food?

LILLIANE: What.

INSPECTOR: Do you get enough food.

LILLIANE: Yes.

Pause.

INSPECTOR: Just a general anxiety then. Like so many of us.

LILLIANE: Yes. I think so.

Pause.

INSPECTOR: I'm afraid I have some bad news for you ... That friend of your brother. Bernard ... He's dead.

She looks at him.

He killed himself. Of course he was not a stable personality. I saw that immediately when I questioned him. He was obviously capable of extreme action. Was that your opinion of him.

LILLIANE: I didn't know him very well.

INSPECTOR: I would say you were fortunate in that.

Pause.

Something else. This might be more painful I'm afraid. He is the one who killed your brother.

LILLIANE: Are you sure.

INSPECTOR: Pretty much. Yes.

LILLIANE: Your investigation proved this?

INSPECTOR: We found a note on his body. A confession. They don't usually lie under those circumstances … Are you all right. I'm sorry, I—

LILLIANE: No. It's just that I don't understand why. I mean—

INSPECTOR: Jealousy. In the note, Bernard said he was jealous of Jean's involvement with some German soldier. You see these friendships, Jean and Bernard, the soldier. They were intimate. You probably didn't know.

LILLIANE: Did the note say anything else.

INSPECTOR: No. Not really.

LILLIANE: Nothing about me.

INSPECTOR: No. Does that surprise you.

LILLIANE: It's just that you say Bernard was unstable. He could have tried to slander me. Perhaps he was jealous of me and Jean as well. I mean, he could have imagined all sorts of things.

INSPECTOR: Perhaps he thought of it. Perhaps he had a moment of generosity and decided to leave you out of it. Such an unstable personality, you see. Unpredictable. Damaged by the war. Severely damaged.

LILLIANE: Yes. I think he was.

INSPECTOR: But now it's over. Tied up. Complete. You must think of the future. I'm sorry about your brother. But think of the future. Eat. Sleep properly …

LILLIANE: Would you like a drink. I'll get one for you if you want.

INSPECTOR: No. Thank you … Here, I have something for you. (*takes out a card*) This is the address of a new company that is going to make films. I have a friend. I talked to him about you. Go and see him.

LILLIANE: I have no experience.

INSPECTOR: This is a new company. No one has any experience. I think you would be good in films.

LILLIANE: I'd like to be in films.

INSPECTOR: Take the address.

She takes the card.

LILLIANE: I'd like to be in films. I really would. I saw one last week. American. No. English ... Anyway, I would have liked to be in it. I sat there thinking that I would like to live in a film. just be alive in a film and nowhere else. I'd like that. I think somehow that would be better.

INSPECTOR: Perhaps it would.

LILLIANE: You've talked to them about me?

INSPECTOR: Yes.

LILLIANE: What did you say. What are they expecting me to be like.

INSPECTOR: Just be yourself.

LILLIANE: Would you like a drink. Maybe we can talk. You can tell me how to behave.

INSPECTOR: No. I have to be going. Just be yourself. You'll be all right.

Stands.

LILLIANE: And that will be enough for them, you think.

INSPECTOR: I'm sure it will. Goodbye.

LILLIANE: Will I see you again.

INSPECTOR: No ... you'll be all right.

He leaves. LILLIANE *takes out a cigarette.*

Blackout.

SCENE TWELVE

Under a streetlamp. INSPECTOR CLAIR. *Hands deep in his pockets.*

INSPECTOR: What you can't make clear, you should at least make complete. Who is responsible for crime when for so long there has been no law. Can there be guilt where there is no innocence. Before the war I had a chief inspector who taught me many things ... including never to ask myself questions like that ... that police work was simply a matter of jurisdiction and enforcement. But that was before the war. Before I met Bernard ... and found myself standing in the darkness of that graveyard listening to his pathetic broken brain with its little pieces talking to each other ... I have decided that the murder I was investigating was just something that happened because of the war. Truth is, I don't know if Bernard killed Jean. Or if Lilliane killed him to protect her lover. Or if the Communists killed him because he was stupid ... I have decided that none of that matters ... because Bernard had to die. He was just a part of what we have become. But it was the saddest most unpredictable part. Where would he go. How would he live. How could the rest of us survive and prosper with him out on the streets making other people sad and unpredictable too ... My behaviour in this matter is obviously open to criticism. (*shrugs*) But I think behaviour depends on circumstance. And circumstance often depends on luck ... Lilliane will go on to become one of this country's most successful film actresses. My luck will be to always see and hear Bernard in the film that runs inside my head ...

He drops his cigarette. Snuffs it out with his foot.

Blackout.

End.

Nothing Sacred

Nothing Sacred was first produced by Centre Stage Company, in the Bluma Appel Theatre of the St. Lawrence Centre for the Arts, Toronto, January 14, 1988, with the following cast:

BAZAROV Robert Bockstael
ARKADY Michael Riley
NIKOLAI (PETROVICH) KIRSANOV David Fox
PAVEL (PETROVICH) KIRSANOV Richard Monette
FENICHKA Beverley Cooper
ANNA Diane D'Aquila
SITNIKOV Ross Manson
PIOTR Peter Blais
BAILIFF Christopher Benson
GREGOR John Dolan
SERGEI Patrick Tierney

Director: Bill Glassco
Set and Costumes: Mary Kerr
Lighting designer: Lynne Hyde
Music composed by: Alan Laing

Persons
YEVGENY (VASSILYICH) BAZAROV, 25
ARKADY (NIKOLAYEVICH) KIRSANOV, 23
NIKOLAI (PETROVICH) KIRSANOV, Arkady's father, 47
PAVEL (PETROVICH) KIRSANOV, Arkady's uncle, 48
FENICHKA (NIKOLAEVNA), 19
ANNA (SERGYEVNA) ODINTSOV, early 30s
VIKTOR SITNIKOV, 25
PIOTR, a servant, an energetic 80 year old
BAILIFF
GREGOR, a young peasant
SERGEI, a large peasant

Place
The play takes place in Russia, in late spring, 1859. The periphery of the set should be a kind of minimalist landscape. Mostly open fields with the occasional slope. A suggestion of forests. The rest is a bare dark hardwood floor. The various locations in the play must be suggested simply with as few pieces of furniture as possible.

Note
Intermission should be placed between Scenes Four and Five.

Nothing Sacred

PROLOGUE

Darkness.

Sounds of someone being beaten.

Lights.

Roadside. A raggedy peasant, GREGOR, *on his knees. His hands held behind his back. Over him stands a* BAILIFF *brandishing a switch.*

Behind them, watching with a bemused expression, is ARKADY KIRSANOV, *twenty-three, a pleasant looking young man in a great coat and a student's hat. He is clutching a carpet bag to his chest.*

BAILIFF: One more for good measure.

GREGOR: Whatever pleases the bailiff.

BAILIFF: In that case four or five.

He hits him.

GREGOR: A little higher please. I think you've opened up a terrible wound in that spot. Feel it. It feels wet and spongy.

BAILIFF: Feel it yourself.

He hits him again.

GREGOR: That wasn't higher at all. I ... I think I'm gonna go fainting here.

BAILIFF: If you pass out it doesn't count. I have to start again after you wake up.

GREGOR: Jesus. (*smiles*)

BAILIFF: What was that?!

He hits him.

GREGOR: Just two more.

BAILIFF: Five more.

GREGOR: No two more. I've been counting.

BAILIFF: You learned to count by stealing things. That reminds me of how much I hate you. Of how much my father hated your father. Another five!

He hits him several times.

GREGOR: Please. Keep count out loud. And stop losing control of yourself or this could go on forever. (*laughs*) You big dumb pig.

The BAILIFF *yells. Starts to beat him wildly.* GREGOR *moans. Mutters. And occasionally smiles.* BAZAROV *wanders on. He is a tall angular man. Unshaven. Wearing a loose-fitting overcoat. Carrying a suitcase on his shoulder. Staring at something he holds in his free hand. He hears the noise. Looks up. Puts down his suitcase. Puts the object in his hand into his pocket. Takes out a cigar. Walks over and stands beside* ARKADY.

BAZAROV: Welcome to the new Russia.

ARKADY: Can you stop this.

BAZAROV: Yes I can. Can you.

ARKADY: Is it my place. That man's a bailiff.

BAZAROV: And the other one's a thief I suppose.

ARKADY: Yes.

BAZAROV: Then they're just doing what they've been doing for hundreds of years ... Cigar?

ARKADY: No ... But we're against this type of thing, aren't we.

BAZAROV: Are we.

ARKADY: This is a form of institutional punishment. One man has power given him by the state ... the institution of serfdom.

BAZAROV: On the other hand, thieves need to be stopped. Right?

ARKADY: Yes. That's what I was thinking while I watched.

BAZAROV: You're a good Russian. You can maintain two political points of view at once ... I think he might be killing him. It could be time to take a stand.

ARKADY looks at *BAZAROV* ... *Then takes a step forward.*

ARKADY: Stop. (*puts down his bag, takes a step forward*) Excuse me.

The BAILIFF *looks at him.*

I've been watching. My opinion is that you've hurt him enough. You should stop now.

BAILIFF: Yes sir. But he's ...

ARKADY: Yes I know. But unless he's stolen someone's entire estate you've beaten him sufficiently.

BAZAROV: (*moving slowly forward*) Unless there is something personal in it. (*to* BAILIFF) Is there something personal in it.

BAILIFF: I'm just doing my job. I'm the bailiff for Nikolai Petrovich Kirsanov. His estate is just two kilometres on.

BAZAROV: Estate? (*laughs*)

ARKADY: (*to* BAZAROV) Farm! It's really just a farm. (*to* BAILIFF) Nikolai Petrovich is my father. And I know he'd want you to stop beating this man right now.

BAZAROV: (*to* BAILIFF) Do you often beat people for this young gentleman's father.

BAILIFF: Hardly ever.

BAZAROV: So this is a special occasion for you.

BAILIFF: Yes ... I mean no. I mean—

BAZAROV: And you must get some pleasure from it.

BAILIFF: Well I—

BAZAROV: There aren't many sources of true pleasure in our world. Justice is one. Justice completely obtained is a joyous vibrant thing. But then you know that. You're a bailiff. But did you know that justice was made to be like a wheel of fire. It turns. And when it turns, it burns!

> BAZAROV *puts his hand around the* BAILIFF'*s neck. He lifts. The* BAILIFF *is on tip-toes.*

I believe there was something personal in this beating. And if that's the case consider that this man might have friends. Yes even this piece of half-eaten garbage might have people who love him and might want to seek their own kind of justice. Love comes quickly to the wretched. Sometimes. I'm beginning to love him myself. I'm beginning to love him quite a lot.

He squeezes. The BAILIFF *gurgles.*

ARKADY: Bazarov.

BAZAROV: What!?

ARKADY: Let him go.

BAZAROV: That's not for you to say. It's for the piece of garbage to say. (*he looks at* GREGOR) Well?

GREGOR: I'm thinking.

> BAZAROV *laughs.*

ARKADY: (*to* GREGOR) Please!

BAZAROV: Don't pressure him now! He's been pressured quite enough for one day.

ARKADY: His face is turning blue.

BAZAROV: (*to* GREGOR) While you're thinking you should be in possession of all the facts. I'm holding his jugular. He'll be dead in one minute if you don't say anything.

GREGOR: Sir. A minute isn't very long to decide something like this. I mean there's a hatred here which is pretty severe. Him for me. Me for him. You know … if I had just a bit more time I could—

ARKADY: Bazarov. Please. This is ridiculous. It's murder.

BAZAROV: It's all right. My friend here and I can take the responsibility. (*to* GREGOR) Can't we.

GREGOR: Can we? (BAZAROV *shrugs*) Let him go.

> BAZAROV *takes his hand off the* BAILIFF*'s neck. The* BAILIFF *doubles up. Wheezing. He drops to his knees.*

ARKADY: Thank you.

BAZAROV: Thank him. (*points to* GREGOR) Go ahead.

> *Pause.* ARKADY *looks puzzled.*

Relax my friend. Would I really make you thank a piece of garbage. It was just a passing thought.

> BAZAROV *goes to retrieve his suitcase.* ARKADY *goes to* GREGOR. *Helps him up.*

The wounds on his back are fairly serious. (*leaving*) Tell him to stay away from those stupid peasant home remedies. Tell him to seek out a chemist for disinfectant. If he can't find one he can visit me at your father's estate.

ARKADY: Farm.

GREGOR: Thank you.

BAZAROV: Tell him it was my pleasure.

> BAZAROV *leaves. Puffing mightily on his cigar.*

ARKADY: Will you be all right.

GREGOR: My mother makes a garlic and fish poultice. We use it all the time.

ARKADY: You heard what he said about that.

GREGOR: Should I believe him.

ARKADY: You should if you're smart. He's a doctor.

BAILIFF: (*through his teeth*) Some doctor.

ARKADY: Well a student actually. (*picking up his bag*) But brilliant ... yes I'd believe him. (*looks at them both*) If I were you. (*leaves*)

> The BAILIFF *and* GREGOR *remain where they are, staring at one another.* GREGOR *laughs.*
>
> *Blackout.*

SCENE ONE

The garden of the Kirsanov house. A couple of benches. A small table. Lilac tree. NIKOLAI KIRSANOV *is pacing. Looking occasionally at his pocket watch. He is a rumpled, pleasant looking man in his mid-forties. Wearing checked trousers and an old sweater.*

PIOTR *comes on carrying a tray of fruit.*

KIRSANOV: Are they here.

PIOTR: No.

KIRSANOV: What do you suppose is keeping them. Why am I asking you that. What do you know about it.

PIOTR: Actually I do have an opinion.

KIRSANOV: Go ahead.

PIOTR: The carriage. It could have broken down. Broke down last week.

KIRSANOV: The carriage was repaired.

PIOTR: Not well.

KIRSANOV: How do you know.

PIOTR: I repaired it.

KIRSANOV: Are you admitting you did a bad job.

PIOTR: I did what I could sir. The front axles were severely warped. There is no money for replacements.

KIRSANOV: Who told you that.

PIOTR: Your brother, sir.

KIRSANOV: Is this my brother's land.

PIOTR: Not to my knowledge, sir.

KIRSANOV: Piotr. Stop assuming that all my questions require answers from you. What's that you're carrying.

PIOTR *just looks at him.*

PIOTR: Is that a question I should answer, sir?

KIRSANOV: Is that insolence, Piotr.

PIOTR: Fruit!

KIRSANOV: What? I see it's fruit. Never mind. What's it for. Never mind. Take it away. Are we Europeans. Never mind. Take it away. We don't eat in the garden. We eat at a table indoors.

ARKADY *enters.*

ARKADY: Of course we do. Are we barbarians, Piotr. No don't answer that.

KIRSANOV: Here's my son. Look at him. Look at him. A university graduate. Come here.

ARKADY *goes to him. They kiss. The Russian style.*

You look well.

ARKADY: I am. You look tired.

KIRSANOV: Oh? Well I … No I feel fine. I was worried about you. You should have been here three hours ago.

ARKADY: Trouble with the carriage. We left it in town with the driver for repairs.

PIOTR: Do you know if the repairs will be expensive, monsieur, sir.

ARKADY: I didn't ask. (*to* KIRSANOV) Should I have found out, Father. Before asking the blacksmith to go ahead.

PIOTR: Yes.

KIRSANOV: No. Of course not. You can leave now Piotr.

ARKADY: You're dressing differently, Piotr. I believe you're speaking differently too.

KIRSANOV: Like a European. That's your Uncle Pavel's doing. He's remodelling the domestic help. Foolishness.

PIOTR: I have an opinion about that, sir.

KIRSANOV: I'm sure you do. But a meal is being prepared inside which needs your supervision so you have to leave here now and … go … into … the … kitchen.

PIOTR *bows. Starts off.* BAZAROV *comes in. Takes an apple off* PIOTR*'s tray as he passes.* PIOTR *bows to* BAZAROV. BAZAROV *smiles. Bows back.* PIOTR *leaves.*

BAZAROV: Why does he bow like that. Is he French.

ARKADY: Bazarov come here. My father. Father. This is my best friend in the world.

They shake hands.

KIRSANOV: Yevgeny Vassilyich, my son has mentioned you often in his letters. It is a pleasure to have you here with us.

BAZAROV: I'm just passing through. I'm on vacation and I have to visit my parents. They live not too far from here. Arkady thought you and I should meet.

KIRSANOV: Of course we should meet. And you must stay with us for awhile.

BAZAROV: We'll see.

ARKADY: Don't try to convince him, Father. He comes and goes for his own reasons. No one can figure them out.

BAZAROV: Why do they try, I wonder. (*bites the apple*) I'm starving. If you don't mind I think I'll wander into the kitchen and pick at things.

KIRSANOV: Oh … You'll do, what? Pick? Oh. Of course. But we'll be eating soon. An enormous meal is being—

BAZAROV: I'm hungry now. I try to eat only when I'm hungry. Sleep only when I'm tired. You and your son the young gentleman graduate here have much to discuss. (*goes off*)

KIRSANOV: An … interesting young man.

ARKADY: You're thinking he's rude. But he's not. He's just practical. And he's brilliant. He's had an enormous influence on me. Please be good to him.

KIRSANOV: In what way has he influenced you.

ARKADY: In how to look at things. Institutions. Traditions … the rest.

KIRSANOV: And how is that.

ARKADY: Critically.

KIRSANOV: I see. Are you looking at me critically now.

ARKADY: You're not an institution, Father. You're a gentleman farmer. Besides I love you faults and all.

KIRSANOV: And I love you friends and all … (*laughs, grabs him*) Come here. Look at you. I'm so proud.

ARKADY: Graduating wasn't difficult. What do I do now.

KIRSANOV: Anything you want. (*He holds him at arm's length*) What do you want by the way.

ARKADY *shrugs.*

He shrugs. He shrugs. But I know he can do better. He's a university graduate. He can use words.

ARKADY: I ... want to change things.

KIRSANOV: Arkady, is that your friend talking.

ARKADY: We can discuss this later. How is farm life.

KIRSANOV: Oh, it's ... No I won't lie to you. Well perhaps a little. (*laughs*) No. Difficult. The new laws. Nobody is sure. I have as you know one of the most liberal practices anywhere. I have turned from serfdom to tenant farming. Some of the ... working tenants ... work. Some ... steal. I haven't a great deal of experience in management so ...

FENICHKA *comes on. A baby wrapped in a blanket in her arms.*

FENICHKA: Oh. Please excuse me. We ... I ... was just getting some ... air. (*leaves*)

ARKADY: Was that your young housekeeper.

KIRSANOV: Fenichka. Yes. Fenichka has—

ARKADY: A baby.

KIRSANOV: Yes! What? Yes. A baby. She has a baby. But—

ARKADY: No husband?

KIRSANOV: What? No. No she has no ...

ARKADY: Husband?

KIRSANOV: But that's a long story. (*looks at his watch*) I think I have something to do now, if I could just remember what it is ... Perhaps later this evening we could sit down and talk about all these things. Your friend. My farm. Fenichka's ... husband. Yes. Now I remember. I have to go. I'm sorry. A matter with my bailiff. (*starts off*)

ARKADY: Oh Father. About your bailiff.

KIRSANOV: Yes?

ARKADY: Perhaps we can discuss him later as well.

KIRSANOV: Certainly. Put him on the list. We'll talk about everything. I promise. (*looks at his watch*) Your Uncle Pavel should be getting up soon.

ARKADY: He's still taking long naps?

KIRSANOV: Longer. Much longer.

> *He leaves.* ARKADY *looks around. Sits.*

> FENICHKA *comes back on. Without the baby.*

ARKADY: (*stands*) Hello.

FENICHKA: Hello.

ARKADY: I'm Arkady. We met briefly last year.

FENICHKA: Yes. Hello …

ARKADY: Hello.

FENICHKA: I believe I was rude earlier. I came to apologize. And to welcome you back to your home properly.

ARKADY: That's not necessary.

FENICHKA: Oh. Yes it is. I'm sorry. And welcome. I mean I'm very pleased that you are here with your father. He needs you desperately. No I shouldn't have said that.

> *She leaves. Shaking her head. Talking to herself. Bumping into* UNCLE PAVEL *on his way on.* PAVEL *is a healthy looking man. Close cropped hair. Clean shaven. Wearing dark suit of English cut. Opal cufflinks. Pink nail polish. He is reading a small book of poetry.*

FENICHKA: (*a gentle scream*) Ohh. It's you. Please excuse me.

PAVEL: No it is you who would direct an honour my way by allowing me to apologize.

FENICHKA: Pardon?

PAVEL: The fault was all mine.

FENICHKA: I hear a baby screaming. (*runs off*)

PAVEL: I hear nothing.

ARKADY: Neither do I.

PAVEL: (*turns*) Ah! You're here. Good. Let's shake hands. (*they do*) You are a splendid young man. I always said so. You have your father's good heart and if you worked at it you could have my good style.

ARKADY: No one has your style, Uncle.

PAVEL: Oh there are two or three Englishmen, and a German baron who do, but otherwise you are quite correct. Let's hug! (*they do.* PAVEL *wipes away a tear*) Have you seen your father.

ARKADY: Yes. He had to run off. Some sort of urgent business.

PAVEL: Poor man. He is always running off. Stumbling back. Falling into bed exhausted. For the most part, his life is a disaster. Poor lovely man … Where's my fruit … He does have one small consolation. You just saw her?

ARKADY: Fenichka? But she's—

PAVEL: A child? A housekeeper? A semi-literate? I thought your generation was above those judgements.

ARKADY: We are. I mean I wasn't … I was just … Why didn't he introduce us properly. Explain.

PAVEL: He's in love. He behaves stupidly around her. Besides, what should he explain to you.

ARKADY: The baby.

PAVEL: Frightened are you, by the notion that you're no longer the only heir?

ARKADY: That never entered my mind, honestly.

PAVEL: Ask him about the baby yourself. I'm saying nothing about it. So tell me about your future. Law? The military? The civil service. I suggest, of course, the military. Like your grandfather, the great general. Like me the not so great captain.

ARKADY: Never the military. It's corrupt from top to bottom.

PAVEL: Really. How did you discover that.

ARKADY: It's a well known fact.

PAVEL: Really. I must be out of touch. Perhaps I've been in the country too long.

ARKADY: I realize you feel a certain loyalty to the army.

PAVEL: Not true. But I do find it necessary from time to time to ask your generation to be more specific with its criticisms.

> BAZAROV *comes on. Munching on a chicken leg.* PAVEL *turns to him abruptly.*

You. The stables are in the rear. Deliver whatever it is you have brought. Then feel free to leave. Thank you very much.

> ARKADY *is in shock, until* BAZAROV *laughs.*

ARKADY: Uncle. I'm sorry. This is my dear friend. Bazarov.

PAVEL *looks at them both.*

PAVEL: I am deeply shamed.

He bows formally.

BAZAROV: So am I.

He bows formally.

PAVEL: I beg your pardon.

BAZAROV: To allow my dress to deteriorate to a point where a gentleman such as yourself could make such a foolish mistake. Please accept my apology.

PAVEL: Well the truth is, I believe I owe you the apology.

BAZAROV: Then let's just say we're both fools and shake hands.

PAVEL: Well … Yes. Of course.

> PAVEL *extends his hand.* BAZAROV *throws away his chicken leg. Extends a hand. They shake.* BAZAROV *raises* PAVEL*'s hand to look at it.*

BAZAROV: Do you have a fungus infection under your fingernails?

PAVEL: No.

BAZAROV: So the pink nail polish is just decoration.

PAVEL: (*withdraws his hand*) You find it … distasteful?

BAZAROV: No. Only superfluous.

ARKADY: My uncle is well known in Moscow and Petersburg as a leader in fashion.

PAVEL: But I'm sure your friend finds fashion superfluous. (*to* BAZAROV) Correct?

BAZAROV: Correct.

PAVEL: Then we should change the subject immediately.

BAZAROV: In a moment, if you don't mind. Is that an English suit.

PAVEL: English cut. Russian cloth.

BAZAROV: So you are leading us into the fashion of the English.

PAVEL: At this moment in our history we could learn much from the English. The aristocracy in particular.

BAZAROV: What exactly.

ARKADY: Yes, Uncle. What?

PAVEL: The English aristocracy never yield one iota of their rights. And for that reason they respect the rights of others. They demand the fulfillment of obligations due to them, and therefore they fulfill their own obligations to others.

BAZAROV: I see we have changed the subject successfully. We're now talking about politics.

ARKADY: Do you resent the new rights for the serfs, Uncle. You've always been so kind to them, I thought.

BAZAROV: My young friend here still has a weak spot in his heart. Excuse me while I cut it out. (*to* ARKADY) What in God's name has kindness to do with justice!? What has attitude of any kind to do with what is natural. Or what is the law!?

ARKADY: I was merely being kind to my uncle.

PAVEL: He's always been a kind boy. Perhaps you didn't know that. Perhaps in Petersburg he pretended not to be kind.

BAZAROV: No he was kind in Petersburg. To people who needed or deserved his kindness.

PAVEL: I think we should stop now. If one gets off on the wrong foot it is necessary to pause before getting back into step. That is perhaps the only useful thing the army taught me. That, and how to shoot with deadly accuracy of course. So I'll retire now and we'll meet later for dinner, when I am less enervated and you are perhaps—

BAZAROV: Better dressed?

PAVEL: Better tempered.

> PAVEL *starts to bow. Stops himself. Shrugs. Leaves.*

ARKADY: Let me explain about my uncle.

BAZAROV: Your uncle is perfectly clear to me.

ARKADY: You're judging just what you see.

BAZAROV: When I see the rest I'll judge the rest. If you are going to tell me he's got a good soul that's not fair. You know I don't understand what that word means.

ARKADY: He's had a difficult life.

BAZAROV: If you continue to say things like that to me one day I might bite your lips off. He's one of the many sorts of country gentry. What could there be in his past to possibly justify his ridiculous clothes and manners.

ARKADY: Love. A great love that wasn't returned.

BAZAROV: So he played his cards with a woman and he lost. And that turned him into a fop.

ARKADY: He … I believe he merely took comfort in what was expected of him. What he had some chance at being successful at.

BAZAROV: You have a poet's understanding of life.

ARKADY: There is no need to be insulting.

BAZAROV: Harden yourself. Or you won't be any use in our kind of work.

ARKADY: So you have decided on a course of action.

BAZAROV: No secret there. I'm going to study medicine and natural science and chemistry and physics as you know. You are going to do … well if you ever get around to choosing a profession, I'm sure you'll be successful at … whatever it is.

ARKADY: Yes. Yes. But what else.

BAZAROV: Ah. You mean actually. Truly. What subversive things will we be doing at night.

ARKADY: I suppose I mean that … in a way. Yes what subversive things will we be doing at night.

BAZAROV *puts his hand on* ARKADY's *chest.*

BAZAROV: Staying alert.

BAZAROV *puts his foot behind* ARKADY's *feet. Pushes.* ARKADY *falls.*

You should start practising immediately, my young friend. (*starts off*)

ARKADY: Why are you always calling me your young friend. We're practically the same age.

BAZAROV *stops.*

BAZAROV: Time means very little. Experience not much more. The important thing is perception. You look at the world and still perceive some kind of future for it with one thing leading to another with a few humane modifications along the way. I look at the world and think of ways of taking it all apart. Starting again from scratch ... But of course you know that ... I think you just like to find new ways of making me say it again ...

He leaves.

ARKADY: Yes ... Until I understand what he actually means by it ... Chemistry ... Physics ... Bombs. Yes ... Or maybe ... No. Bombs. He's going to blow things up. Churches. Government buildings. Military headquarters. I couldn't ... Well I could ... yes I could do that too ... If there was no other way ... Banks ... Luxury hotels ... Libraries ... (*looks around*) Farms?

Blackout.

SCENE TWO

Begin in darkness.

The sound of several people arguing loudly. Lights up.

The Kirsanov drawing room. A small supper table. The meal is over.
KIRSANOV, ARKADY, BAZAROV, *and* FENICHKA *are seated.* PAVEL *is
pacing a few feet away.* PIOTR *is standing upstage of them. Hands
behind his back. Expressionless.*

PAVEL: All right! All right, please!! Please let me speak.

ARKADY: (*stands*) I think you're wrong. Simply wrong!

KIRSANOV: A little respect! Please the supper is ruined!

FENICHKA: I hear the baby.

KIRSANOV: You see you've woken the baby!

PAVEL: To hell with the baby!

KIRSANOV: Pavel!

PAVEL: Let me speak!

ARKADY: I was speaking! You interrupted!

PAVEL: Well let me interrupt then! Please!

FENICHKA: Please! I should go to the baby!

KIRSANOV: The baby has a nurse doesn't he!

FENICHKA: Why are you yelling at me Nikolai.

KIRSANOV: Oh. I'm sorry. (*to the others*) You see. I'm yelling at
her!

ARKADY: I was simply trying to say that respect is not something
you take for granted!

PAVEL: Principles! I want to talk about principles.

ARKADY: Yes there's the problem, Uncle. You think I don't
respect your principles. What I actually said was that your
principles are linked to certain traditions—

PAVEL: If you ignore tradition you ignore what we are made of.
You don't know the Russian people. They hold tradition
sacred. How can you work for them if you don't know them.
But that's not my point. Please please I beg you let me make
my point!!

BAZAROV *has just finished eating.*

BAZAROV: Cigar?

KIRSANOV / PAVEL / ARKADY: No!

BAZAROV: Let him make his point, Arkady. All this shouting is upsetting this young woman.

BAZAROV *lights a cigar.*

FENICHKA: No I'm all right. Thank you. But I'm worried—

KIRSANOV: Honestly, Fenichka. The baby will survive without you for an evening. You should be here with us.

ARKADY: I think so too. in fact, I'm the one who insisted that you dine with us.

KIRSANOV: There. You see?

FENICHKA: (*to* ARKADY) I'm grateful, believe me.

BAZAROV: You need his permission to eat, do you.

ARKADY: Please Bazarov. Of course not. What she meant—What I meant—

PAVEL: What he meant was, he doesn't care about your station in life one way or the other, Fenichka. He loves his father. If his father is happy, he's happy.

BAZAROV: What is all this about.

KIRSANOV: Pavel.

PAVEL: Oh for God's sake. Can't we air this thing.

KIRSANOV: (*to* BAZAROV) A family matter.

BAZAROV: I'll leave.

KIRSANOV: No please. I believe we were talking about principles.

PAVEL: That's the ticket! Now to our young friends here, I am simply an empty poseur.

ARKADY: Uncle.

PAVEL: I know you love me. But we're not speaking of love. We're speaking of beliefs. Of dignity.

BAZAROV: No. Principles, remember?

PAVEL: I remember better than you. We were eating a few moments ago. You asked me to explain my earlier comments about the English aristocracy. I explained that what I meant by that was that—simply put—if you don't respect yourself you cannot respect others.

ARKADY: Yes. And I said—no, Bazarov said that it didn't matter if you respected yourself or not—that it would have the same impact on the population at large. Namely none—

PAVEL: Yes. Because we of the aristocracy are the men of folded arms, aren't we. Big gaudy do-nothings.

ARKADY: But what I said after that was—

PAVEL: A simple addendum to what your friend had already said. Be still Arkady. My quarrel is with the man in black here.

BAZAROV: You don't like my clothes. I'm sorry. It's the closest I have to something decent to eat in. Besides it was the only thing that was clean.

PAVEL: It is the uniform of a nihilist.

   Pause.

KIRSANOV: A what.

ARKADY: Nihilist. It comes from the Latin. Nihil. It means—

PAVEL: Nothing.

ARKADY: Exactly. (*to* KIRSANOV) The word is now used in the cities mostly to describe a kind of man. A man who recognizes nothing.

PAVEL: Or respects nothing.

ARKADY: A man who … looks at everything critically. Takes no principles for granted.

PAVEL: Principles! What do you know—

ARKADY: Please I was going to say that we don't recognize authority and to be 'principled' as you say—

KIRSANOV: You said 'we,' son. Are you a what's-it-called too.

ARKADY: Nihilist. Well … Yes.

PAVEL: Doctrine. They think they've invented it. The philosophy of disrespect has been here before. It always proves to be bankrupt.

BAZAROV: If I may—

PAVEL: Yes.

BAZAROV: The baby *is* crying. And coughing too.

FENICHKA: (*to* KIRSANOV) Please let me go to him.

KIRSANOV: Certainly.

BAZAROV: I might be of help.

FENICHKA: No that's not necessary.

BAZAROV: I know some medicine.

KIRSANOV: Then please go with her.

> BAZAROV *stands.*

FENICHKA: Excuse me.

> *She leaves.*

BAZAROV: Fine dinner. Especially the soup. Very much like my mother makes. And she is an excellent cook.

PAVEL: We'll continue this later.

BAZAROV: I don't think so. I think you enjoy debating too much for my taste.

PAVEL: Well if there's a reason I do—

BAZAROV: I believe you should state your case if you're asked, then leave it. Thoughts aren't like laundry. They don't need to be hung out to dry.

> KIRSANOV *is gesturing* PAVEL *to sit down.*

PAVEL: But ... but I would ... Please humour an old ... older man. I would simply like to know what you are planning to do after you have torn everything down.

BAZAROV: Seriously?

PAVEL: Of course!

BAZAROV: Nothing.

PAVEL: What?

> BAZAROV *goes to* PAVEL.

BAZAROV: I'll do nothing. The tearing down is sufficient. In fact an entire life's work. The next generation can do the building. As for your earlier comments. Principles mean nothing to me. Neither as an idea nor a word. Other words. Aristocratism, liberalism, progress. Just empty words. Useless words. And foreign words to boot. I simply base my conduct on what is useful … Oh a few years ago we young people were saying that our officials took bribes, that we had no roads, no trade, no impartial courts of justice—

PAVEL: Of course, I understand those accusations. In fact, I agree with many of your criticisms but—

BAZAROV: Then we realized that just to keep on talking about our social diseases was a waste of time, and merely led to a trivial doctrinaire attitude. We saw that our clever men, our so-called progressives and reformers never accomplished anything, that we were concerning ourselves with a lot of nonsense, discussing art, abstract creative work, parliamentarianism, the law and the devil knows what, while all the while the real question was getting daily bread to eat, stopping the vulgar superstitions of our church, preventing our fledgling industries from coming to grief because of the crooks who run them, and realizing that the government's so-called emancipation of the serfs will do us no good because the serfs are so without pride that they spend most of their time robbing each other and drinking themselves into oblivion.

PAVEL: And so knowing all this convinced you to become a nihilist. In effect, to do nothing.

    BAZAROV *stiffens. Then smiles crookedly. Shakes his head.*

BAZAROV: Well at least nothing I could describe to you. Or nothing you could understand. (*leaves*)

PAVEL: Arrogant, arrogant man! (*pounds the table*) Arrogant! (*points at* KIRSANOV) And if I were you I'd think twice about letting a man who respects nothing, fears nothing, feels nothing, be alone with that young girl! (*starts off. Stops*) That's what I say.

    PAVEL *leaves. Pause.* KIRSANOV *and* ARKADY *look at each other. Both smiling weakly.*

KIRSANOV: Some of what he said I agree with.

ARKADY: Who.

KIRSANOV: Bazarov. The superstitions in our culture do a great deal of damage … Almost everything else he said made me sad. I'm not at all like your Uncle Pavel. Not so firmly rooted in the past. Nevertheless ... Actually I thought I saw a look of sadness on your face when your friend was speaking at one point.

ARKADY: Maybe you did. Maybe I wasn't thinking about what Bazarov was saying though. I was probably thinking about you, Papa.

KIRSANOV: You've looked around the farm. Yes I know things don't look so good. When I moved back here three years ago I had such high hopes. But I have to tell you, Arkasha, that in spite of the unpaid bills, the workers who hate me for not paying them enough, the workers who steal, my bailiff who is a drunk and a bully and who scares me a little—I'm happy. No well not exactly. Yes yes I have to be honest, I'm a bit happy.

ARKADY: Well I won't assume you're happy at being a total failure as a farmer and a businessman. I'll have to guess there's some other reason.

KIRSANOV: Fenichka.

> KIRSANOV *looks at* PIOTR. PIOTR *nods. Turns around so that his back is to them.*

ARKADY: Fenichka. And her baby.

KIRSANOV: My baby.

ARKADY: My brother.

KIRSANOV: Your brother. Yes. You see I hope you ... Well you know what I hope ... You see, Fenichka's mother died. You knew that?

ARKADY: No.

KIRSANOV: Oh. But you know it was her mother who I hired to be my housekeeper. Naturally she brought Fenichka to live here with her.

ARKADY: Naturally. Certainly.

KIRSANOV: When her mother died ... You see Fenichka knew the house by then. How to keep it ordered ... But that's not ... When her mother died she was alone. I felt a kind of sympathy ... at first. She's ... well, you can tell, a gentle person. The sympathy became ... became ...

ARKADY: I should be making this easier for you. But I—

KIRSANOV: You don't approve.

ARKADY: Oh no. It's not that. I just want you to tell me in your own way. You must have some reason for not having told me before.

KIRSANOV: In a letter? No I couldn't. You see … I loved your mother. You know that. We don't have to discuss your mother. This is …

ARKADY: You should marry her, Papa.

KIRSANOV: I love her.

ARKADY: The baby should have your name.

KIRSANOV: And yours.

ARKADY: Yes.

KIRSANOV: That's all right with you?

ARKADY: You thought it wouldn't be?

KIRSANOV: Well I didn't presume. No that's not the truth. It's not about you. You see, I try to put a foot in the right direction but the other foot won't move with it. I'm afraid there's still something from the old world in me.

ARKADY: If you make love to a housekeeper's daughter … If you love a housekeeper's daughter … If you're … a bit happy with her now you'll be happy if you're married to her.

KIRSANOV: Marriage is … it becomes … a mixture of personal histories. How can you tell if the mixture …

> ARKADY *gets up. Goes behind his father. Puts his arms around his neck.*

ARKADY: You're a good man. You'll do the right thing.

KIRSANOV: Perhaps. But how would she feel about being in my world. I don't know how she feels even now. I don't think so but it's possible she only took me … I mean she could have been afraid of losing her place in the house. What am I saying.

ARKADY: She loves you. Believe me. Everybody loves you.

KIRSANOV: (*sighs*) Just as long as you love me.

> BAZAROV *comes on.*

KIRSANOV: Is the baby all right.

BAZAROV: Yes.

KIRSANOV: Nothing to be concerned about?

BAZAROV: A chill maybe. I left him slurping happily at his mother's breast.

KIRSANOV: She nursed the baby in front of you?

BAZAROV: That's the way they do things in the country Nikolai Petrovich. She's a very fine young woman. Healthy. Intelligent. Direct.

KIRSANOV: Direct?

BAZAROV: She opened up. We had a good little talk. Wouldn't tell me who the father was though. I assume it is you sir. I couldn't stomach the idea of it being your brother.

KIRSANOV: Excuse me!? Yes … (*awkwardly*) Excuse me. (*leaves*)

ARKADY: That was grotesque! Grotesque and heartless!

BAZAROV: Oh let's strip the veneer from these gentle country barons, my friend. Let's clear the air and see where we really are. Or aren't you up to it.

ARKADY: So that was a test for my sake.

BAZAROV: Or maybe mine. Who knows. Or maybe I just spoke the truth. As simple as that.

> *A commotion.* PIOTR *faces out again. The* BAILIFF *staggers on. Followed by* KIRSANOV, *trying to restrain him. The* BAILIFF *is drunk. Carrying a large board.*

KIRSANOV: What are you doing here? Who do you think you are brushing past me like that.

> *The* BAILIFF *shakes* KIRSANOV's *arm off.*

BAILIFF: Out of my way.

KIRSANOV: But I own this farm. I'm the owner. I can't believe you're talking to me this way.

BAILIFF: Am I a human being. Are you a human being. Can't human beings talk.

KIRSANOV: Of course. But not like this! I mean you shouldn't be here. And that's final!

> KIRSANOV *grabs the* BAILIFF's *arm again. The* BAILIFF *shakes him off.* KIRSANOV *falls.* ARKADY *goes to help him up.*

BAILIFF: Get off me! I've got business here all right. (*to* BAZAROV) So you tricked me before. But I don't forget. I never forget. I checked around. You're nothing special. You're not an official person. I can fix you all right. And nothing happens.

BAZAROV: Officially, you mean.

BAILIFF: You tricked me. I wasn't ready for ya. (*advances*) I'm ready now.

He swings the board at BAZAROV. BAZAROV *ducks under the board. Throws the* BAILIFF *forward. The* BAILIFF *falls on his face.* BAZAROV *grabs a plate from the table. The* BAILIFF *is on his knees now.* BAZAROV *breaks the plate across the back of the* BAILIFF*'s head. The* BAILIFF *falls unconscious.*

PIOTR: That plate was over two hundred years old!

KIRSANOV: Bazarov!

ARKADY: Bazarov.

BAZAROV: (*to* ARKADY) Oh I forgot. We've got an invitation to stay with a mutual friend in town. His father owns a hotel. I think it was time we were moving on anyway.

Blackout.

SCENE THREE

The sitting room of a hotel suite.

A couch, a chair. A large floral arrangement.

BAZAROV, ARKADY, *and* SITNIKOV *are drinking champagne.*
BAZAROV *is smoking a cigar. Chuckling at* SITNIKOV. *Throwing back
glass after glass. Lounging on the couch.* ARKADY *is reading a book.
Sipping.* SITNIKOV *is on his feet telling a story which he finds
particularly funny. He wears a Slavic jacket. And European trousers.
He has a strange laugh which could be something he accomplishes by
expelling air and somehow producing an extended 'ee' sound.*

SITNIKOV: Eeeeeee. But the governor says to my father, 'This is
my province, if you want to do business here you have to
make me feel that you like me.' So ... my father kissed him.
Eeeeeee. That's funny. I know that's funny. But this is
funnier. My father meant it. He told me later that he did like
the governor, that he thought, all in all, he was a pleasant
man. So he ... eeeeee, kissed him with genuine warmth.
Needless to say the governor looked on my father from that
moment on as a potentially unstable business partner and my
father was not allowed to establish the system of trade he
wanted, so he sought my advice. 'Buy a hotel,' I said ... eeee.
I was joking you see. It was the first thing that came into my
head. So he did ... eeeeee. And here we are. Drinking his
champagne. Eeeeeee.

BAZAROV *sits up suddenly.*

BAZAROV: Viktor! If the point of that amazingly long and only
mildly amusing story was merely to demonstrate that your
father is a fool, I will ... rip out your tonsils.

SITNIKOV *sobers immediately.*

SITNIKOV: Yes. And you'd be quite right too. No of course the
point of the story is ... is ... this—even though good things
can sometimes come from bad practices we must always be
attempting to turn those good things back—

BAZAROV: Into a joke.

SITNIKOV: Well no ... But Yevgeny you used to enjoy a good joke.

BAZAROV: I still do.

SITNIKOV: I see but now is not the time. I see. We are graduates now. Yes. The time now and the time ahead is serious business. If that's what you say, I am your disciple and that is how I shall start behaving immediately—

BAZAROV: Good. Here is the first piece of serious business I wish you to undertake. Go get more champagne.

SITNIKOV: Of course. (*starts off. Stops. Points at* BAZAROV) Eeeeee. You tricked me.

BAZAROV: Eeeeeee. A little.

SITNIKOV: Never mind. I am your disciple truly. I don't mind.

He leaves. BAZAROV *practices* SITNIKOV*'s laugh.*

ARKADY: (*still reading*) When did he become your disciple.

BAZAROV: You'd have to say it was a gradual process. Almost imperceptible. Or else I would have put a stop to it.

ARKADY: Would you.

BAZAROV: There is not much to be gained by having imbeciles as disciples.

ARKADY: But you don't object to the notion of having disciples as a rule.

BAZAROV: What are you reading.

ARKADY: Nothing you'd find very interesting.

BAZAROV sits up. Grabs the book.

BAZAROV: A manual on agricultural management. A German manual?

ARKADY: I'm sorry but they happen to be the foremost experts on the subject. I'm looking for ways of advising my father.

BAZAROV: Really! (*throws the book back*) I liked your father more or less.

ARKADY: How generous of you to say so.

BAZAROV: Now don't get in a snit. I was being honest. I found him to be intelligent and kind. I wasn't too happy about the way he's keeping that girl—his young flame—flickering in the corner.

ARKADY: You don't understand that. So we shouldn't talk about it. My father has some problems regarding his feelings. I think that's quite common in men his age.

BAZAROV: Oh come now. His problems there are about class. His class. Her class. The 'indecent' distance between the two. You know that as well as I. And if you're going to be blind stupid, sentimental and obstinate about it, then you're right we shouldn't talk!

ARKADY: (*stands*) I've changed my mind. I think this is politically important. One strong piece of rope ... together is stronger than a bunch of smaller ropes tied ... together.

BAZAROV: The poet is struggling to find his metaphor here. Be careful.

ARKADY: If you take a generation ... or if a generation is taken and ... or not taken, if you don't attempt to heal the ... (*sits*)

BAZAROV: Simply please. Just say it.

ARKADY: It's better ... to educate these old fellows and thereby enlist their help for the future.

BAZAROV: No time. Not enough energy. Much more difficult than you could imagine. Basically unnecessary.

ARKADY: Take my father and my uncle as examples—

BAZAROV: (*stands*) Your uncle is absurd. He embodies much of what is wrong with this country. He lusts after foreign influences. He wears clothes that allow him to pretend he is actually living somewhere else. He uses make-up to contour his broad Russian face into something like an English ferret. He can't look simple peasants in the eye because they terrify him. Not because of what they might do to him someday but because of what they are. And what they are is Russian! Russian. For better or worse! Russian! ... (*takes a drink*) As for your father. The merciful thing is to let him alone. Let him die as he lived. Don't go trying to fill his head with bright new ideas. Unless you want him to stumble to his grave in chaos.

They are looking at one another. SITNIKOV *comes on. Three bottles of champagne.*

SITNIKOV: Mission accomplished.

They ignore him.

ARKADY: But what about love.

BAZAROV: What about it.

ARKADY: Are you against love.

BAZAROV: What kind of a question is that.

ARKADY: We've never really talked about it before. Seeing my father again, I realize how much I love him.

BAZAROV: I love my father as well. So?

ARKADY: So what is it? Love. Is it a kind of social necessity under certain circumstances. In a family for example. Or something else.

BAZAROV: Something else, probably. Since your first definition doesn't make any sense.

SITNIKOV: I'd have to agree with that.

ARKADY: Shut up.

SITNIKOV: You can't tell me to shut up.

BAZAROV: Can I tell you to shut up, Viktor.

ARKADY: Would it be a kind of elemental human characteristic for example. Something untouchable. Incomprehensible?

BAZAROV: Everything is comprehensible. You take the conditions. And measure them against the facts.

ARKADY: Like a science.

BAZAROV: Listen friend. If you're searching for some rationale for excusing certain kinds of behaviour you don't need my help. There are hundreds of novels, thousands of poems, in fact an entire world of art that will allow you to do that. You'll probably turn to them eventually. You might as well do it now.

ARKADY: You don't believe I have the stomach for hard choices, do you.

BAZAROV: This is the last summer vacation Arkady. Use it. I'm using it. Drink champagne. I'm drinking champagne. Spend time with fools. (*puts his arm around* SITNIKOV) I'm spending time with fools. Be as natural as you want. Autumn comes soon enough. When the leaves change you can change with them if you decide. Come on. That's as close to poetry as you'll ever get from me. And I did it just for you.

   He hugs ARKADY.

SITNIKOV: Do you truly think I'm a fool Yevgeny. I know you use humour as a cruel weapon. To cut to the truth. But … I can't stay, here in the room with you if that is your true opinion of me. I have a little pride, you know.

BAZAROV: Then it's a precious commodity. I suggest you save it by finding the door.

SITNIKOV *starts off.*

Viktor.

SITNIKOV *stops.*

SITNIKOV: Yes Yevgeny.

BAZAROV: Eeeeeee. (*he smiles*)

SITNIKOV: Another trick. Eeeeeee. God bless you. If he existed, of course. (*rushes to them. Awkwardly hugs them both*) Three friends embrace. They drink they think they quarrel. But eventually they embrace. It's summer. Let things occur they say. Autumn will come. Then we'll see if the world's safe. Eeeeeeeee.

Pause.

ANNA ODINTSOV *comes on. She is about thirty. Tall, wealthy, sparkling ironic expression. They don't see her.* SERGEI *comes on carrying two suitcases. Stands beside her.*

ANNA: Gentlemen.

They turn.

Young gentlemen. Excuse me.

They look at her. They are impressed. They look at each other. SITNIKOV *breaks away first.*

You are in my room.

SITNIKOV: What was that.

ANNA: This room. The bedrooms. The entire suite … is mine.

SITNIKOV: Madame Odintsov?

ANNA: Correct.

SITNIKOV: No it wasn't a question. I know your name of course. Let me explain.

BAZAROV: Yes please let him explain. It's bound to be a treat to watch.

SITNIKOV: I am Viktor Sitnikov. We have met on several occasions.

ANNA: Strange. I have no recollection of you.

SITNIKOV: No? Well no. Why should you. Who am I.

ANNA: Very well. Who are you.

BAZAROV: Continue Viktor. No disappointment so far.

SITNIKOV: My father owns this hotel.

ANNA: Is that an important fact.

SITNIKOV: Well no. Not in itself. How do you mean. I'm not a status seeker.

BAZAROV: Ouch. (*to* ARKADY) The man is a comic genius.

ANNA: Does the fact that your father owns the hotel somehow give you permission to occupy my rooms when I'm not here.

SITNIKOV: Good heavens. Do you think I do this on a regular basis.

BAZAROV: Good boy Viktor. Go blindly to the offensive.

SITNIKOV: Please, Bazarov.

SERGEI: Do you want me to throw them out ma'am.

ANNA: Yes after they've explained what they're doing here you can throw them out.

SITNIKOV: Who is that. Who are you. You're not one of our porters.

ANNA: Sergei works for me.

BAZAROV: A bodyguard. (*to* ARKADY) Quite a body too.

SERGEI: She heard that. Didn't you, ma'am.

ANNA: No.

BAZAROV: Do you want me to repeat it.

SITNIKOV: Oh dear. Things are getting worse. Listen. (*begins to gather the glasses and empty bottles*) Why don't we just leave and I'll explain later. It's a small misunderstanding. Perhaps I misread the calendar.

BAZAROV: I'm staying—

SITNIKOV: Bazarov.

BAZAROV: No I'm definitely staying. There's something about this woman that attracts me.

SERGEI: Do you want me to hit him hard, ma'am.

ANNA: No. Perhaps later I'll let you hit him hard. In the meantime please take my luggage into the bedroom.

SERGEI: Whatever you say.

> *He goes.*

ANNA: (*to* SITNIKOV) You may leave now.

SITNIKOV: Of course. Come on friends.

ANNA: Just you. This rude one here and his silent friend can stay awhile … if they wish.

ARKADY: Oh no that—

BAZAROV: Shush.

> ANNA *stares at* SITNIKOV. *He leaves.*
>
> ANNA *and* BAZAROV *stare at one another.* BAZAROV *walks to her slowly. Puts his hand on her cheek. Kisses her. Embraces her. She returns the embrace. The kiss becomes passionate.* ARKADY *is frozen. His eyes wide. Still kissing* ANNA, BAZAROV *puts out a hand to* ARKADY. ARKADY's *eyes get even wider. He backs off.* BAZAROV *snaps his fingers.* ARKADY *slowly moves in. Takes* BAZAROV's *hand.*
>
> BAZAROV *steps back. Puts* ARKADY's *hand in* ANNA's *hand.*

BAZAROV: Arkady Nikolayevich Kirsanov please meet my old friend Anna Sergyevna Odintsov.

> ANNA *gives a gentle laugh.*

ANNA: I've heard so much about you, Arkady.

ARKADY: You … You're, you're his—

ANNA: His friend the widow. The one with the reputation.

ARKADY: No. I meant I've heard so much about you as well. Everything except your name … no not everything … I mean—

BAZAROV: Please Arkady you're beginning to sound like Viktor. (*to* ANNA) Speaking of Viktor, you were very cruel to him Anna.

ANNA: I got the distinct impression you wanted me to be even crueler.

BAZAROV: I don't know what it is about him that stirs malice in me. I'd like to be philosophical and think it's his manner or his attitude, but I think it's actually his face.

ARKADY: You planned this?

BAZAROV: Haphazardly. When Viktor suggested we make ourselves comfortable somewhere in the hotel I bribed a porter into delivering us here. Then I bribed him to tell Viktor that Anna wasn't expected for a week. The rest I left to Madame Odintsov's wonderful sense of occasion.

ARKADY: I'll go find Viktor. He could be slitting his wrists.

ANNA: Over something so small.

ARKADY: Not that you found him here. But that he wasn't allowed to stay. Like we were.

BAZAROV: Yes. His manhood has been questioned. He won't actually understand that. But he'll be deeply depressed nonetheless. My fault ... I'll go fix it. You two get acquainted.

    BAZAROV *leaves.*

ANNA: Please sit.

ARKADY: May I help you with your cloak.

ANNA: Thank you.

    He does. SERGEI *comes on.*

SERGEI: That's done, ma'am.

ANNA: Thank you, Sergei.

SERGEI: I'm new at this remember, ma'am. What should I do now. Should I prepare your bath? Polish furniture?

ANNA: I prepare my own bath Sergei. That's not part of your job. What I wish you to do is make a bed of sorts for yourself outside my door.

SERGEI: And stay there? And guard it?

ANNA: Yes.

SERGEI: Yes. I can do that ... No problem.

    He leaves.

ARKADY: So he is a body guard then?

ANNA: Yes.

ARKADY: But why—

ANNA: Oh the usual reasons.

ARKADY: Sergei. Just ... Sergei?

ANNA: We don't use his other name. Sheep-in-a-ditch-in-love or something like that. Hideous. (*sits*) Please sit down. Here beside me.

ARKADY: There ... beside you?

ANNA: Please. (*he does*) You're staring.

ARKADY: I was afraid of that.

ANNA: I just thought I should let you know.

ARKADY: Thank you. Excuse me. (*lowers his head*) You're beautiful.

ANNA: So are you.

ARKADY: What?

ANNA: So have you decided what you're going to do with your life yet?

ARKADY: Well I ... How did—

ANNA: Bazarov says he's going to hire a band when you make a decision. I would have suggested law from what he told me of your ambitions. Law is the surest route to power unfortunately. But now that I've met you I don't think law is right for you at all. You're far too shy.

ARKADY: No ... No ... Not as a rule ... But when I saw you ... I became ... No it's too embarrassing to talk about.

ANNA: So we won't.

ARKADY: Thank you. So ... you've come to this hotel to be with Bazarov. Actually I'd like to rephrase that if you don't mind.

ANNA: You know Bazarov and I have been having an affair for a number of years. We don't have to be coy about that. We can be coy about other things if you wish ...

ARKADY: I ... well ... I've often asked to meet you.

ANNA: He likes his life compartmentalized. Have you ever met his parents.

ARKADY: No.

ANNA: Neither have I. He's kept us all separated. At first I believed that he was ashamed of every one of us. But later I understood ...

ARKADY: Focus.

ANNA: Yes. Exactly. Full attention to each at all times. No compromises for social reasons only.

ARKADY: And besides it wasn't necessary.

ANNA: (*smiles*) I see we have been reading the same book.

ARKADY: Yes he's quite a book our friend. Very demanding.

ANNA: And this is precisely the sort of conversation he has prevented us from having.

ARKADY: Until now for some reason.

ANNA: That was my idea. In fact I insisted upon it. I need help from both of you. (ARKADY *stands*)

ARKADY: I am at your service, till death if need be! (*he sits. Lowers his head*) I'm sorry. What a stupid thing to say.

ANNA: Like something out of a romance novel, wasn't it?

ARKADY: I used to read those books when I was young. I'm afraid little pieces of them are still attached to my brain.

A commotion outside. Two voices. Then a loud noise. BAZAROV *comes on. Adjusting his clothes.*

BAZAROV: (*to* ANNA) Please explain to that moron out there that if a person has already been in the room it poses no danger to let him return.

ANNA: Did you hurt him badly.

BAZAROV: He's ten feet high and weighs as much as a horse. The best I could do was put a finger in his eye. He'll be fine ... (*sits*) So will Viktor. And to prove he's a man of spirit and balance he sent us another bottle of his father's best.

BAZAROV opens the champagne. Serves.

ARKADY: None for me, please ... It ... makes me foolish.

BAZAROV: Really? Since when.

ARKADY: Please, no.

BAZAROV: Very well. (*to* ANNA) Have you two become intimate friends yet. Or was he dumbstruck by your appearance.

ARKADY: Yes. I behaved like a total ass, you'll be glad to hear.

BAZAROV: She has the same effect on all men.

ANNA: Not on you, as I remember.

ARKADY: But he's not a man. He's a primal force.

BAZAROV: I'll take that as a compliment.

ARKADY: It was meant as one. Surely you don't believe I enjoy behaving like a total ass. I'd much rather be a primal force.

ANNA: I thank heaven there is a Bazarov in my life. Although, heaven knows, one is quite enough.

BAZAROV: He won't know how to take that. Arkady is a primal force in training.

ANNA: That's too bad. You make a much more potent team the way you are. (*to* BAZAROV) That is the way you are. (*to* ARKADY) And ... the way ... you are.

BAZAROV: More champagne?

ANNA: Yes, please.

ARKADY: I'll join you.

BAZAROV: Really. Found your footing again, have you? (*pours*) Go ahead, Anna.

ANNA: Yes?

BAZAROV: The reason we're all here. You are going to tell us aren't you. Or do we have to guess ... Very well. You want us to murder someone.

> ARKADY *laughs.*

ANNA: Yes. Exactly. Good for Bazarov.

> ARKADY *looks at* BAZAROV.

BAZAROV: Who is it this time. One of those badgering old lechers who are always chasing you all over Russia.

ANNA: He's not a lecher. He's a deeply disturbed man. His name is Pavel Petrovich Kirsanov. And I would like him dead within the week.

ARKADY / BAZAROV: But—

BAZAROV: But that's his ... No! Consider it done.

ANNA: Then let's drink to it.

ARKADY: But that's my uncle.

ANNA: We know.

BAZAROV: Let's drink to it!

> BAZAROV *and* ANNA *raise glasses. Look at* ARKADY. *He looks at them.*
> *Blackout.*

A country road.

GREGOR *sitting on the ground. Fiddling with a pistol. Hears people approaching. Pulls a kerchief up to cover his lower face. Hides.*

BAZAROV *and* ARKADY *come on. Carrying suitcases.*

BAZAROV: I've told you she doesn't really want us to kill him. We're to talk to him about her, that's all.

ARKADY: That in itself might kill him. He'd be appalled. I'm a bit appalled just thinking about it.

BAZAROV: Your uncle has made a serious mistake. Anna is a woman of the new age. She has no time for fending off crazed suitors. She has ambitions. She intends to become politically influential.

ARKADY: A woman?

BAZAROV: Would you say that to her face.

ARKADY: I mean the odds against that would be astronomical.

BAZAROV: Would you say that to her face.

ARKADY: I have to sit down. (*he does*) I'm tired. Why do we have to walk everywhere.

BAZAROV: Saves money. Keeps us fit. Get up.

ARKADY: No. Besides I'm in no hurry to face my uncle. Honestly, I just don't think it my place to give him romantic advice.

BAZAROV: I'll do it.

ARKADY: Oh yes. And gently too I imagine.

BAZAROV: I'll state the case. I won't stammer. There'll be no emotion. A simple understanding will be reached.

ARKADY: He'll slap your face or something. That's what his generation does you know.

BAZAROV: Well then I'll slap him back. And I'll keep slapping him till he listens to reason.

ARKADY: Bazarov please. He's my father's brother after all. This once have pity.

BAZAROV: No time for that. Pity excuses weakness.

BAZAROV / ARKADY: Confuses the strong.

ARKADY: Oh please.

BAZAROV: Listen. (*sits beside him*) The truth is it might be better if I do it anyway. I know things you don't.

ARKADY: Yes I know. Only God knows more than you. And just barely.

BAZAROV: Shut up. I know things about your uncle and Anna. Things she told me in confidence just before we left.

ARKADY: Are they … sordid. I don't want to know.

BAZAROV: Anna didn't want you to know either. But I think it's better if you do. Considering how weak you're being. Sometimes a little dose of the truth …

ARKADY: Please just tell me if you're going to tell me.

BAZAROV: It appears your uncle, besides being a superfluous human being, is an extremely unhealthy one as well. This great unrequited love of his you mentioned to me … Well it turns out to have been Anna's mother.

ARKADY: Is that possible.

BAZAROV: One of life's cruel circular jokes … He pursued her mother for over a decade through Russia, Italy, France …

ARKADY: England. Scandinavia. He resigned his commission in the army. He spent his entire inheritance. He—

BAZAROV: Yes. But for the moment we're telling this story from Anna's point of view. Her mother was married. Happily says Anna, so we'll give her the benefit of the doubt. And your uncle made her life tragic. Letters. Hired informants. Public scenes. Well you know how that crowd responds to those things. Badly. The husband behaved badly. Anna's mother behaved badly. All their friends behaved badly. It became a bad life all around. Five years ago Anna's mother died. After that nothing was heard of Pavel Petrovich. Until three months ago … You see he's started it all over again. But now he's directing his obsession towards Anna. And something definitely unhealthy is playing havoc with his brain cells. Anna believes your uncle thinks she is, in fact, her mother … It has to be stopped. Under any other circumstances I could not care less about something like this. The mad dog ruling class insanely sniffing at each other.

ARKADY: I think Anna was right not to tell me. You have no compassion. Can't you imagine how great a love that must have been to have driven my uncle into this state.

BAZAROV: Romantic bilge. As I've already told you, Anna has other things on her mind. And she is too important to us to be diverted by this kind of thing.

ARKADY: And there it is again. 'Important to us.' Us? What are we? Are we a populist movement. Are we a political party. Are we an underground army.

BAZAROV: Pick one. Your favourite.

ARKADY: I'm serious.

BAZAROV: So am I. We could be any of those things. We'll have to see which one is the most useful.

ARKADY: And in the meantime we traipse around the countryside stomping on people's dreams.

BAZAROV: (*smiles*) Small tasks. Easily undertaken. Summer drags along. We go about our business like good citizens.

ARKADY: You go about. I'm staying here.

BAZAROV: Get up.

ARKADY: No. You don't need me. I'm weak. I'm distracted.

BAZAROV: But you've got potential. Anna saw it too.

ARKADY: I love her.

BAZAROV: What.

ARKADY: I love her. I loved her from the moment I saw her.

BAZAROV: Please don't say things like that without a knowing smile. They make me nauseous.

ARKADY: I could have been more abstract. I could have couched it in acceptable words. I could have said I felt a bond or something like that … but I …

BAZAROV: Give it up. She's not for you. She's too worldly. Too cynical. Dead cold at the core. I know …

ARKADY: How do you know. You've told me that your … friendship was only physical.

BAZAROV: Only physical? Friendship? What else do you suppose there is.

ARKADY: What are you saving.

BAZAROV: She's not for you. She's … for me.

ARKADY: (*stands*) You love her!?

BAZAROV: Yes I guess that would be your word for it.

ARKADY: All of a sudden you love someone!? And it has to be her!? (*he lets himself collapse*)

BAZAROV: Are you all right … Arkady?

ARKADY: I don't know how long I can take the stress of being your friend. (*puts his head in his hands*)

BAZAROV: Get up. Let's go.

ARKADY: Yes. Why not.

BAZAROV: Arkady?

ARKADY: (*standing*) Yes. Head on. I'll follow. Why not. I've got nothing else to do with my life.

> They start off. GREGOR *jumps out behind them. Pointing his pistol.*

GREGOR: Stop! Hands up! Don't turn around.

> ARKADY *obeys.* BAZAROV *turns around.*

I said don't turn around.

BAZAROV: And who are you to tell me what to do.

GREGOR: Can't you see I've got a pistol.

BAZAROV: Do I look like I'm blind. (*to* ARKADY) Turn around. And look at the wretched little thing who wants to rob us.

GREGOR: Be careful what you say.

BAZAROV: Shut up. (*to* ARKADY) Turn around.

ARKADY: (*sighs*) Certainly. Whatever you say. (*turns around*)

BAZAROV: Imposing, isn't he. This is where the country is going, I tell you.

GREGOR: Give me money.

BAZAROV: How much.

GREGOR: How much? How much do you have.

BAZAROV: Why? Do you just want a portion of it. Not the whole amount?

GREGOR: Yes. No. Give me the whole amount.

BAZAROV: (*to* ARKADY) You see? They do respond if you give them attention. They can be educated.

GREGOR: And your clothes. I want your clothes too. And our suitcases.

BAZAROV: Yes that's the problem, all right. Knowing something leads to wanting something leads to wanting everything. (*to* GREGOR) Slow down my friend. It's a long way to the revolution yet. How about a coin or two to help you get a decent meal.

GREGOR: I don't see how you can be so brave when I've got a pistol. Maybe you think I won't use it.

BAZAROV: Actually I think you can't use it. I can see from here that it's broken. The screw must have fallen away. The trigger is limp.

> GREGOR *checks. Immediately grabs the barrel of the pistol. Holds it up like a club.*

GREGOR: (*backing up*) Stay away from me. I warn you. I'm a cornered rat. I'm a cornered rat.

BAZAROV: Such amazing self-esteem. No don't run away. I like you.

GREGOR: What did you say.

BAZAROV: Don't you remember me … I like you … Actually I love you. (*to* ARKADY) I usually use the word ironically as you know. But this fellow I genuinely love. Remember, friend? The piece of garbage your father's bailiff was beating to a pulp.

GREGOR: No that's not me. That's … someone else. You don't recognize me. I'm wearing a mask.

BAZAROV: But you haven't changed your clothes.

> GREGOR *looks down. Pause. Pulls down the mask.*

GREGOR: These are the only clothes I've got.

BAZAROV: I'm sorry.

GREGOR: This is my first robbery. I was going to dress myself in your clothes for my second one. If I'd gotten that far.

ARKADY: (*to* BAZAROV) Let's go.

BAZAROV: Good idea. (*They start off. To* GREGOR) Come on ...
Come on, we're leaving.

GREGOR: You want me to come with you.

BAZAROV: Of course.

GREGOR: To turn me in.

BAZAROV: No. No why would I do that. You're one of us. (*to*
ARKADY) Isn't he.

ARKADY: If you say so.

BAZAROV: Come on.

GREGOR: (*to* ARKADY) Should I do what he says.

ARKADY: Do you have anything better to do.

> GREGOR *runs over.* BAZAROV *puts his arm around him.*

BAZAROV: Good man. Here we are then. Together. You'll be all
right now. You'll be fed. You'll be clothed. You'll have a nice
bed at the house of our friend here. Your future is secure.
(*looks up*) One down. One hundred million to go.

> *They start off.*

GREGOR: Why are you doing this.

BAZAROV: Because I love you.

> *They leave.*

> *Blackout.*

> *Intermission.*

SCENE FIVE

The Kirsanov garden. PAVEL *and* PIOTR.

PAVEL is more done-up than before. He sits in a wicker chair smoking a cigarette. PIOTR *stands beside him. Holding a tray with two glasses of sherry on it.*

PAVEL: This will be interesting to us both, Piotr. For different reasons of course.

PIOTR: Yes sir.

PAVEL: Imagine we are in a salon in Paris. Surrounded by intriguing people. Over there the Countess What's-her-name, on my right the Earl of Gloucester or Leicester or Alabaster, on my left the Baron and Baroness Von Somewhere … You get the picture?

PIOTR: Very clearly, sir.

PAVEL: You are at my side. You are always at my side … in the European fashion. Not so close!

PIOTR backs up a step.

Good. Our relationship is formal but cordial. Your attitude is one of muted insouciance. Mine, of amused tolerance. I banter with the guests. The topic of conversation changes quickly and often, without warning. I follow easily. And you in your own way do the same. And even if you don't you appear to. You accomplish this with the eyebrows …

PAVEL demonstrates. PIOTR *copies him badly.*

I'll teach you later. In the European fashion I occasionally ask you to remark. For example, I am asked about my home. I say it is comfortable but simple and quaint in the style of my country. Isn't that right, Pierre? You say something appropriate.

PIOTR: Home is where the sheep graze. But the heart … stays?

PAVEL: Too much. But the tone is right. And the tone is just about everything in Paris. We move on. I make a comment about servants. You know, the usual complaint. You could say something witty here, Piotr. Nothing too witty or you'll appear to have been coached beyond your class.

PIOTR: Sir, with indulgence, wit has nothing to do with class. It's a gift. I've got it.

PAVEL: Suppress it … Or at least mute it. Mutation is the essence of good conversation.

PIOTR: Is mutation the correct word there, sir?

> KIRSANOV *and* BAILIFF *come on arguing.*

KIRSANOV: Leave me alone. Stop pestering me.

BAILIFF: I need more authority. That's what it comes down to. The serfs are running amok.

KIRSANOV: Stop thinking of them as serfs. They're not, you know. They're tenants actually.

BAILIFF: They'll always be serfs to me.

KIRSANOV: Yes. Yes. Well this is an experimental situation here. And in order for the … experiment to succeed, certain … certain … concessions have to be made. Among them … well you just have to stop beating them all the time. Beatings. Beatings. Everywhere I go I see the results of your rod or your club. Sometimes it seems half the estate is bleeding to death.

BAILIFF: You know the truth is I think they enjoy it as much as I do. It's habit forming, I think.

KIRSANOV: What? So you admit you enjoy it.

BAILIFF: Sure.

KIRSANOV: But … but don't you think … Aren't you worried that might make you … well a bit mentally unstable.

BAILIFF: Have you ever beaten anyone.

KIRSANOV: No.

BAILIFF: You should try it. I bet you'd enjoy it too. It's a good thing. It feels good. I don't know why. I didn't make human beings. Human beings enjoy beating other human beings. That's a fact.

KIRSANOV: Well … well try to stop please. Try to find your pleasure somewhere else … I'll give you a raise in pay if you cut your beatings in half this month.

BAILIFF: They'll rob you blind. They'll get drunk and do damage to the machinery. They'll eat their children …

KIRSANOV: Just try. Think of it as an experiment.

BAILIFF: Sure. But you'll see. I'm warning you. Consider yourself warned, all right?

KIRSANOV: Yes. Thank you. Goodbye.

BAILIFF *leaves.*

(*sitting*) Could I have one of those glasses.

PIOTR *hands him one.*

PAVEL: Did it ever occur to you, brother, that you weren't cut out for this work.

KIRSANOV: Every day ... But I feel something important needs to be done here. I feel I ...

PAVEL: Let others do it.

KIRSANOV: Men like our bailiff? Men like our corrupt governor? (*drinks. Groans loudly. Looks at* PIOTR)

PIOTR: English sherry, sir.

PAVEL: I'll be packing soon. Leaving on a great adventure. You're welcome to come with me.

KIRSANOV: Oh don't leave again, Pavel. You know you always return in disrepair.

PAVEL: There is a lady who needs my attention, my devotion, my ... protection.

KIRSANOV: There's no one ... nothing out there for you anymore.

PAVEL: I'm too old for adventure, you think.

KIRSANOV: Well no ... Yes. Yes I can't let you go on thinking ... look at you. Why are you wearing all that powder!?

PAVEL: It suits me!

KIRSANOV: It ... Piotr, go away. (PIOTR *turns around*) No, Piotr. Go. Away! (PIOTR *leaves*) People laugh at you behind your back.

PAVEL: What people. There's no one here except us. And Fenichka. Does she laugh at me.

KIRSANOV: No. The others.

PAVEL: The help? Do I care what the help thinks about me. Really, brother, let's not allow this democratic strain to become ridiculous. Anyway I'm not the problem. You're the problem!

KIRSANOV: I'll be fine when I develop a system of management. You're the problem, actually!

PAVEL: Very well. Let's agree to leave each other to our own hell. You to sink like compost into the earth! Me to search for a style of life beyond my grasp!

KIRSANOV: But …

PAVEL: What?

KIRSANOV: Yes but—

PAVEL: What!?

KIRSANOV: Well the truth is I don't want you to go! I need you here. I need someone.

Pause.

PAVEL: You have Fenichka.

KIRSANOV: I do?

PAVEL: You could.

KIRSANOV: Yes well … I tried to talk to her last night. We … well we're so very different.

PAVEL: Do you know something. I've become quite fond of her. I think she's a rare exception to the rule.

KIRSANOV: What rule.

PAVEL: The rule. The one which keeps everyone and everything in its place. I think she'll be good for you.

KIRSANOV: Perhaps. But … I need … Arkady. I need him to be with me. Especially if you're leaving. I want what I do here to mean more than myself … Or perhaps I just want to be close to him again for awhile. Before he leaves me forever.

PAVEL: Tell him that. He's a generous boy. Always was. Talk to him when he returns.

KIRSANOV: They returned late last night. They're still asleep.

PAVEL: They? He brought that son of darkness with him.

KIRSANOV: Yes. And someone else.

PAVEL: Oh wonderful. An invasion. (*he stands*) In that case I'd better go prepare for battle. Excuse me.

He leaves. A rustling.

KIRSANOV: Who's there.

FENICHKA *steps out from behind a tree or a bush or something.*

FENICHKA: Only me. I was walking.

KIRSANOV: (*standing*) Where's the baby.

FENICHKA: Asleep.

KIRSANOV: Good. That's good. So you're walking by yourself these days. I'm glad. It's good to get away from him sometimes.

FENICHKA: You think so? Why?

KIRSANOV: Yes. No ... Well don't you?

FENICHKA: I love him very much. I like being with him.

KIRSANOV: Of course. I know ... I wasn't suggesting ... I love him too, you know ... If you don't believe me ... I ... Well perhaps I should spend more time with him myself. But I'm so awfully busy.

FENICHKA: Nikolai, may I sit down.

KIRSANOV: Of course. Didn't I offer you a seat. I'm sure I meant to ... Please. There. No here. Yes here beside me. (*sits*)

Pause.

KIRSANOV: So ... this is pleasant. A pleasant morning.

FENICHKA: I overheard you talking to your brother about you and ... me.

KIRSANOV: Oh. Well whatever I said about that I didn't mean. Well I meant it but I didn't explain it. Not properly.

FENICHKA: I think I should go away.

KIRSANOV: You do?

FENICHKA: I don't exactly have a place to go but maybe you could arrange work for me somewhere.

KIRSANOV: No place to go? And you still want to leave. Do you hate me Fenichka ... for what happened.

FENICHKA: You gave me a beautiful baby ... I don't hate you.

KIRSANOV: You think I hate you?

FENICHKA: I believe you are trapped inside a terrible problem. With no way out unless I help you … by leaving.

KIRSANOV: But that's not … I don't want you to go away … Fenichka I know I'm an old man. Believe me, I feel it. With all the problems on the farm—the workers, the bailiff—but what has that to do with you … We were talking about … Then there's my brother. And my son … Arkady. Oh I love him so much.

FENICHKA: Excuse me. (*stands*) I hear my baby crying.

She leaves.

KIRSANOV: Why is it I never hear the baby crying when she does. Am I going deaf … I should have just said something affectionate to her. Fenichka I love you. I love you Fenichka. Just like that. She'd stay if I said that simple thing to her. So it's up to me. All right then I'll do it … (*starts off*) But not now. I have to supervise the distribution of fertilizer. (*turns, starts off in the other direction*) Yes, one of the highlights of my day. Distributing fertilizer.

He is gone. FENICHKA *comes back. Sits. Looking off in the direction* KIRSANOV *went.* BAZAROV *comes on. Eating an apple.*

BAZAROV: Hello there.

FENICHKA: (*stands*) Excuse me.

BAZAROV: (*grabs her arm*) Not so fast. The baby's not crying. You can't fool me there. I just came from his room. He's sound asleep.

FENICHKA: Oh I thought I heard—

She is trying to remove his hand, with no success.

But if you say you saw him. And that he's fine …

BAZAROV: Will you sit down with me.

FENICHKA: If you take away your hand.

BAZAROV: If you promise not to run away.

FENICHKA: Why would I run away. I'm not afraid of you.

BAZAROV *smiles. Takes his hand off her arm. Sits.*

FENICHKA *sits. Pause.*

What were you doing in the baby's room.

BAZAROV: Looking. I like babies.

FENICHKA: All of them.

BAZAROV: Yes. As a matter of fact, I do.

FENICHKA: For scientific reasons?

BAZAROV: Oh. So you think you know me, do you.

FENICHKA: I listened when you were here before … talking about various things.

BAZAROV: And now you're an expert on my motives.

FENICHKA: I don't know how to argue with you. I'll just say you struck me as a harsh person.

BAZAROV: Really. Didn't I help you when the baby had a chill.

FENICHKA: I watched you then. You examined him like a … a …

BAZAROV: Specimen.

FENICHKA: Yes! Not that I wasn't grateful.

BAZAROV: Should I have made baby jokes. Laughed. Perhaps even cried. For God's sake. He was sick. I was trying to make him well. Don't be stupid.

FENICHKA: I am stupid. I can't help it.

She stands. He stands. Puts a hand on her shoulder.

BAZAROV: You're not stupid. I'm rude sometimes. An old habit. I apologize.

FENICHKA: That's not necessary.

BAZAROV: Good. Let's keep talking. (*they sit*) Tell me everything you think about life. Be honest. Take all the time you need.

FENICHKA: Why.

BAZAROV: You need a reason to talk about what you think?

FENICHKA: I need to know why you want to listen.

BAZAROV: I could lie. I could make something up about curiosity. But the truth is I'd like an opportunity to just … look at you. I find you very attractive.

Pause.

FENICHKA: Thank you.

BAZAROV: Do you find me attractive. (*Pause*) Well.

FENICHKA: I am … not in a position to …

He is reaching for her hand. The sound of people coming. She pushes his hand away. ARKADY *comes on.* GREGOR *is close behind him.*

ARKADY: Good morning, Fenichka.

FENICHKA: Good morning.

GREGOR: Good morning, Fenichka.

FENICHKA: Good morning. Do I know you.

ARKADY: No. Pretend he isn't here. Bazarov will you tell him to stop following me around.

BAZAROV: But I've told him that's exactly what he has to do if he wants to learn how to behave like a gentleman. And that is what he wants.

ARKADY: (*to* GREGOR) Is it?

GREGOR: (*to* BAZAROV) Is it.

BAZAROV: Yes.

GREGOR: (*to* ARKADY) Yes.

ARKADY: Well then let him follow you around.

BAZAROV: I'm no gentleman. (*to* FENICHKA) Am I?

FENICHKA: Aren't you.

ARKADY: Bazarov, what does that mean.

BAZAROV: Ask her.

ARKADY: Fenichka?

FENICHKA: He's a … perfect gentleman. I think he's teasing you. (*stands*)

ARKADY: Why are you leaving.

BAZAROV: The baby is screaming his lungs out. Can't you hear him.

ARKADY: No …

FENICHKA: The baby is asleep. I just want to look in on him. (*to* BAZAROV) If that's all right with you.

BAZAROV *smiles.*

ARKADY: I'll come with you. This would be a good time to have a long look at my little brother, wouldn't it.

FENICHKA: You call him your brother?

BAZAROV: Yes. And his kindness in doing so is an inspiration to us all.

ARKADY: Mind your own business.

BAZAROV: Why do people think that what goes on in a family is somehow beyond the criticism of society in general. Is a family above the civil law? No. Then should it be above the natural law, the laws of behaviour?

ARKADY: Only when those laws are being imposed by a man who is not only outside the family but outside of society as well.

BAZAROV: You're criticizing me a lot these days. Why is that.

ARKADY: I'm only trying to be an intelligent disciple. Besides, I still agree with you about all of the big things.

BAZAROV: So your patronizing attitude toward this young woman is a little thing.

ARKADY: I think you've misread me on that. If you need an example of a patronizing attitude, examine the way you talk to young Gregor here.

BAZAROV: (*to* GREGOR) Do I condesc—Do I talk down to you.

GREGOR: What?

BAZAROV: Do I talk to you like you're stupid.

GREGOR: But I am stupid. Why shouldn't you talk to me like that.

BAZAROV: (*sighs, puts his head in his hands*) But what about the famous earthy common sense of the peasant. Don't you think you have that.

GREGOR: Maybe. But a lot of good it's done me. No sir, you just keep talking to me like I'm stupid and then maybe I'll learn something.

ARKADY: He could have a point there.

BAZAROV: But it's so deeply buried in the misery of his self-contempt we might never find it.

ARKADY: (*to* FENICHKA) Come on. We'll go look at the baby. And we'll have a good talk too.

They start off. GREGOR *starts off too.*

(*to* GREGOR) Stay put.

They leave. GREGOR *shoves his hands in his pockets.*

BAZAROV: Come sit here by me, old friend.

> GREGOR *obeys.* BAZAROV *puts an arm around him.*

So how do you like your new life so far. Is it everything you imagined.

GREGOR: Breakfast was good. I ate like a pig.

BAZAROV: Well these things take time. At lunch try to eat like a monkey. By supper time we'll have you eating like a human being. No I'm sorry I said that.

GREGOR: Why?

> PAVEL *comes on. A bit more done-up. He is wearing his most dandified outfit.*

PAVEL: Ah here you are.

BAZAROV: Yes. And there you are. Incredible as it may seem.

PAVEL: Take your time now. Look me over closely. Examine every excess. Savor me. Then attack. I'm ready.

BAZAROV: Before you came out I was sitting here wondering what exactly it is about this place that makes me so wretched. Makes me rude to pleasant young women, cruel to my best friends … and then here you are. The essential truth. The disease in its most virulent form. The extreme edge so to speak.

PAVEL: You and I have unfinished business. My style is at stake. I have prepared a lengthy verbal lesson in history for you.

BAZAROV: That will have to wait. I have a message for you from Anna Odintsov.

> *Pause.* PAVEL *is still.*

PAVEL: How do you know this lady.

BAZAROV: That's none of your business. I'm more concerned with how you think you know her. But we should discuss this in private. I'll send young Gregor here away.

PAVEL: Who is he to me. An empty space. Going or staying he remains an empty space. I'll show you how it is done, (*to* GREGOR) You, beggar boy. This man and I are about to have a discussion. You won't hear it. Do you understand?

GREGOR: Yes sir.

PAVEL: (*to* BAZAROV) Speak.

BAZAROV *approaches him. Takes a pack of letters from his pocket.*

BAZAROV: These belong to you.

PAVEL *looks at them.*

PAVEL: No. They belong to the dear lady.

BAZAROV: They are your letters. She doesn't want them.

PAVEL: Then have her return them herself.

BAZAROV *throws the letters down.*

PAVEL *stiffens.*

BAZAROV: I don't really wish to be cruel to you, you know.

PAVEL: Be cruel. That might be easier for both of us.

BAZAROV: You are deluded. You believe this woman is her mother.

PAVEL: What I believe is beyond your comprehension.

BAZAROV: In some stupid abstract way that might be true. But the simple truth is, these letters prove that you think she's her mother. It's possible that you're only playing at this delusion, in a kind of semi-conscious way. You don't strike me as being insane.

PAVEL: What would you know about insanity. Only extremely sensitive people reach that exalted state.

BAZAROV: That is dangerous romantic garbage. It is dangerous for the lady in question, for the ones who care for you and for yourself I advise you to stop giving in to this notion. You are not in an exalted state. You are in a feverish state similar to the ones we all experience in adolescence. In short it is simply time to grow up.

PAVEL *picks up the letters.*

PAVEL: If you were a sensitive man I would tell you that I love the lady. I ... loved the lady very much. Her daughter reminds me so much ... What possible harm can I do with such a love.

BAZAROV: For one thing you bring unwanted attention on her. I'm talking to you now like you're sane. I'm giving you the benefit of the doubt ... If you listen like a sane person should, it can stop here. If it doesn't stop, I will be forced to take action.

PAVEL: A threat. Good.

BAZAROV: Believe it or not, except for this matter, I have no real quarrel with you.

PAVEL: That's not true. We are enemies!

BAZAROV: You are no threat to me, I'm sorry. There is only the matter of your obsessive behaviour toward my friend Anna Odintsov.

PAVEL: And other than that, no threat? I don't believe it!

BAZAROV: Believe it.

> *Pause.*

PAVEL: I see ... Well you have spoken clearly ... I can assure you of one thing at least. The lady has nothing to fear from me. (*starts off. Stops*) As for the motives behind my obsessive behaviour as you call it—

BAZAROV: No explanation please.

PAVEL: No, of course not. That would be totally absurd anyway. Almost as absurd as the way I dress.

> *He bows. Leaves.*

BAZAROV: Sad.

GREGOR: Sad?

> BAZAROV *looks at* GREGOR. *Goes to him. Takes him by the shoulders.*

BAZAROV: I'm sorry if I've been cruel to you. I don't mean to be cruel ... Honestly.

> *He pulls* GREGOR *to him.* GREGOR *puts his head on* BAZAROV's *chest.*
>
> *Blackout.*

Begins in darkness. With a crash.

Then the loud sustained sound of eeeeeeeeeee. Lights.

The Kirsanov supper table. KIRSANOV, ARKADY, PAVEL, *and* FENICHKA *are seated. Watching* SITNIKOV *in a desultory manner.* SITNIKOV *is standing next to the table.* GREGOR *sits silently beside* BAZAROV *throughout the entire scene. Eating slowly. Carefully.*

BAZAROV *is smiling broadly at* SITNIKOV.

SITNIKOV: Well of course this could be an extremely embarrassing moment if we don't look for the humour in it. Eeeeee. I mean I barge in here uninvited. I interrupt your supper. I stumble in my awkwardness and break a decanter—

PIOTR *rises from behind the table. Holding the broken pieces.*

PIOTR: A decanter. And a two-hundred-year-old bowl.

SITNIKOV: Oh a bowl too. I'm so sorry. I apologize. Arkady, who should I be apologizing to.

ARKADY: This is my father.

SITNIKOV: I apologize, sir. For the bowl. For the interruption.

BAZAROV: Quick Viktor. The humour. Get to the humour of it.

SITNIKOV: Well the truth is ... You see I did see the possibility of humour a moment ago. But it seems to have slipped away.

PIOTR *leaves.*

ARKADY: I don't suppose you could manage to do the same thing.

SITNIKOV: Oh I see. I'm not wanted here. How was I to know.

ARKADY: The fact that you weren't invited could have served as a hint.

SITNIKOV: Well you might like to know that I'm on a mission of honour. (*to* BAZAROV) Not that honour means anything to me. (*to* KIRSANOV) Not that I have anything against honour.

ANNA *comes on. Followed by* SERGEI.

ANNA: I asked him to bring me. Arkady, I didn't know where you lived.

SITNIKOV: Madame Odintsov. I was about to explain.

The men stand. Except BAZAROV.

ANNA: Yes Viktor. But now I'm putting you out of your misery. Please gentlemen. Sit.

Only GREGOR *sits. Then* GREGOR *rises.*

No. Sit!

They all sit except ARKADY.

ARKADY: Ah. Father. Uncle. This is—

ANNA: Anna Odintsov.

She goes to KIRSANOV. *Puts out her hand. He takes it awkwardly.*

KIRSANOV: It is a pleasure to have—

ANNA: Yes yes pleasure. I'm sorry to interrupt your supper but I have some urgent business here. (*to* BAZAROV) I realized after all, that it required my personal attention.

BAZAROV: That might not be necessary.

ANNA *takes out a letter. Shows it to* BAZAROV.

ANNA: I received that this morning. (*points to* PAVEL) From him.

BAZAROV *looks at it. At* PAVEL.

KIRSANOV: What's going on here.

PAVEL: Nothing to do with you Nikolai. (*stands*) Madame I am at your disposal.

ANNA: Somewhere quiet please.

PAVEL: The garden should do. (*to others*) Excuse me.

They start off.

ANNA: (*over her shoulder*) Oh. And me.

PAVEL *points the way.* ANNA *goes.* PAVEL *follows her.* SERGEI *follows him.*

KIRSANOV: Arkady, do you know what this is about.

ARKADY: I think you should ask Uncle Pavel, Father.

BAZAROV: That would not be wise. It's quite crowded in the labyrinth already. (*laughs*)

KIRSANOV: So you know about this too? So this is just something else beyond my knowledge. Why am I in the dark about so many things. Am I prematurely senile.

FENICHKA: Perhaps it doesn't concern you, Nikolai.

KIRSANOV: He's my brother, isn't he. Obviously he's in some kind of dilemma. If I'd had my eyes open I would have seen it ... but ... Fenichka—

FENICHKA: What?

KIRSANOV: Nothing.

SITNIKOV: Excuse me. I seem to have been left dangling here. It's rather awkward.

KIRSANOV: (*to* FENICHKA) You. You're the problem.

SITNIKOV: Me?

KIRSANOV: No not you. Her. Who are you anyway. Never mind. (*to* FENICHKA) My senility. It's because of you Fenichka. You're all I see—what should I do about you.

FENICHKA: Please Nikolai. Not now.

BAZAROV: Why ask her what you should do anyway.

ARKADY: Bazarov.

BAZAROV: She's not your conscience. She may be your responsibility but—

KIRSANOV: Oh an opinion about that too.

ARKADY: Bazarov you have no right to be involved.

BAZAROV: But I do.

SITNIKOV: Perhaps I could just sit down.

BAZAROV: I have a deep and perfect right.

ARKADY: And what is it.

KIRSANOV: Yes what.

SITNIKOV: So no one objects then. (*sits*)

BAZAROV *stands.*

BAZAROV: I love her.

KIRSANOV: What?

FENICHKA: (*to* BAZAROV) Please. Stop.

BAZAROV: I love her. And I want to marry her.

ARKADY: Bazarov what is this about.

BAZAROV: Are you asking me to explain love to you. Very well. It's a kind of deep abiding passion. It makes the earth tremble. It glows in the dark.

FENICHKA: Sir. You are going too far. I think you misunderstood my openness.

KIRSANOV: What openness? Oh … I see. Now I finally see something. And it's awful. He's young isn't he. That's the whole truth.

FENICHKA: Nikolai, you're being stupid.

BAZAROV: Marry me. I'm not stupid.

KIRSANOV: I'm dying here. My chest feels like it's twisting inside my skin. I can't breathe.

ARKADY: Father.

KIRSANOV: No leave me alone … I'm too old to live.

> KIRSANOV *goes out.* ARKADY *starts to follow.*

BAZAROV: Stay here. He'll be fine. He's just had a shock.

ARKADY: You don't have to tell me what he's just had. You have just ended our friendship.

BAZAROV: But I thought you loved me. I thought our bond was unbreakable. Beyond the reach of history, politics, religion, family.

ARKADY: But not cruelty. Or … disloyalty.

BAZAROV: Fenichka tell our friend here that nothing happened between us.

FENICHKA: Yes. Nothing, Arkasha. It was a misuse of words on my part.

BAZAROV: I do love you, though. In a way. You remind me of the sister I never had.

SITNIKOV: Eeeeeeeee.

BAZAROV: You find that funny, Viktor?!

SITNIKOV: (*sobers immediately*) Not if it wasn't a joke.

BAZAROV: Fenichka. You know I don't want to marry you.

FENICHKA: Why should you.

BAZAROV: Well that's another question. I probably should. But I'm hard at the core. Love for just one person isn't strong enough to penetrate.

ARKADY: Besides, it's actually only the idea of you he loves. (*to* BAZAROV) Correct?

BAZAROV: I suppose so.

ARKADY: Grotesque. You become more inhuman every day. Some perverse idea enters your head and you just spew it out and let it bounce off anyone who happens to be there. You toy with the idea of a kind of love for her and you bounce it off my father's skull!

BAZAROV: You know I believe that's an accurate observation. I do things like that often. I wonder why. Do you have any ideas?

ARKADY: None at all.

BAZAROV: Well, in any event you're wrong about me this time. I had an 'honourable' motive. I thought your father just needed a good shock about this young woman here and his true feelings toward her. A little challenge to bring him to his senses.

ARKADY: What a brazen reckless thing to do.

BAZAROV: I'll bet good money he proposes to her before the night is through.

ARKADY: Not if he believes there's something between the two of you.

BAZAROV: Don't worry. Fenichka will go tell him the truth about that … Won't you?

FENICHKA: Yes.

> BAZAROV *helps her up.*

BAZAROV: She'll gaze lovingly into his eyes and he'll believe every word she says … Won't he.

FENICHKA: Yes.

BAZAROV: And she'll do it right now. Very quickly. Before he does something foolish to himself … Won't you.

FENICHKA: Yes! (*starts off*) And if he believes … and if that makes him think … I'll be grateful to you forever. (*runs off*)

ARKADY: And if it fails I'll cut out your heart.

BAZAROV: There's always a risk in meddling in other people's affairs. If you meddle deeply enough. Cut right into the heartland of hypocrisy.

ARKADY: That's what you think you've done to my father, is it.

BAZAROV: If it turns out well, does it matter. Listen. That thing between them was not going in the direction of resolution.

    ARKADY *sits.*

ARKADY: I'd feel better if I thought you did these things out of concern and not just to exercise your brain.

BAZAROV: Drink? Come on, drink. A few vodkas will take the hard edge off the argument I know we are about to have.

ARKADY: I've decided never to drink with you again.

    BAZAROV *fills two glasses with vodka. Lights fade in the drawing room. Lights up in the garden.*

    PAVEL *is sitting.* ANNA *is pacing slowly.*

ANNA: … and so when I received your letter this morning my heart sank. I was sure that when Bazarov had explained to you how I felt I would hear nothing more from you. This has to stop. You have terrorized and destroyed my family. And I won't let you terrorize and destroy me.

PAVEL: Please. I have to interrupt. I am extremely uncomfortable with this situation.

ANNA: You are responsible for this situation.

PAVEL: I meant our physical situation. I am sitting while you stand. Perhaps if you sat or if you allowed me to join—

ANNA: Never mind that. You are fine where you are. I am fine where I am.

PAVEL: Well at least I can see the moonlight in your hair.

ANNA: Please.

PAVEL: Your sparkling eyes, the fluidity of your movements.

ANNA: Please!

PAVEL: I only wish to add that you dress well. You dress with simplicity and style.

ANNA: Have you no sense at all!? Are you totally incapable of having a reasonable conversation!? Of receiving information!?

PAVEL: I … didn't mean to be disrespectful.

ANNA: That's not the point. (*pause*) Listen to me. Perhaps you think my objections to the ... attention you're giving me aren't serious enough. That they are only signs of girlish coyness.

PAVEL: You are not a girl. I know that.

ANNA: But do you know that the difficulties you are causing me are not ones that I can just casually dismiss. What I am doing with my life now is full of risk ... I wish I could trust you enough to tell you the truth about myself ... if you knew the truth you'd hate me. No! What I really want to say to you, what you should be able to understand, is that I'm afraid. To be the object of your desire against my will, is in some way I can't quite explain, terrifying. Do you want to terrify me, Pavel Petrovich.

PAVEL: No of course not.

ANNA: Then stop this immediately.

PAVEL: If I could ... but—

ANNA: Are you admitting that you are too weak to stop.

PAVEL: Weak? I feel a great strength in my feelings toward you.

ANNA: Perhaps you need an even greater strength to control your feelings.

PAVEL: Perhaps. But did you read my last letter?

ANNA: Of course.

PAVEL: Carefully?

ANNA: Carefully? No. I was only looking for an apology.

PAVEL: Ah. But I wasn't offering an apology. I was offering an explanation. May I have it.

ANNA: (*sighs*) If you wish.

She hands it to him. He unfolds it.

PAVEL: Yes here it is. Perhaps this might explain for you. (*reading*) 'And yet there's something about me you cannot know. The love I felt for your mother was my life. It came to be my entire life. No thoughts in my head. No world in front of my eyes. No friends. Or family. Or profession. I only lived in my love for your mother. Which drew me to her, so close that everything in the world came through her and I was just an aura, not solid, not heard ... and finally not felt. And when she was gone from me ... I began to dissolve ...' (*looks at her*) And then I saw you and I stopped dissolving and after I stopped dissolving I began to hope that I could become real again. To let the force of love make me ... real.

He drops the letter. He puts his hand over his eyes.

I'm sorry.

ANNA: If you have the strength to love that way, you have the strength to attract a love in return someday that is also ... real.

PAVEL: Unfortunately that's not how it works ... I'm too old ... too unhealthy in my mind. Too weak, yes I know that. And I'm dissolving again.

He sits. Lowers his head. ANNA *sits. Pause.*

ANNA: You could read me more of the letter. If you want to. I mean that might help you.

PAVEL: How?

ANNA: To understand your state of mind. Or it might help me to understand ... or maybe we could find someone who'd understand. And then we could talk again. (*picks up the letter. Sits again. Hands it to him*) Go ahead.

Lights fade. Lights up in the drawing room.

BAZAROV *and* ARKADY *seem more relaxed. A bit drunk. So are* GREGOR *and* SITNIKOV.

BAZAROV: Go ahead. Say it.

ARKADY: No you go ahead.

BAZAROV: Just say it. Go on—

SITNIKOV *jumps to his feet.*

SITNIKOV: I have to say that even though I'm ignorant of many of the specific details, that is, when one of you says 'he' and the other one 'she' I don't know who you are talking about, nevertheless I've found the conversation so far, very stimulating. I have to agree with Bazarov of course.

BAZAROV / ARKADY: of course.

SITNIKOV: Eeeeeeee. No seriously. I mean ... take hypocrisy as an example. It's everywhere isn't it. It's one of the things we'll always have to be on guard against. Treat it like an enemy. Show no mercy. Never bend. Difficult, to say the least. But we'll manage as long as we stick together. We'll be a force of truth and courage. And honesty.

BAZAROV: Where did you get that fancy new coat.

SITNIKOV: I stole it from my father. Eeeeeee. No I made that up. You see I can make a joke as well as anyone. You have to stop under estimating me. No the coat was a gift from Madame Odintsov. It belonged to her late husband.

BAZAROV: The one who died of leprosy?

SITNIKOV: (*stiffens*) Eeeeeeeee. I knew you were joking that time. I warn you. I'm getting harder to trick every day.

BAZAROV *smiles.*

ARKADY: Why would the lady give you a coat, Viktor.

SITNIKOV: I asked for it … Well people were always making fun of my other coat. I found it difficult to get them to take me seriously.

BAZAROV: Coward. You always told us you were a Slavic nationalist. And it was your duty to dress like a Slav.

SITNIKOV: But the truth is I'm not a Slav. And now I have the courage to admit it.

ARKADY: So why were you pretending to be one in the first place.

SITNIKOV: Because they were the only ones who invited me to join their political party. Yes. And now I have the courage to admit that too … I think I'm making great strides don't you.

BAZAROV: (*stands*) But in what direction, Viktor!?

ANNA *comes on. She looks shaken.*

ANNA: Pour me something to drink please.

ARKADY *obliges.* ANNA *sits.*

I feel as if I've just done something very cruel. And I'm not sure why.

BAZAROV: I take it he didn't respond well.

ANNA: He wouldn't—

ARKADY: Excuse me. Viktor this is personal business we are going to discuss.

SITNIKOV: Of course. I'll be discreet.

ARKADY: You'll leave the room.

SITNIKOV: Of course. (*stands*) Where am I going. Am I staying the night. Am I going somewhere else for the night.

ARKADY: You're just leaving the room.

SITNIKOV: Of course.

> *He leaves.*

ANNA: What about him. (*points to* GREGOR)

BAZAROV: He stays at my side. Forever. He is my future. Continue.

ANNA: He wouldn't listen to me at first. But at some point I thought we'd reached an agreement of sorts. Then ... the letter. He read it to me ... It was ... It was all of his heart I think. And his soul and his life. It just poured out. Page after page of excruciating personal disclosure and pleading for my love. In language I have never heard before. So tightly strung ... emotional ... almost raving ... building to some kind of terrifying climax. I could feel it coming like a wind. Like energy. I felt as if it was going to leap off the page and kill one of us ... both of us ... but suddenly he ... just stopped ... Then he ran off.

> *Pause.* ARKADY *stands.*

ARKADY: I should go find him.

ANNA: I told Sergei to follow him. And to make sure he did no harm to himself.

> ARKADY *sits.*

BAZAROV: Your uncle might be insane.

ARKADY: You'd say that, I know.

BAZAROV: (*to* ANNA) What would you say.

ANNA: He scares me. I know that. But I don't think he's insane. He has a pure obsession and he's let it take him away.

ARKADY: It's only love. A little thing. Not a nightmare. Not a huge screaming storm. It's a little precious feeling. I understand him I think.

BAZAROV: Not now, Arkady. Save that talk for when there's less at stake. Anna's safety for example.

ARKADY: When is there ever anything not at stake. When can you have a feeling and not put something at risk. If you keep denying the true passion in people, Bazarov, you'll never be the great leader all your friends expect. If you can't forgive my uncle, how will you be able to forgive the hundred million.

BAZAROV: But it's not a matter of forgiving your uncle. I'm trying to protect Anna.

ARKADY: I don't entirely believe that. What's burning in my uncle will dissolve eventually and I think you know that. You see again, it's what you call the general idea behind his feelings you want to destroy. An idea which you find very threatening because it's beyond your own comprehension.

BAZAROV: (*stands*) This is getting us nowhere. We still have a problem. If you have a problem. Solve it. I thought I taught you that much.

ARKADY: Oh. Very well. Anna. This will be totally unexpected. Perhaps shocking. Perhaps absurd. Will you marry me.

ANNA: I beg your pardon.

BAZAROV: Come on, Arkady. Doesn't she have enough of that to deal with already.

ARKADY: (*to* ANNA) I don't think you are your mother. I know exactly who you are. And who I am. And what I feel.

BAZAROV: Stop this, now.

ARKADY: Shush! I feel something special for you, Anna. I felt it immediately. Yes. Like they do in those silly romantic novels. I think I could make you happy. I'm different from Bazarov in important ways. I know that now. I could be a healthy strong anchor for you. I respect everything you are trying to do and will offer any assistance I can. As well as a life-long devotion to your happiness and well-being. So I am asking you to marry me even if you don't love me because much good will come to both of us if you do.

BAZAROV: Wonderful. And what do you possibly expect her to say to something like that.

ANNA: I'll think it over.

They both look at her.

I mean he makes perfect sense when you listen to him closely.

BAZAROV: Are you serious.

ANNA: Serious enough to give it some consideration. I know Bazarov that you and I could never be happy. And you know that too.

BAZAROV: I do?

ANNA: We have too much in common. A history together which was both too frivolous and intense. Besides marriage might be a good thing for me. My current status in society seems to be making me vulnerable in many ways. (*to* ARKADY) I'm much older than you.

> BAZAROV *has moved away a few feet. He is staring off.*

ARKADY: A few years. It means nothing.

ANNA: Oh it could mean something. We would just have to turn it to our advantage.

BAZAROV: (*to* GREGOR) I feel a certain kind of justice taking place here.

ARKADY: I'm in shock. I never imagined you'd say yes.

ANNA: I haven't said yes.

ARKADY: I know. But now I can imagine that you will.

BAZAROV: I could have imagined it easily, if I'd taken the time. Another one of life's cruel circular jokes.

ARKADY: Do you think you'll be taking a long time to make up your mind.

ANNA: Oh no. A few days at the most. Now I warn you not to get your hopes up. I'm not a fickle person but I could be swayed by practicalities beyond your control.

ARKADY: If it's all right with you, I think I'll get my hopes up anyway. It will be a new sensation for me.

BAZAROV: Well I can learn to live with it. In fact, I'm starting to enjoy the idea already a bit. (*looks at them*) Of course you'll have children. And name one after me.

ARKADY: Of course.

ANNA: If you wish.

BAZAROV: That was a joke actually.

ANNA: Oh.

ARKADY: Oh.

> FENICHKA *comes on.*

FENICHKA: He's disappeared. Nikolai. I couldn't find him anywhere. He's wandering around thinking I've been unfaithful to him. What do you think he'll do. No don't tell me.

> SERGEI *comes on.*

SERGEI: That man you had me following ma'am. Well I didn't do so good a job. Gone like a puff of smoke. (*to* GREGOR) I think the wood demons got him.

> GREGOR *stands, knocking over his chair.* BAZAROV *stares off.*

BAZAROV: Pile them on. One after the other. If fate's a comedian we've got one hell of a big laugh in store. If he's feeling tragic well ... what can I say.

ARKADY: I don't understand what you're talking about. Or why you're talking about it at this particular moment. (*to others*) Come on. We'll organize a search party.

> GREGOR *and* SERGEI *don't move.*

Come on!

SERGEI: No. I ain't goin' up against the wood demons.

> ARKADY *groans. Grabs them. And they all rush off. Except* ANNA *and* BAZAROV.

> BAZAROV *goes to the table. Stands behind* ANNA. *She hands him her drink.*

ANNA: (*laughs*) Chaos in the country. This is just the sort of thing we should enjoy.

BAZAROV: I'd prefer their world to crumble without causing pain. I find no pleasure in human misery.

ANNA: Perhaps that's because you haven't met the true enemy yet. He's waiting for us in the cities.

BAZAROV: Are you seriously considering Arkady's proposal.

ANNA: Which one of us are you worried about.

BAZAROV: You see the thing we both find attractive about him, the thing that makes him different from you and me, is his ability to let his heart make little compromises with the truth … Will you tell him that you are planning to use bombs, Anna … that you've already used one or two.

ANNA: Of course.

BAZAROV: What do you suppose he'll do then.

ANNA: Choose.

BAZAROV: (*laughs*) Now that will be hard won't it. Because I believe he really loves you. Yes, that will be a hard choice. Or a hard compromise. (*shakes his head*) Excuse me. I've never seen a search party organized before. (*starts off*) And I've always wondered how it was done. Oh, by the way. (*stops*) I love you too.

  Pause.

ANNA: Am I supposed to say something now.

BAZAROV: Well it occurred to me … that … you might not have known that.

ANNA: (*stands*) So you actually believe I am considering marriage to Arkady because I think you don't love me. I explained to you why I might marry him. I thought my reasons were both personally and politically clear. If the same sort of thing had come from your mouth there would have been no further questions … You have to start listening to me. And you have to start believing what I say!

  Pause.

BAZAROV: Yes. You're right. I'm sorry.

ANNA: (*smiles*) So do you still love me.

BAZAROV: More than ever.

ANNA: If it's important to you, we could talk about it sometime.

BAZAROV: Anna. I said I loved you. I never said it was important.

  He leaves.

  Blackout.

SCENE SEVEN

Midnight.

In the woods. The light of a full moon.

PIOTR, GREGOR, SERGEI, *and the* BAILIFF *come on. Carrying torches.*

PIOTR: Watch where you're walking, fool. You'll set someone on fire.

SERGEI: Is he talking to me.

GREGOR: No I think he's talking to me.

PIOTR: Shush … Stop!

SERGEI: He is talking to me.

GREGOR: No he's—

PIOTR: Listen! (*they do*) Who hears what I hear.

GREGOR: What do you hear.

SERGEI: Is it the sound of someone being eaten alive?

PIOTR: Silence.

GREGOR: He hears silence.

SERGEI: The wood demons and the shadow monsters all eat people whole. Is it a crunching sound.

PIOTR: Nothing. All right. Everyone spread out.

BAILIFF: I say if they wanted to get lost we should leave them lost. Who cares about those two snotty old guys, anyway.

PIOTR: I do. You should too. They pay your wages.

BAILIFF: I've got talent. I can get a job anywhere.

SERGEI: The moon is full. But it's yellow. That's a kinda unnatural colour for a moon isn't it.

GREGOR: Is it.

BAILIFF: Maybe. Maybe not. I'm not saying.

PIOTR: I said spread out. Why isn't anyone spreading out.

GREGOR: I think you have to tell us more than that. Suppose we all spread out the same way.

PIOTR: God help us all.

SERGEI: Yeah, let's pray. I know one that keeps the spirits of the undead from sneaking into you through your mouth. They go in that way cause a man's mouth is always wide open when he meets the undead.

PIOTR: Spread out! You that way. You that way. You this way.

They begin to move off. Slowly fanning out.

GREGOR: If I find them what do I say. I can't just tell them to go home. Who am I to tell them where to go or not to go.

PIOTR: Just say that supper is ready. They'll get the hint.

GREGOR: What hint. If that's a hint I don't get it myself.

PIOTR: It's a discreet way of saying people are worried about them.

BAILIFF: I'm not worried about them. They're nothing to me. Like I'm nothing to them. We're two halves of a thing that doesn't exist … And I still don't see why we have to be doing this anyway.

PIOTR: I volunteered us.

BAILIFF: Typical. One go-getter always volunteers. And he always takes a few lackeys with him, against their will. That's how go-getters get things. And that's how lackeys get to stay lackeys.

PIOTR: (*backing off*) Spread out! And keep spreading out until you disappear from the face of the earth!!

They are all offstage now. Except SERGEI *who has paused briefly.*

SERGEI: I see a terrible darkness. I feel a frightful stillness. Oh oh, now I hear it … I hear … the silence. (*starts off slowly*) Demons be kind. I'm big … but I'm confused.

And SERGEI *is off now too. Silence.*

A lamp is lit behind a tree. PAVEL *steps out. Holding the lamp and a flask of vodka. He is a bit drunk.*

PAVEL: My life just stumbled across my eyes. All Russia is searching for her wayward son. I am moved by her concern. Worried a bit about her competence. (*sits against a tree*) I was right behind this tree you pitiful collection of half-eaten non-entities!! Ah … but I love you still a bit. Do you still love me a bit. Does anyone love me. Ah that's too sad a question … If you think that's sad imagine the answer … Oh no keep the mouth closed or the undead will be climbing in by the droves. (*falls over laughing*) If she could see me now. (*sits up*) Maybe she should see me now. A little pity goes a long way for a woman. But not her. God, she is hard. Is she some new invention. Yes she is a hard new thing. Ah forget her. Who can I love instead.

> KIRSANOV *comes on wrapped in a horse blanket.*

KIRSANOV: Pavel?

PAVEL: I know this man. I knew him in better times.

KIRSANOV: Pavel. Is that you.

PAVEL: Forget you saw me. Spread a rumour that I'm dead. Go get your supper. Tell them to call in the search party.

KIRSANOV: The search party is for me.

PAVEL: Me as well! Why are you wearing a horse blanket.

KIRSANOV: Cold.

PAVEL: And sad?

KIRSANOV: Can I join you.

PAVEL: You are my brother. I love you. Yes! You are one of the things I love. Come here. Sit down. (KIRSANOV *obeys*) Let me hug you.

KIRSANOV: Are you drunk, Pavel.

> PAVEL *passes him the flask.* KIRSANOV *drinks.*

PAVEL: What is Russia. No what is the world. Is the world just … future. Is the future a hard place to be.

KIRSANOV: Probably. Yes.

PAVEL: Not for you. You have love.

KIRSANOV: So you haven't heard what's happened.

PAVEL: News doesn't travel very fast in the forest. I've tried to keep up but—No, I'm sorry. I'm drunk. Tell me.

KIRSANOV: Fenichka loves Bazarov.

PAVEL: Don't be stupid. She loves you.

KIRSANOV: She feels obligated to me. She loves Bazarov.

PAVEL: He's a disease. No one loves a disease. Trust me. I'm an expert on love. Actually that's not true is it. I'm more an expert on the absence of love. Go away, I can't help you. You're just making me sadder than I already was.

KIRSANOV: I'm sorry.

PAVEL: No. Stay put. What are brothers for. Tell me all the sordid details. He molested her, didn't he.

KIRSANOV: No I don't think so.

PAVEL: Nothing you say will convince me that he didn't, in some cunning nihilistic way, molest her.

KIRSANOV: I think they merely found one another. Shared something. I have a vague picture in my mind of how it happened. I've been wandering around for hours picturing it ... vaguely.

PAVEL: If it's true, it's too sad to even think about. I don't want you to think about it ... Oh damn the way things are ... if this is how they are ... damn them to hell.

KIRSANOV: Yes. Damn the women and children. Damn the serfs. Damn the farm.

PAVEL: I know. Let's kill each other. One final noble act. I'll make all the arrangements.

KIRSANOV: I appreciate the gesture. But ... I'm not sure I want to die.

PAVEL: Of course you do. What have you got to live for.

KIRSANOV: Well ... there's my son.

PAVEL: He's part of the army of darkness. Do you think he'll have time for you when he's busy setting fire to all the beautiful buildings in Moscow. And Petersburg. Ah that architecture. How can they even consider destroying things of such monumental grace and strength.

KIRSANOV: The thing is ... I think all this is my own fault. Fenichka and I could have been married months ago if I weren't so foolish.

PAVEL: Marriage is just another institution to our friend Bazarov. He would have knocked it down if it was in his way ... Remember the way father conducted his business ...

KIRSANOV: Business? Father was a general in the army, Pavel.

PAVEL: The business of his life. He conducted it with dignity. He behaved well because he knew what he came from. And he knew what he came from was respected. And so it followed that he showed respect ... but I've made this argument before. Who listens.

KIRSANOV: I do.

PAVEL: Remember the holidays. Each holiday marked by the same traditional routine. It gave you strength. It gave you memory ... Oh I ruined that part of my life myself. Ruined any chance to have a real family. I got carried away by love. I couldn't help myself.

KIRSANOV: You could have if you'd wanted to.

PAVEL: Yes. You're right. I enjoyed very much the feeling of being carried away. But only at the beginning. Does everything turn dark in this world, Nikolai.

KIRSANOV: Yes. Darkness. Then ... what?

PAVEL: Death ... Can I hug you again, Nikolai.

KIRSANOV: Yes.

> PAVEL *puts his arms around* KIRSANOV. *Puts* KIRSANOV*'s head on his chest.*

All I have to stay alive for is my farm.

PAVEL: (*laughs, sighs*) Your pathetic farm.

KIRSANOV: I know now that I wanted a wife and child to live for. Too late though.

PAVEL: Too late. For you. And for me.

KIRSANOV: There's a world of difference between living for something and just staying alive for something.

PAVEL: I'd settle for a reason for staying alive.

KIRSANOV: Promise me you won't kill yourself Pavel. I couldn't stand it. That would be the last straw for me.

PAVEL: Maybe that's reason enough. At least for now. For tonight. Under this tree ... Are you crying, Nikolai ... There. There. (*rocking slowly back and forth*) Please don't. Please ... Nikolai ... Shush ... there, there ... I think the world should be kinder to fools.

> *Blackout.*

SCENE EIGHT

Dawn.

An open field. BAZAROV *and* GREGOR *are sitting. Talking. Chuckling. Eating apples.* PAVEL *and* PIOTR *come on.* PAVEL *in shirt, trousers, and boots.* PIOTR *is carrying a case.* BAZAROV *and* GREGOR *stand.*

PAVEL: Ah you're here. I'm so glad.

> PAVEL *goes to* BAZAROV. *Extends a hand.* BAZAROV *hesitates. Then takes it. They shake.*

I was worried that you might not see the note.

BAZAROV: You could have knocked. You didn't have to leave an envelope under my door.

PAVEL: It was late. You were asleep. I am, believe it or not, a considerate man.

BAZAROV: Yes. Well here I am. You wanted to talk?

PAVEL: This is a bit irregular, I realize. These things are usually discussed well in advance. What are your feelings about the old way of settling accounts.

BAZAROV: Excuse me?

PAVEL: Duelling.

BAZAROV: Ah. I see. (*looks around*) Yes. Dawn. An open field. Your second.

PAVEL: Usually one uses a gentleman as a second. But under the circumstances, Piotr will have to do.

> PIOTR *bows deeply.*

BAZAROV: And the circumstances are?

PAVEL: A need for a quick resolution.

BAZAROV: To what?

PAVEL: In a moment. First. Are you opposed to duelling.

BAZAROV: I don't see how that matters much. If there are things which must be settled they'll be settled somehow.

PAVEL: Glad to hear that. Saves me the indignity of having to whack you about a bit to force your hand.

BAZAROV: You want to kill me for some reason, I take it.

PAVEL: Please. Killing you isn't the object here. This is a matter of honour.

BAZAROV: Yours?

PAVEL: This is not about me. You have dishonoured my brother. How shall I put this delicately.

BAZAROV: Why bother.

PAVEL: Please. Let me keep some things in my world intact. This is about you and … the girl. Fenichka.

BAZAROV: But there's nothing …

PAVEL: Yes?

BAZAROV: Not really. This is not really about that at all for you. Be honest now. If you're honest with me, I might oblige.

PAVEL: But this is for my brother. And yes! For myself as well. I have to show you somehow that my belief in certain traditions is not just decoration.

BAZAROV: Why.

PAVEL: Because I *am* a threat to you. I must be a threat to you. I owe it to Russia.

BAZAROV: No. You owe it to your father. You owe it to your family, your class, your history. I have absolutely no respect for any of those things. But I have boundless respect for the inevitable. And for Russia. Let's do it!

> BAZAROV *moves toward* PIOTR.

Now I take it Piotr has the weapons in this case.

PAVEL: Can you shoot well.

BAZAROV: I can do everything well.

PAVEL: I am a crack shot.

BAZAROV: Yes you've told me that before. But you told me so many preposterous things, it's difficult for me to get impressed.

PAVEL: Choose your weapon.

BAZAROV: There are four pistols here. Are we expecting company.

PAVEL: Piotr will explain. Just choose one.

> BAZAROV *does*.

BAZAROV: Gregor. Go stand opposite Piotr.

GREGOR: Why.

BAZAROV: (*to* PAVEL) Can you tell him.

PAVEL: The form of it. That's all. The form of it.

BAZAROV: Yes the form of it, Gregor. Now get over there.

   GREGOR *obeys.*

Now isn't there something about paces involved here.

PAVEL: It is Piotr's duty to explain the rest.

PIOTR: My pleasure. I have made a mark on the ground. There. That is the centre. The two gentlemen can then mark off eight or ten paces from that mark. There must be an agreement here.

PAVEL: Eight?

BAZAROV: Eight is fine.

PAVEL: (*to* PIOTR) Go on.

PIOTR: (*to* BAZAROV) The two gentlemen then raise their weapons. And shoot when they wish. That should be the end of you … it.

PAVEL: You forgot the reason for the other two pistols.

PIOTR: Sorry, sir. If that is not the end of it the two gentlemen have the option to take another pistol and fire again.

BAZAROV: In the meantime, Piotr, are you reloading the original pistols. Is this meant to go on all day? There was an interesting natural science textbook I was hoping to finish this afternoon.

PAVEL: There will be a maximum of four shots.

BAZAROV: Well I suppose someone should be dead by then.

PAVEL: (*taking his position*) Please honour me by taking this a little more seriously.

BAZAROV: (*taking his position*) Please honour me by allowing me to take it any damn way I choose.

   They are back to back. They move to PIOTR'*s command.*

PIOTR: One … Two … Three … Four—

GREGOR: I can't watch this.

BAZAROV: Is it necessary that he watch.

PAVEL: Under proper circumstances yes. But I think we can make an exception here.

BAZAROV: Close your eyes, Gregor.

GREGOR: Thank you, sir. (*does*)

PIOTR: Five ... Six ... Seven ... Eight ...

PAVEL: (*stopping*) Are you there yet.

BAZAROV: Yes. What about one more. Would you mind just one more.

PAVEL: Fine.

PIOTR: Nine.

> *They both turn.* PAVEL *shoots instantly.*

BAZAROV: Missed. You were aiming for my head. I felt the bullet whiz by my ear.

PAVEL: Shoot.

BAZAROV: Not satisfied yet?

PAVEL: You must shoot ... and you must do it seriously.

BAZAROV: Seriously.

> BAZAROV *looks away. Shoots without aiming.* PAVEL *grabs his leg and falls to the ground.*

Oh damn. (*runs to* PAVEL) Here let me help you up.

PAVEL: I can manage. (*struggles to his feet*)

BAZAROV: Well, honour is served then. Now let's get you home and I'll bandage that leg and arrange for a doctor.

> PAVEL *is limping towards* PIOTR.

BAZAROV: Where are you going.

> PAVEL *takes another pistol.*

Oh I see. Honour really does need to kill someone.

PAVEL: Arm yourself.

> BAZAROV *shrugs. Goes and gets a pistol.* PAVEL *has taken his centre position mark again.*

BAZAROV: Can't we dispense with the pacing this time.

PAVEL: No! We'll do it right!

> BAZAROV *takes his position.*

PIOTR: (*more quickly*) One … two … three … four …

BAZAROV: This joke is out of control.

PIOTR: Five … six …

BAZAROV: I think something nasty is going to happen here now.

PIOTR: Seven … eight.

PAVEL: We have to do it right. I have to do something right don't you see.

> PAVEL *turns.*

BAZAROV: God you're pathetic! (*turns, gesturing*) Can't you see I've just been trying—

> PAVEL *shoots.* BAZAROV *is thrown back a step. Clutches his chest. Looks down.*

Oh wonderful.

> BAZAROV *falls.* GREGOR *rushes to him.* PAVEL *rushes to him, holding his leg.*

BAZAROV: You … interrupted what I was trying to say.

PAVEL: I thought you were going to shoot. I didn't mean to do this. I was going to fire wide. You startled me.

BAZAROV: I'm sorry.

PAVEL: This looks like a serious wound.

BAZAROV: Serious? (*chuckles*) Well I'm glad I was finally able to … enter into the spirit of the thing. I'm losing … consciousness now …

> *He passes out.*

PAVEL: Quickly. The two of you. Get him back to the house.

> GREGOR *and* PIOTR *are picking* BAZAROV *up.*

Careful. Careful.

PIOTR: Good shot, sir.

PAVEL: Shut up.

GREGOR: Is he dying.

PIOTR: Serves him right.

GREGOR: Shut up.

PAVEL: Quickly. Quickly.

They leave. PAVEL *stares after them a moment.*

I didn't mean to do that.

He limps off.

Blackout.

A bedroom.

A bed, a chair, a small table with a lamp on it. BAZAROV *is propped up in bed. His chest bandaged. Blood seeping through.*

ANNA *sits on the edge of the bed. Applying cold compresses to his forehead.* ARKADY *is in the chair. His head in his hands.*

ANNA: I can't get the fever down this way. I think that doctor was a quack. I think we should send to town for silver nitrate.

ARKADY: Yes. I'll go myself.

BAZAROV *opens his eyes. He speaks slowly, softly.*

BAZAROV: Stupid. All wrong. Silver nitrate is for infections in the blood. My diagnosis is … a collapsed lung. Ruptured artery …

ANNA: Don't talk.

BAZAROV: Then stop playing doctor. Let me die in peace. Silver nitrate. (*laughs*) Ahh. That hurts.

ARKADY: We're worried that the doctor was incompetent.

BAZAROV: He was trained by barbarians. Our medical profession is still in the dark ages. I was hoping to help change—

ARKADY: You will …

BAZAROV: Please. Try this once only to say useful non-sentimental things. I'm worried about your father.

ARKADY: Fenichka found him and they had a long talk. You were right. He's changed somehow.

BAZAROV: Oh … I doubt that. He's going to marry her though.

ARKADY: Yes. Probably.

BAZAROV: Well that's change enough. Fathers. Did I ever tell you about my father.

ARKADY: Never.

BAZAROV: Did I ever tell you about him, Anna.

ANNA: No.

BAZAROV: Well I don't see why I should start now … No that was a joke … My father loves me. He's a good man. Retired army

doctor ... good doctor ... limited knowledge ... and my
mother, she's there still. Good woman. Good cook. But all I
really know about them is ... they love me.

He passes out.

ARKADY: Is he dead. God. Is he dead.

ANNA: Unconscious ... This is a waste. He's going to die and it's
such a waste.

FENICHKA *and* KIRSANOV *come on.*

KIRSANOV: How is he doing.

No response.

I'm sorry for you, son.

BAZAROV *opens his eyes.*

BAZAROV: It's getting crowded in here ... Oh look two pairs of
soon to be newlyweds ... a matched set ...

KIRSANOV: He's delirious. He's seeing double.

ARKADY: No. He means Anna and me. I'll explain later.

ARKADY *goes off.*

BAZAROV: I wish I could be there to hear it. Nikolai Petrovich.
Can you hear me.

KIRSANOV: Yes.

BAZAROV: My brain is a step behind my mouth. I'm afraid I'm
not coherent.

KIRSANOV: You're speaking well.

BAZAROV: Good. Anna here is a fine woman. Ignore everything
you hear about her reputation. In fact ignore what I just said.
I'm delirious.

ARKADY *comes back on.*

ARKADY: Bazarov. My uncle is outside. He wants something from
you.

BAZAROV: I think I've given your uncle enough for one lifetime.
No, I'm wrong. Let him in.

ARKADY *goes out.*

Hello, Fenichka.

FENICHKA: I'm sorry. (*to* KIRSANOV) I don't know what to say to him. (*to* BAZAROV) Can I get you anything.

BAZAROV: Yes. Another death. Any other death but this will do. You look wonderful Fenichka. Oh I hear the baby crying.

FENICHKA: You do?

KIRSANOV: Never mind. He's delirious.

BAZAROV: No one ever gets my best jokes … Oh that reminds me. Where's Viktor.

ANNA: Out in the hall. He's afraid to come in. He's worried he'll make a fool of himself.

BAZAROV: But that's exactly what he's supposed to do. Please someone … get him.

FENICHKA: I'll go.

> FENICHKA *goes out.* ARKADY *and* PAVEL *come in.*

BAZAROV: People coming in. Going out. Better actually. Less like a death bed. More like a train station.

KIRSANOV: (*laughs loudly*) Very funny, Bazarov.

BAZAROV: Thank you.

> KIRSANOV *bows.*

ARKADY: My uncle is here, Yevgeny.

PAVEL: (*to* BAZAROV) Sir. Young gentleman … I'm … leaving here soon. Off on another great journey. My bags are packed … but … I find I'm missing something. (*sits on the edge of the bed head bowed*) I need your forgiveness, I'm afraid.

BAZAROV: I have something better for you. A job. My friend Gregor. I want you to turn him into a … gentleman. Think of it as an interesting experiment … Teach him to disappear into your world …

PAVEL: But why?

BAZAROV: Just a notion … But nevertheless, promise.

PAVEL: No, I can't. Is there something else I can do for you instead. Anything.

KIRSANOV: Pavel. That is the wish of a … a man who is … You can't refuse.

PAVEL: But what about my beliefs. Doing what he asks would make a mockery of my life. I want Bazarov to go to his death knowing that I meant my life ... Bazarov. I still need your forgiveness. Will you give it to me.

BAZAROV: For shooting me? Yes. For your beliefs? No.

PAVEL *stands.*

PAVEL: What you understand is what you come to believe in. That is the quality in life. And the comfort in death. God help us both.

He bows. Leaves.

BAZAROV: Arkady come here. Close to my mouth.

ARKADY *bends down.* BAZAROV *begins to whisper in his ear.*

FENICHKA *leads* SITNIKOV *in. He looks terrified.*

SITNIKOV: Oh I don't know. I don't know how to behave. I've never seen anyone die. I might do something inappropriate.

BAZAROV *pushes* ARKADY *away. Sits up a bit.*

BAZAROV: Oh my God. I'm dying? I'm dying? Why didn't anyone tell me!?

SITNIKOV *looks around in horror.*

SITNIKOV: Oh my God!

BAZAROV: Oh my God!

SITNIKOV: I'm sorry. So—

BAZAROV: I'm dying. Did you hear him. I'm dying.

SITNIKOV: Oh no. I thought he knew. Oh my God, this is awful. This is hell. I'm—

BAZAROV: Viktor?

SITNIKOV: Yes.

SITNIKOV *leans close to him.*

BAZAROV *leans back. Closes his eyes.*

BAZAROV: Eeeeeeee. (*opens his eyes. Smiles*)

SITNIKOV: Oh ... What. Oh. Yes ... a joke. Of course ... you're dying and you knew it all the time ... You'll be dead within the hour, you old joker ... I'm—

They all look at SITNIKOV. *He sees this.*

SITNIKOV: Sorry.

ARKADY: We have to get out now. He asked to clear the room.
(*to* KIRSANOV) Are the servants close at hand.

KIRSANOV: Just outside.

> *They all start off. Except* ANNA, *who goes to a corner of the room, in the half-light, and watches* BAZAROV.

BAZAROV: Arkady.

> ARKADY *stops.*

ARKADY: Yes.

BAZAROV: Stop there a moment. (*pause*) Seriously now, Arkady. What are you going to do with your life.

ARKADY: Stay here for now ... Wait for Anna to make up her mind. Help my father manage things. The truth is I might belong here ... forever.

BAZAROV: I liked our friendship ... very much. I found it useful.

> BAZAROV *holds out a hand.* ARKADY *takes it.*

ARKADY: Are you afraid.

BAZAROV: Well ... Oh yes. I am.

ARKADY: I'll be back soon. Get some rest.

> ARKADY *leaves.*

BAZAROV: People are odd about death ... I'm not afraid at all ... Disappointed ... but not afraid. He'd want me to be though ... that would make me more human. Am I conscious ... Oh, I meant to ask someone to kiss my parents for me.

ANNA: I'll do it.

BAZAROV: Thank you ... Who said that.

ANNA: Go to sleep.

> PIOTR, GREGOR, SERGEI, *and the* BAILIFF *come in.*

GREGOR: They told us you wanted us in here, sir.

BAZAROV: Yes.

GREGOR: Is there something we can do.

BAZAROV: Just stand there. Let me look at you all.

> *They look at one another.*

Yes. I was right. You are the ... (*closes his eyes. Dies*)

Long pause.

PIOTR *goes close. Takes his pulse.*

PIOTR: He's dead.

SERGEI: We are the what. He didn't finish. We are the what.

GREGOR: The future.

BAILIFF: The dirt under his shoe.

GREGOR: No the future.

BAILIFF: Come off it. He was going to insult us something awful. One last great kick in the teeth.

SERGEI: It's bad luck to be in the same room with a corpse if you don't have any coins in your pocket.

PIOTR: Stupid man!

SERGEI: You talking to me?

PIOTR: It's superstitions like that that hold us all down, you moron.

SERGEI: So you are talking to me, eh!! I'd watch out if I were you.

PIOTR: Moron! Imbecile.

PIOTR *leaves.*

BAILIFF: That's it. That's what he wanted from us. A good fight! One last spectacle from the rabble before he kissed off. I tell you, we were the dirt in his fingernails! (*leaves*)

GREGOR *shouts after him.*

GREGOR: No! The future!

GREGOR *turns to* SERGEI.

The future … He told me. He took time and told me all about it. If I explain it to you, will you listen.

SERGEI: I'll try.

Lights begin to fade. ANNA *laughs. Sadly at first. Then with a kind of light joyful recognition. Brief blackout.*

Then flash back up to a dazzling white light which throws people into silhouette. BAZAROV *has gone.*

All the other characters are on the periphery of the stage watching.
GREGOR *and* SERGEI *walk off.* GREGOR *gesturing his explanation.*
SERGEI *just listening.*

Blackout.

End.